THE REWARD PLAN ADVANTAGE

THE REWARD PLAN ADVANTAGE

A Manager's Guide to
Improving Business Performance
Through People

Jerry L. McAdams

Foreword by Jack Stack

Jossey-Bass Publishers • San Francisco

Substantial discounts on bulk quantities of Jossey-Bass books are available to corporations, professional associations, and other organizations. For details and discount information, contact the special sales department at Jossey-Bass Inc., Publishers (415) 433–1740; Fax (800) 605–2665.

For sales outside the United States, please contact your local Simon & Schuster International Office.

Interior Design by Gary Head

Manufactured in the United States of America on acid-free paper containing 80 percent recycled fiber of which a minimum of 20 percent is postconsumer.

Library of Congress Cataloging-in-Publication Data

McAdams, Jerry.
The reward plan advantage: a manager's guide to improving business performance through people / Jerry L. McAdams.
      p.   cm.—(The Jossey-Bass business and management series)
   Includes bibliographical references and index.
   ISBN 0-7879-0232-2 (alk. paper)
   1. Incentives in industry—United States. 2. Performance awards—United States. I. Title. II Series.
HF5549.5.I5M39 1996
658.3'225—dc20   96-461

FIRST EDITION
HB Printing   10 9 8 7 6 5 4 3 2 1

The Jossey-Bass
Business & Management Series

Contents

Foreword

It's the last half of the last decade of the century, and by the numbers the United States economy is on fire. All the economic indicators would lead us to believe that we are headed for some of the best years of our lives.

Yet this is not the first time in my life that the economic outlook seemed so bright. Twice before the stage was set, but we blew it. How were we to know the reliance our economy had on oil and its relationships in the Middle East? We thought we were self-reliant. How were we to know that the Japanese would have a major impact on our marketplace and blast us into global competition?

How do we know now what today's rosy outlook will deliver? Granted, we've accumulated capital—and a lot of it. But do we really know how to keep it this time? Where will the other shoe fall? I'm afraid it will fall between labor and management. I'm afraid that we haven't learned our lessons from the past and that we haven't learned how to win with a lead—that we are a come-from-behind society. We have an incredible ability to pull together in a life raft, yet ignore each other on a luxury liner.

It seems as though every time the economy gets going, we can't figure out how to bring everyone along for the ride. It seems as though the only thing that stops us is the friction that the success creates. The very core of capitalism is that those who create wealth should get to keep it. However, whenever it comes time to share that wealth, there is an imbalance between the workers' rewards and the owners' rewards. After all, the story goes, it is the owners who take the risks. And *this* is our weakness. How do we make everyone feel like they can make a difference? How do we adequately reward everyone who has contributed to company success? How do we balance the risks and the rewards and keep our global edge?

Is there a middle-ground approach that will not only prevent the labor-management shoe from falling, but also will keep us from shooting ourselves in the foot? I believe so, and I believe Jerry McAdams comes about as close as anyone to presenting a clear path for achieving these goals in *The Reward Plan Advantage*.

No one has all the answers, but Jerry does show us how we can put in place incentives that reward people for initiative, hard work, and productivity while keeping us competitive in the global arena.

Jerry addresses "the middle," that gap between the haves and have-nots, and makes a convincing argument that if everyone understands the economic situations of the business, a compensation system can be implemented that provides job security, variable pay, and a chance at the brass ring—equity. Jerry believes as I do that if we don't address "the middle" we will be faced with turmoil and discontent, and we will ultimately lose the competitive edge we have today.

This book presents a structure that allows owners to be competitive in the market while rewarding all participants if they do better than the market expects. These ideas may just be scratching the surface, but wouldn't it be exciting if everyone had a role in building our future? *The Reward Plan Advantage* shows us how.

Springfield, Missouri   JACK STACK
February 1996   *President and CEO*
                              Springfield Remanufacturing Company

Acknowledgments

It takes a year to write a book. It also takes a lot of help. The people who read every word and gave me their feedback based on their own years of experience made the project seem worthwhile. Jane Bjorndal McAdams, my partner, is an expert in compensation; she made sure that what I wrote was clear and correct. Roger Stotz and Nancy Ogden of Maritz Performance Improvement Company, Maritz Inc., critically focused on the recognition and group-based incentive portion of the book. Elizabeth Hawk of Sibson & Company and my co-director of the Consortium for Alternative Reward Strategies Research (CARS) gave me input with her usual thoroughness and thoughtfulness. Don Barry of Chase Manhattan Bank stretched my thinking and enhanced my sense of humor. May Eagle Seyle refined my scattered words into a logical and understandable format. I cannot thank these good friends enough for their support and expertise.

A number of other people lent their expertise to more specific areas of the book. Jamie Hale, Andy West, Ed Bancroft, and Rick Beal (all of Watson Wyatt Worldwide) shared their experience and perspective. So did Sherry Tucker of Towers Perrin; Bob Holben of Westinghouse Energy Systems Business Unit; Bob Pike of the Lord Corporation; Melinda Branchini of VHA, Dallas; Mike Higgins of BankOne, Dallas; Roy Baum, Mike Lockwood, Bob Mai, Jeff Sherk, and Mary Anne Walton, all of Maritz Inc.; Pat Rowell and Nina Rappaport of Chase Bankcard Systems, Chase Manhattan Bank; Walter Nord of Florida State University; Dick Beatty and Charles Fay of Rutgers University; Laura Popo of Washington University, St. Louis; Brian Riedy of Hewitt; and Stephen B. Knouse of Southern State University. The Jossey-Bass professionals made the process much more interesting through their expertise: Byron Schneider, Mary Douglas, Alice Rowan, and Mary O'Briant.

To those at Maritz Inc. who believed that I could make a contribution to the body of knowledge, a special thanks. Their support of the CARS project and of my research was critical. In particular, William E. Maritz, Norm Schwesig, Dan Westrich, and Steve Maritz created an atmosphere that allows this kind of research to continue. Jeff Reinberg was instrumental in getting support for my work and provided unique and practical insight during the writing process. Phil Moses and Charlie Vogt regularly demonstrated how to use the language in an effective way.

The members of the CARS project, particularly the American Compensation Association, in addition to those already mentioned, contributed their time, money, and expertise to make the research possible.

We all owe a debt of gratitude to the leaders and reporters of open-book management: Jack Stack of SRC and author of *The Great Game of Business*, who was kind enough to write the foreword of this book, and John Case and Bo Burlington of *Inc.* magazine. They are spreading the word and deed of making people a competitive advantage.

Finally, my thanks go to Gina Breadon, my friend and associate at Maritz, who kept things in order and made my working life considerably more productive and pleasant.

St. Louis, Missouri   JERRY MCADAMS
February 1996

The Author

Since June of 1995, **Jerry McAdams** has been the national practice leader for Reward and Recognition Systems, Watson Wyatt Worldwide, an international consulting firm specializing in human resources, systems, and financial management. Prior to joining Watson Wyatt, McAdams was the vice president for performance improvement resources at Maritz Inc., in St. Louis. Before joining Maritz, McAdams held a variety of positions with General Electric, working in the United States and Europe. McAdams also served as a member of the Reward Systems Committee of the White House Conference on Productivity in 1984, and more recently, in November of 1994, he testified about organizational performance's link to rewards and possible tax code changes before the House of Representatives Committee of the U.S. Congress.

McAdams is also a founder and co-director of the nonprofit Consortium for Alternative Reward Strategies Research (CARS). He is a member of the certification faculty of the American Compensation Association (ACA) on alternative reward strategies, and for several years he has taught a "soup to nuts" course in Europe, Central and South America, and Australia on reward and recognition plans and improving customer service. McAdams has worked with AT&T, Rockwell Automation, Johnson & Johnson, Xerox, Chase Manhattan Bank, McDonald's, and health care institutions. He has directed the design and installation of all forms of reward systems for sales and marketing, manufacturing, health care, and service firms.

A leading thinker in the research, design, as well as the implementation of reward and recognition systems, McAdams is the co-author of *People, Performance and Pay* (1987, with Carla O'Dell), *Capitalizing on Human Assets* (1992, with Elizabeth Hawk) and *Organizational Performance and Rewards: 663 Experiences in Making the Link* (1994, with Elizabeth Hawk). In addition, he has collaborated with Robert Mai on *Learning Partnerships* (1995), a book about reward systems and the learning organization. He was a contributor to *The Performance Imperative* (1995).

McAdams lives in St. Louis with his wife, Jane, and their two sons, Ryan and Mitchell.

To my wife, Jane, for her invaluable expert contribution to this work, and to Jane and our sons, Ryan and Mitchell, for their support and love

THE REWARD PLAN ADVANTAGE

PART ONE

THE FUNDAMENTALS

Almost nothing makes me skip a part of a business book like the title, "The Fundamentals." The more accurate description of "book overview, background, everything starts with objectives and measurements, and assessment of what you have now" is just too long. I've tried to put thoughts into this first part that you can use for each type of performance improvement reward plan you may wish to design and implement.

"Getting Something Useful out of This Book—Quickly" (Chapter One) gives you a brief overview of the contents. *The Reward Plan Advantage* is anything but a novel, so I expect you will jump around to your areas of interest. This chapter should help that process by laying some context for the book, explaining why open-book management (OBM) is so important, and then describing each chapter. There is also a discussion of rules, or, more accurately, the lack of them. "How We Got Here" (Chapter Two) is my journey from teachings of Frederick Taylor to our present view of employees as assets. The real fundamentals for improving your organization's performance through people are laid down in "Objectives and Measurements" (Chapter Three)—everything starts with them—and "Assessing Your Current Situation" (Chapter Four), which helps you get a clear picture of how your organization presently reinforces employees.

I wouldn't skip Part One. The rest of the book will be of greater use to you if you are clear on the fundamentals.

CHAPTER 1

Getting Something Useful out of This Book—Quickly

It took about eighty years after the onset of the industrial revolution for management to discover the customer, and it has taken about ninety years to discover the employee. Management thought leaders had already figured out how to calculate the lifetime value of a customer, and we are now trying to figure out how to calculate the value of employee contributions to organizational success.

The importance of the employee to the company can be seen in the experience of Springfield Remanufacturing Company (SRC), an engine remanufacturing company located in Springfield, Missouri. In the early 1980s, CEO Jack Stack and his management team bought the operation from International Harvester with the highest leveraged loan I'd ever heard of—eighty-nine to one—at an 18 percent interest rate. Not having the money to invest in capital improvements (or anything else for that matter), Jack had to rely on his employees. He taught them how the financial game is played—by the use of financial measures and attention to performance—engaged them, and made them accountable for winning. His bonus plan and partial employee ownership gave them a financial stake in the game, and it worked. Sales have risen from $16 million to over $90 million among their nine companies. The 10-cents-a-share stock price is now over $20. SRC is a compelling example of how an organization's performance can be improved by improving its people through financial literacy, trust, engagement of all employees, and a customized reward system. These are all elements of "open-book management," or OBM, as John Case of *INC*. magazine coined it in an article titled "The Open-Book Managers," in September of 1990.

While SRC was toiling away in obscurity in Springfield, I was equally obscurely toiling away at Maritz Inc., a performance improvement agency in St. Louis specializing in the use of incentives. As were a lot of other researchers in business, labor, and academia around the country, I was trying to discover what human resource practices, particularly reward systems, can make a difference in an organization's performance. (Chapter Two describes that journey.) In the early 1990s, national focus came to rest on SRC's success through Stack's book, *The Great Game of Business,* and on the research that was being done on reward systems with the publication of *Capitalizing on Human Assets,* which I coauthored with Elizabeth Hawk. Jack and I had both discovered the power of employees at about the same time, gotten to know each other, and found that our experiences dovetailed.

This book is about using rewards to get employees to contribute to an organization's success. You do not have to work in an "open-book" managed organization to use this book. Most companies won't ever be as open with and engaging of their employees as OBM companies are, but the reward plans described here can make a big difference anyway. If, however, you are or are becoming a practitioner of OBM, the plans and processes described here will show you how to develop a reward plan for your organization.

Use Every Asset You Have

Competitiveness demands that organizations get the best possible return on their assets. If you believe that people are assets and not solely a cost of doing business, this book will show you how to get a better return on these employed assets. Most companies spend a good deal of money, time, and energy on all kinds of reward plans, in addition to base pay, with little understanding of what they are getting in return. It is often possible to put a dollar value on that return, but sometimes it isn't. Such plans can make good business sense even without providing a dollar return, such as rewarding for customer satisfaction improvement. In any case, when organizations want employees to make a difference, they must be clear about their objectives, and they must make their reward plans *positively reinforcing* to employees. In addition, if organizations want to maximize the return on their investment, they must have the courage to unleash the creative energy of employees, enabling them to become contributing stakeholders.

What You Will Find in This Book

- A means for line and staff management to gain an understanding of reward plan options and of how to use education, communications, and assessment to make these options work most effectively.

- An argument for using group-based reward plans in addition to or in place of a portion of traditional compensation, to enable and reinforce employees at all levels to become more effective contributing stakeholders.

- An approach to improving the return on your investment in all your reward plans.

- A guide for involving all employees in improving organizational performance.

- A presentation of "best principles" rather than "best practices." There are few, if any, "best practices." Improving performance through people demands that you create plans for the unique needs of your organization. There is danger in trendy, cookie-cutter answers. I have used examples only to better describe how an approach works, not to suggest that any particular method will be successful for your organization—although it may well be.

- An enjoyable read, a unique view, a "how to" book when you need it to be.

Most managers have a basic understanding of how pay systems work, and organizations are probably not going to change fundamentally the way they pay people. The focus of this book, therefore, is on improving understanding of what employers can get from existing systems and on using additional (or redirected) funds to launch plans more directly aligned with their organization's objectives.

Compensation can become a little exclusionary in its language. But you don't have to know much about the technical aspects of compensation to make this book work for you. In fact, it may be better if you don't. The book is addressed to all managers in the organization—top, line, or staff—rather than strictly to human resources (HR) personnel. While most HR functions serve the critical function of attracting, developing, maintaining, and retaining individuals, they have rarely addressed improving the organization's performance. Line managers are becoming more responsible for improving performance through employees, while HR is being reengineered into teams of consultants dedicated to supporting (and getting out of the way of) line management.

The Reinforcement Model

The framework for this book is the *Reinforcement Model* shown in Figure 1.1. In this model, *business objectives and desired culture* drive the design of the *total reward opportunity,* which is made up of *individual compensation, capability, recognition, group incentive,* and *project team incentive* plans.

In the model, the plans are ordered from left to right on a continuum from their individual to group focus and according to their potential for contributing to results (that is, the degree to which performance improvement can be attributed to the plan). I have labeled the compensation end of the continuum (which includes base pay, benefits, and most adjustments to base pay) *cost of doing business,* because it is most difficult to attribute business results to these plans; I have labeled the project team incentive end *business results,* because these plans only reward when the result of the contribution is measurable and valuable.

Moving from left to right on the continuum also represents an evolution from an administrative mind-set to a creative one. Beginning with capability plans, the creative demand placed on an organization is for imaginative approaches to a constantly changing environment. The need for creativity grows as does the need for alignment between employees and as the objectives that determine organizational success increase. The ability of an organization to meet those objectives in a cost-effective manner requires creativity. Creativity can open up the organization's systems to allow employees to move from job-bound, narrowly focused, micromanaged cost centers to become engaged, contributing stakeholders with both accountability and reward opportunity.

If they were easy, you'd already be doing them.

My objective in this book is to make the model complete rather than complex. But paying, rewarding, and recognizing people for the right things and the right results are not easy. If they were easy, you'd already be doing them.

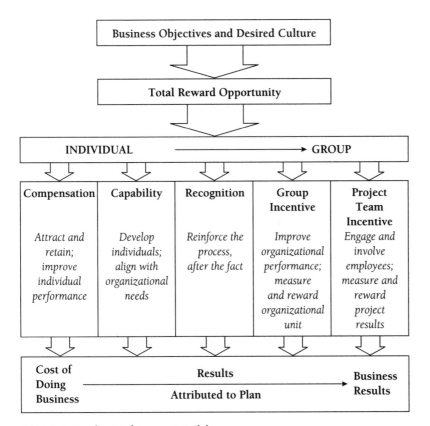

FIGURE 1.1. *The Reinforcement Model.*

It is critical to realize that the reinforcement model is just part of the picture. The real power comes from *performance management, assessment, education, communication, feedback, employee involvement, reassessment,* and *some fun.* These processes support the reward plans and create an environment of alignment and focus.

Results Through Individual Improvement

Most managers think that proper administration of individual compensation plans is their primary tool for performance improvement through people and that it can (or should) do it all. I disagree.

A good deal is already known about improving performance by focusing on the individual employee. This *bottom-up* approach is the primary focus of individual compensation plans. It assumes that improvement of each person's performance (assuming that improvement could be measured) will add up to organizational improvement. This book argues that while that may be the case, it can never be known for sure whether it works. With the possible exception of sales, it cannot be proved that a 10 percent improvement in individual productivity, for example, will result in a cumulative 10 percent productivity gain for the entire organization—or any gain for that matter. The accounting, measurement, job, and operational systems are too complex for such a simplistic approach.

The inability to assess the impact of individual improvement does not relieve organizations of the job of improving each employee's performance, however. How to do that is the subject of hundreds of books and seminars. This book touches on the subject by reviewing individual-based compensation plans, but it argues that this is not the only road to measurable, justifiable performance improvement on an organizational level.

Improvement Through Group Focus

Competitiveness demands that all employees be engaged in making a business successful. That engagement requires everyone to know, understand, focus, and act on the objectives that determine organizational success. Group-based plans, in the broadest terms, are designed expressly to improve organizational success by combining a *top-down* and a *bottom-up* approach.

At a conference in San Francisco, one of my audience members argued against rewarding everyone in a group for improving performance. He didn't believe a file clerk could influence the measurements. I pointed out that he was right—if the person is seen as just a file clerk, whose role is confined to filing. But if you view the clerk as an intelligent human being and allow him or her to contribute more broadly, he or she could make a difference. The challenge is to engage that file clerk in collaboration with others to make a contribution and be rewarded for the result or recognized for the effort.

The goal of adding a group focus is to create an environment that unleashes the creativity of employees. When channeled through clear direction and engaging processes, that creativity is one of an organization's most effective competitive elements.

Reinforcement Isn't Everything

I do not believe that reward plans are the *only* way to improve an organization's performance. Far from it. Financial literacy, organizational redesign, reengineering, systems and process development, new products and services, quality becoming "customer-driven," along with hiring, orientation, and career development practices and all kinds of other interventions are destined to affect performance.

Reward plans can precede the improvement process or follow it, but they absolutely must reinforce it. The problem is that most experts in improving organizational performance only pay lip service to reward plans, and that is a lost opportunity. Those who, without reinforcement, have participated in their umpteenth management-by-objectives (MBO) process or reengineering know what I mean. I believe that what gets measured gets managed, and what gets rewarded gets done.

Another caveat: I believe in intrinsic as well as extrinsic rewards. Both are needed. No reward plan will offset a lousy supervisor who makes your job painful. Nor will it offset a job you hate. By the same token, to rely solely on intrinsic rewards is a mistake. It does not take long for employees to say, "I really like working on this special team to improve the process, but what else is in it for me?" As in all matters, a balance must be struck.

As my father, a tough depression-era realist, used to say, "If you want to get people really involved, get them to put some skin in the game." In this context, "skin" is employees sharing risk *and* reward with the organization in the game of business.

> **What gets measured gets managed, and what gets rewarded gets done.**

Organization of This Book

This book is organized according to the reinforcement model, with a few additions. Chapter Two presents an overview of how I have watched U.S. businesses use the principles of Frederick Taylor, the father of standardized work tasks through scientific management. Those principles have shaped management's attitude toward and treatment of people, and that system is still prevalent in employee practices. The chapter follows my learning from the traditional practices of the 1960s through the experimentation of the 1980s

Business Objectives and Desired Culture

and the broad applications of the 1990s. Chapter Three describes a straightforward process for gaining consensus on an organization's *business objectives* and discusses how to know when you are successful in improving those objectives. Chapter Four addresses the first complete and really useful assessment process I have seen in action. It is a simple method of assessing the plans you have now, what they do for you, what they cost, what return you get, and the messages they send to employees. The method will help you to articulate a clear statement of your present culture. The chapter also discusses how to assess what your employees *really* think about the organization and how it operates.

Part Two contains two chapters on *individual compensation*. These chapters describe individually focused, bottom-up approaches. They are overviews, but they include some ideas for making the elements of these plans more effective. For those of you without a background in compensation, this part is a helpful, nontechnical briefing. If you have heard of "skill-based" or "competency-based" pay but are not clear on their meanings, this section will bring you up to speed.

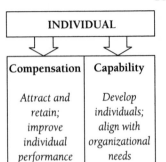

Chapter Five deals with the theory and science of behavioral modification that is behind the traditional approach to individual compensation and discusses how to use it—and not to use it. Chapter Six gives an overview of each of the elements of the individual compensation side of the model, *compensation* and *capability*. Compensation includes base pay, adjustments to base pay, individual incentives, promotions, variable entitlements, and benefit plans. These approaches are designed to be (or they have become) entitlements, or costs of doing business. Capability plans focus on developing the individual's ability to do the job, to make a contribution to the organization, and to make the process more meaningful than the traditional merit increase review. These plans are currently taking the form of competency-based plans, and they are changing the way we think about individual development and the importance of linking it with the core competencies required by the organization. My objective in these chapters is not to discuss each plan in detail but to comment on each plan's evolving role in the total reward opportunity.

The chapters in Part Three, which make up the bulk of the book, explore recognition, group incentive, and project team incentive plans. These plans call for adjustments in management's leadership role. These chapters posit, that as leaders, managers need to tell people what to accomplish, give them the tools and time they need to get the job done, and then get out of the way. The rest of managing is knowing how to make sure that what people do when managers get out of the way is effective. Recognition, group incentive, and project team incentive plans incorporate both bottom-up and top-down processes.

Chapter Seven discusses reward and recognition plans that reinforce the process itself more than the outcome. These plans celebrate the importance of individual, team, and organizational accomplishments. Their outcomes are "after the fact." They are a formalized way for the organization to show appreciation, as opposed to being an incentive. Recognition plans include celebrating organizational objectives, reinforcing extraordinary people, recognizing activities and contributions, reinforcing demonstrated desired behaviors, recognizing service, and recognizing the needs of employees.

Chapter Eight deals with group incentive plans that educate and reward employees based on how the organizational unit performs against specific measures. It shows how to design and operate a plan that will give you a real return on your investment. These plans are technically called "organizational performance reward plans." Some of the terms that are used more often are current profit sharing, gainsharing, winsharing, success sharing, and goal sharing. All are variations on the same theme. Work teams (self-directed or not) are covered here, for they are organizational units. This is a "how to" chapter. It follows a design process that I've been using for years and have found to be complete, consultative with top management, and nonthreatening to the design team.

Chapter Nine addresses the need for bottom-up plans to reward team performance on projects they choose or those chosen for them. These teams are not business or organizational units, but are cross-functional, possibly made up of a few employees within an organizational unit. I cover individual suggestion plans, team idea plans, ad hoc problem solving, and project team plans, as well as continuous quality improvement process team plans. I spend most of the chapter discussing team idea plans, which are the most dynamic of the project team incentive plans. These plans can also save a lot of money, and they can improve customer satisfaction and company processes.

Chapter Ten explains how to choose the type of award. Discussion of this topic often surprises people. The general assumption is that cash is used for all plans except recognition. This is not the case. Plans can be energized by using a wider variety of awards, selected to fit each type of plan.

Chapter Eleven discusses implementation of reward plans, particularly those focused on groups. Topics include approval, management ownership, employee involvement, education, introduction, communication, promotion, reassessment, and renewal. The chapter focuses on all the steps after design and type of award selection. These steps are business strategy tools for improving performance, and they must be dynamic. Designing plans, therefore, is 25 percent of the job, and implementing, operating, and reassessing plans are 75 percent. This is the most important chapter, because it addresses how to get the most out of your plan investment. Poorly designed plans well implemented do better than well-designed plans poorly implemented. However, there is never a reason to settle for bad design—particularly if you read and use this book.

The final chapter, Chapter Twelve, is a summary of thoughts and observations on tying together all of the ideas presented in the book. There is never one answer; there are no silver bullets. You probably will need more than one type of reward plan, just as you have a number of compensation plans. People need to be motivated and engaged, not overloaded, and this can be done with deliberative thought and a little planning.

What Else You Can Expect, or Not

There is only one rule: people are an asset, not just a cost.

What you won't find in this book are a lot of rules. In fact, there is only one: people are assets and not solely a cost of doing business. This perspective is in contrast to the view that labor is a cost and costs are to be controlled or reduced. Businesses have tended to look at people as a cost, so when they run into trouble, they lay people off, often with unfortunate personal and organizational results. Clearly, there are situations in which reducing workforce is the only intelligent business strategy, such as in times of reduced demand and changes in the line of business, product, or market. However, laying people off solely as a way to reduce costs (with the assumption that they will be hired back when things get better) is an expensive decision for a company. It is also a very difficult and complex situation for the person affected by the layoff—not to mention those who survive the cut.

Organizations also have a problem with laying off the right people. Seniority is often a guide. But seniority does not guarantee or preclude that an employee will have a new idea or improve his or her performance. Yet, senior employees are often the highest paid employees, with commensurate benefits. This often leads to the decision to lay off more of the lower seniority employees to achieve a targeted savings. It also means it will be harder to balance new processes and business requirements with the available people.

The idea that people are an asset is growing. You don't lay off an asset to save money. You grow it. You get a return on it. You make the assets you have more productive. And although you may not be able to calculate a return on each individual asset, you just might be able to get a return on your whole portfolio. People assets appreciate. Most others depreciate.

Beyond "people as assets," a few other rules of thumb may be used for guidance. Organizations are different in almost every dimension. I regularly get calls from people who want the names of companies that have plans they can "learn from." My concern is that what they really want is to learn and then replicate. First of all, there *are* a lot of organizations with plans, but just because they're doing it does not necessarily mean the plans are working. Practice does not automatically mean *best* practice. Second, plans are difficult to transplant. A best practice in one organization may work because it meshes with that organization's unique culture and organizational climate. There has been precious little benchmarking in this area. Good benchmarking requires a diagnosis of *why* something works, as well as of *what* works.

Practice does not automatically mean "best" practice.

This news is frustrating to people who want a stock or cookie-cutter design answer or who want to copy a practice used by a recognized leader in their market. Traditional compensation practices tend to be "formula-ized," to conform to legal requirements, and to be directly transferable between dissimilar organizations. But with the revitalized need for employees to be contributors, organization-specific performance improvement plans are essential.

By their very nature, performance improvement plans must take into account the unique characteristics of an organization. As organizations become flatter and are forced to become more flexible, even more attention will have to be paid to the unique cultural side of this process, while still making money at it. That can be a hard concept for traditional managers in command-and-control organizations.

When I use examples in this book, they are of real companies that have allowed me to use their names and relate their designs. When I haven't named names, it is because the companies preferred that I didn't, often because they consider their practice a competitive advantage. In this book, examples are for understanding, not to present successful or "best" practices.

Adding to and Drawing from the Body of Knowledge

This book is an admittedly personal view, but it is based on my own experience and extensive research, much of which has been published previously. I also draw on and recommend the variety of tools that are available to help managers manage business and lead people. Among them are some excellent books and studies on each element of this process—education, communications, feedback, involvement, and reward systems. This book is somewhere between Edward Lawler's benchmark work *Strategic Pay* (1990), which primarily focuses on person-based (as opposed to job-based) pay plans, and John Belcher's excellent *Gain Sharing* (1987), which presents a specific type of reward plan and is primarily aimed at the manufacturing sector. *The New Pay* (1992), by Jay Schuster and Patricia Zingheim, is an excellent overview of all forms of compensation plans, with an emphasis on variable pay.

My book takes a different approach than those I have just named, and it provides more detailed guidance on how to design, implement, value, and reassess plans. It complements Jack Stack's *The Great Game of Business* (1994) and John Case's *Open-Book Management* (1995) by providing the process necessary to design and implement the reward portion of the OBM strategy.

CHAPTER 2

How We Got Here

To one who has been educated as an engineer, as I was, everything in business can look like a system. My work in sales, marketing, strategy, human resources, compensation, education, and assessment seemed to me to be just systematic ways of improving performance. It's no surprise, then, that my approach was to create a model—a template. A model can be applied to each situation as a way to map what action is needed, and the kinks can be worked out as necessary. The reinforcement model introduced in Chapter One, combined with assessment and implementation methodology, is an example of such a process.

What You Will Find in This Chapter

What follows is a personal, three-decade view of how organizations have attempted to engage people in improving organizational performance. The chapter describes:

- Frederick Taylor's influence on how we think about our employees

- Rewarding employees at General Electric in the 1960s and 1970s

- What sales incentives taught me about improving organizational performance through nonsales employees

- American business's initial experience with Japanese quality movements

- The emerging awareness of productivity and quality as operational measures of success

- Problems with the first approach to group and team incentives

- Research on reward systems and initial insights it provided

- National awareness of open-book management and the importance of employees as assets

This chain of events and developments is the path I took to arrive at the reinforcement model and my awareness of its value and effectiveness in describing reward systems. I also discuss the findings of three benchmark studies on reward systems and my connection with open-book management.

The Influence of Frederick Taylor

Oklahoma State University (OSU) in the 1960s was a hotbed for Frederick Taylor's principles of scientific management. I earned my industrial engineering degree primarily by learning and applying Taylor's philosophy. In his book, *The Principles of Scientific Management* (1911, p. 85), he explained his method using the example of a bricklayer:

> *First.* The development (by management, not the worker) of the science of bricklaying, with rigid rules for each motion of every man, and the perfection and standardization of all implements and working conditions.
> *Second.* The careful selection and subsequent training of the bricklayers into first-class men. . . .
> *Third.* Bringing the first-class bricklayer and the science of bricklaying together, through the constant help and watchfulness of the management, and through paying each man a large daily bonus for working fast and doing what he is told to do.
> *Fourth.* An almost equal division of the work and responsibility between the workman and the management. All day long the management work almost side by side with the men, helping, encouraging, and smoothing the way for them. . . .

Before Taylor, many American workers were craftsmen, with their own way of doing their work. This was inefficient and costly.

As more work began to be done in factories or at large building sites, it was critical to take the best practices from each craftsman, document them, and create standards for each task. This procedure moved the Industrial Revolution into high gear, and with it, the entire manufacturing economy.

This thought process was also the basis for the development of human resource (personnel) management, which held that people were elements of the production process, just like the machines that stamped out the metal parts for high-finned cars or applied Teflon to pots and pans. After all, that's what Taylor's book taught: "The greatest prosperity can exist only as the result of the greatest possible productivity of the men and machines of the establishment—that is, when each man and each machine are turning out the largest possible output" (p. 27).

Taylor was not insensitive to the needs of the worker. He believed that scientific management was the best way both to improve organizational performance *and* to maximize the employee's daily wage. The valuable practices of task definition, training, efficient methods, and assuring employees that they have all the resources necessary to do the job, all of which derive from Taylor's theory, are integrated into current management practices. The employee's role, however, is defined by the job and its component tasks, not by his or her value as a person. Craftsmanship without coordination and standardization was just what they were trying to eliminate.

Scientific management was the best way to improve organizational performance.

Rewarding Employees at General Electric

Being Taylor trained and indoctrinated, I was a perfect fit for my first employer, General Electric (GE). Taylor's book rested quite comfortably next to my GE manuals on technical marketing and management. In those days (the early 1960s), GE was a directive, top-down organization that served as a prime example and training ground for a good part of the U.S. industrial community. GE was typical of most larger U.S. companies and considerably more successful than many of them.

GE's focus was on process, cost reduction, market penetration, legal compliance (the company was still reeling from the price-fixing scandals), and manufacturing excellence. The company went from centralized to decentralized operations and back again. It was a great place to learn.

GE's approach to developing and improving the performance of employees at that time was limited to individual performance reviews and training. Human resource and compensation practice was administered on a local level by the employee and community relations department (E&CR). E&CR considered and rewarded nonsales employees as if they were interchangeable cogs in a manufacturing process—whether they were actually in manufacturing or not. The "mushroom theory" often prevailed. It is: "keep 'em in the dark, cover them with s——, and cut their heads off when you need to."

This approach was the natural outcome of scientific management at work. People, particularly those in nonmanagement jobs, were valued in terms of the job description they fulfilled and what tasks they performed, not what additional contributions they made or could make, if given the chance. Or as Taylor said, "Perhaps the most prominent single element in modern scientific management is the task idea. . . . This task specifies not only what is to be done but how it is to be done and the exact time allowed for doing it" (Taylor, 1911, p. 39).

Job descriptions operated just like machine specifications, but for humans. These descriptions defined the job, its range of control, responsibilities, and tasks, and often the experience necessary to do the job. There was little or no discussion of how performance was to be measured or what was to be accomplished. The job evaluation process gave value to jobs by assigning points to each aspect of the job, and the point total translated into a job value. This work was done by a job evaluation committee with the help of compensation consultants. The point totals were compared to the competitive labor market through standard or customized salary surveys.

Human resource management continues to measure the imprecise with great precision.

Perhaps the leading thinker today (and certainly the most articulate) on pay systems is Edward Lawler, founder of the Center for Effective Organizations at the University of Southern California. In *Strategic Pay* (1984), Lawler comments on job evaluations: "Through a series of subjective decisions, an organization can translate the tasks that it asks individuals to perform into an 'objective,' quantified result and a pay level. This is often facilitated by some moderately complex mathematical manipulations of the data, which give the results an appearance of scientific objectivity" (p. 136). In its compulsion for exactness and data in support (and defense) of its recommendations and actions, human resource management continues to measure the imprecise with great precision.

Nonexempt, hourly workers at GE were either on a straight hourly rate or were measured and rewarded with an hourly incentive that would vary with each person's production or piece rate. The harder and faster a person worked, the more he or she made. Negotiations determined most aspects of labor's role in an organization. That role was codified and written up, and it became the bible that controlled employees' activities through job description, allowing for little focus on organizational performance.

As is the case today, everyone else was on salary, but the process of determining those salaries was centrally controlled at GE, as was each person's job and level, regardless of the location or the nature of business. No matter what one did or where one worked, everyone fell into a defined job level. Every manager above a certain level carried a small white card with salary grades printed on the back showing the range of pay for all employees.

Nonunion employees usually received annual cost-of-living adjustments and/or annual merit increases. The individual performance review (often called "pay for performance" or, incorrectly, "performance management") was an attempt to connect the person's performance with the merit increase. It was hard to effectively and accurately measure the performance of individuals. Employee reviews were almost solely based on activities or traits rather than on results, in the opinion of management. Quite often, the bell curve tolled, forcing the ratings into a "normal distribution," whether the employee work group was "normal" or not.

The bell curve tolls, forcing ratings into "normal distribution" whether the work group was "normal" or not.

In the sixties, most management training sessions were about how to *lead* the troops. But the subtext was *micromanagement*. In addition, there was always the subtle statement that if managers were just "better people"—more reinforcing, considerate, sensitive, and better communicators—direct reports would improve their performance. This was valuable training for me personally, but I saw little chance to practice it upon returning the training retreat to the real world. Even the management team that sent me to the training in the first place offered little support for change.

Again, the scientific management approach became the inadvertent driver for individual performance reviews and/or performance management. Forms ("Are blue forms more effective for nonexempt workers than yellow ones?"), base pay increase matrixes ("If you are 5 percent over midpoint and have a 3 rating, you get between a 3.6 percent and a 4.2 percent increase"), and forced distribution ("You must stack rank your people, forcing 10 percent with a 1 rating, 20 percent with a 2 rating . . .") were the primary tools. If you were lucky, you worked for a manager who really worked the system, giving you opportunities for growth. My best manager, Andy Walsh, did just that. He was charismatic and was the exception to the rule.

Everything was laid out precisely, using simple mathematical procedures to provide control and limit discretion. But because of the inability to measure individual performance, because of managers' unwillingness to differentiate among individuals, and because of the limited pool of funds, performance reviews for the most part became a maintenance exercise for the organization and an entitlement for the person. Day-to-day performance had little to do with financial reward. Real differentiation between people went out the window.

Even career planning was somewhat mechanistic and not necessarily tied to performance or potential for performance. I actually had a ten-year career path laid out for me by my first manager. The basic assumption was that the organization was static and the market was ever expanding. Charles Handy's wonderful book *The Age of Unreason* (1989) tells of his experience with this process, which was much the same as mine:

> Thirty years ago I started work in a world-famous multinational company. By way of encouragement, my employer produced an outline of my future career—"This will be your life," they said—with titles of likely jobs. The outline ended, I remember, with myself a chief executive of a particular company in a particular far-off country. I was, at the time, suitably flattered. I left them long before I reached the heights they planned for me, and by then I knew that not only did the job they had picked out no longer exist, neither did the company I would have directed nor even the country in which I would have operated [p. 6].

While GE was not promising me a career path anything like Charles Handy's, I too was programmed on a clear channel to success.

Rewarding Sales Partnerships

In the sixties, the closest thing to aligning employees with business objectives was the sales commission plan. Sales was an important

---

Performance reviews became a maintenance exercise for the organization and an entitlement for the person.

objective. It was easy to measure on an individual level, so rewarding salespeople for improving their performance was (and is) a commonly accepted practice.

During this period, GE began to appreciate the importance of resale distributors in its marketing effort. It created a plan to reward these distributors for buying, stocking, and selling more GE products (electrical distribution and control equipment) than the previous year. The company didn't tamper with what each distributor earned in profit margin. It did realize that to develop an exciting partnership, it had to be creative enough to accelerate and reward distributors' incremental efforts.

GE could measure its distributors' performance in a number of ways. Sales, sales by product line, shelf space, sales by salesperson, training, and end-market penetration were all used as measurements. GE was creative with the awards as well. It took a page from the automotive dealership experience and improved upon it by offering awards like trips and merchandise, both to distributors and to the distributors' salespeople who improved their performance.

Much to everyone's surprise and delight, GE had tapped into an incremental business gold mine. The company found that its customers had ideas on how to sell more, improve the products, and increase the company's visibility in the marketplace. The "loyalty thing" developed on the beaches of Hawaii and the golf courses of Florida. Dealer networks naturally developed on these trips, through which information and sales techniques were shared. Merchandise ranging in value from $100 to $10,000 or more was earned and enjoyed by the distributors, owners, and salespeople and their families.

There was no scientific management at work here. GE had unleashed its customers—the distributors—to contribute to everyone's success. These new and exciting reward plans led to a profound change in the way GE did business with these customers. GE was treating them as valued partners in improving organizational performance.

Although sales employees were treated considerably better than employees in nonsales jobs, GE had not included them in the distributor performance reward plans. The general manager regularly said that the only incentive employees needed was to have a job. But when management saw the power of the distributor reward mechanisms, they began to include the GE salespeople in the plans. By adding this group, the programs became even more successful.

What impressed me most was the power that all forms of reward plans had in improving individual and group performance. These plans seemed to align the efforts of the salespeople and distributors in a way that was good not only for the organization but also for the sales force and distributors. GE's experience was not unique. In the sixties, these kinds of reward strategies were being replicated (and they still are) in almost every large marketing organization in the United States.

What About the Nonsales Majority?

If sales people and top management are successfully rewarded for performance, wouldn't it make sense for other employees as well?

As I moved from a marketing to a strategic role within GE, I began to see some hypocrisy in the oft-repeated company slogans on the importance of people as assets. As the previous discussion illustrates, the company was certainly beginning to treat its salespeople as if they were a real contributory asset, and top management had always been treated that way. But wouldn't it make sense for the organization to focus on reinforcing the positive contributions of nonsales employees as well? These people were slotted, described, reviewed, and controlled. Clearly, there were a lot more people in the organization supporting sales than actually making them. Top management's behavior, actions, and focus were aligned with the organization's strategic objectives. But for middle management, there were relatively few opportunities to contribute to and be rewarded for organizational performance improvement, and almost none for the rank and file. Employees improved organizational performance by doing their jobs better. The rest was left to management. Taylor's scientific "bricklaying" influence was alive and thriving.

This attitude is surprisingly still present in many organizations. Lawler (1984, p. 3) argues that "many organizations are more concerned with doing the wrong things right than searching for the right pay practices. . . . [These systems] are driven more by history and what other organizations do than by a strategic analysis of organizational needs." Traditional pay systems are much more than means of paying people. They are "a way of thinking about work and organizing people. Inherent in any job description is a statement to individuals about what is *not* included in their responsibilities. . . . [This way of thinking] does not fit well, however, with an orientation that says an individual should jump in and do what is right in the situation rather than what is called for by the job description."

Evolution Stumbles a Bit . . . at First

In the mid 1970s, I moved from GE to Maritz, the company that had designed and operated the sales incentive plans for GE, because I wanted to learn how to improve performance for a broader range of people. It appeared to me that all the principles that apply to salespeople could also apply to nonsales people and nonexecutives. The style would have to be different, and the measurement would be more difficult to determine and to track. But it stood to reason that organizations could see improved performance from all employees through the proper utilization of performance improvement plans.

Lots of people were looking for solutions to the problems facing the United States in the competitive world market. The American Productivity Center (APC) (which later became the American Productivity and Quality Center, or the APQC) was established in 1977 to promote awareness and conduct research on how to improve organizational performance, primarily through productivity improvement. The center's founder, C. Jackson Grayson, constantly talked about the employee as the critical success factor. The APC also worked to incorporate the quality methods of W. Edwards Deming and Joseph M. Juran into their message.

In the early 1980s, the documentary *If Japan Can, Why Can't We?* was aired on U.S. television, increasing national awareness of global competitiveness. Management became enamored of Japanese processes. The initial import from this chief competitor—quality circles—gave employees a blank sheet of paper, some training, and said, "Go make things better."

Employees in quality circles made recommendations and management may or may not have acted on them, but most managers assumed that the people in quality circles were reinforced by the sheer joy of participation and by being able to talk directly to top executives. It wasn't necessarily so. Quality circles were permitted, even encouraged, to present the results of their work to management. There were instances of real success. Recommendations were often well received, and many a management team saw what the rank and file could do when given the chance. In many cases, however, presenting to the management group made some circle team members very nervous. Others just didn't want to talk to the president because in certain environments it isn't a good thing to be singled out from your fellow workers.

Managers assumed people in quality circles were reinforced by the sheer joy of participation.

There were other reasons why quality circles more often than not didn't live up to expectations. While it was possible to import the Japanese *process,* American business didn't have the same cultural underpinnings that made quality circles work in Japan. Japan's ancient Shinto religion or their holistic culture could not be imported. The lack of management support over the long haul, the absence of awards for quality circle contributions, and the inability of the organization to follow through, implement, and value the recommendations are reasons quality circles had a life span of about eighteen months in an organization. The business community just wasn't ready for an engaged workforce.

Getting Down to Business

In 1984, the White House Conference on Productivity, coordinated by the APQC, identified new methods of meeting the emerging global competitive challenge. Six hundred thought leaders from all sectors of the economy worked for eighteen months to present recommendations to President Reagan and his cabinet. (We met primarily by computer conference using new technology—a PC.) Many of the conference participants believed that U.S. businesses needed to rethink quality from the American cultural point of view. More education and clearer processes were needed, as were management support and an environment that encouraged people to participate and reinforced them for results. The most significant contributions made by the conference were related to human resource practices and quality. The conference also led to the genesis of the now-influential Malcolm Baldrige Award, and the needs identified by its participants were later validated by the process contributions of Juran and Deming. (I was honored to be a part of the conference as a primary contributor to the subconference on reward systems and nontraditional human resource practices, which was chaired by Carla O'Dell from the APQC.)

What my colleagues and I learned by participating in the Washington conference were the critical elements of effective human resource practice: a lot of communication, a lot more feedback, employee involvement, some sense of security, and rewards actually based on measurable performance. We also found that companies were experimenting with non-traditional human resource practices, T-groups, and information sharing. They were starting to get people to work in teams and reward the team's performance. The companies that had incorporated these practices into their day-to-day operations were the exceptions, and they became the fodder for many a best-selling book.

As a natural outcome of these developments, narrowly focused reward plans were getting a lot more attention. It looked as if there might be another way to answer the battle cry of the competition. One such plan was trademarked as GainSharing,® followed by ImproShare® and Rucker.® These plans were limited to productivity measures, primarily in factories. The APQC expanded the scope of such plans by popularizing the "family of measures," originated by the Oregon Center for Productivity in 1983. Interestingly enough, these were not considered compensation plans. The American Compensation Association (ACA), the major force in the compensation field, began to take note. They co-sponsored research with the APQC and added a course on nontraditional reward systems for the compensation community through their extensive certification program in 1987.

Companies were also recognizing the opportunity to save huge amounts of money through rank-and-file team suggestion plans, a new and improved team version of the suggestion box of old. Other kinds of recognition plans were being used, too, with the knowledge that people could be motivated by being recognized. All of these plans tended to operate independently, however, with little common direction or coordination.

One thing was abundantly clear: there was a lot of activity out there. In an effort to capture what was going on and to put some structure to it, Carla O'Dell and I worked together from 1985 to 1987. We collaborated on *People, Performance, and Pay* (1987), a study of 1,600 organizations and their nontraditional reward and human resource practices. The study was sponsored by ACA and APQC, and it established a baseline for future research in this area. Our conclusion was that the 1980s was a decade of experimentation, and the 1990s would be a critical period of widespread implementation.

> *The 1980s was a decade of experimentation, and the 1990s would be a critical period of widespread implementation.*

The Evolution Picks Up Steam

By the late 1980s, quality rather than productivity had the full attention of American business. Productivity just didn't sell to the rank and file. Productivity improvements were being reengineered into the workplace through technology, and this explosion of technology allowed the ranks of middle management and white-collar jobs to be thinned, at great savings to the companies and at great cost to employees. It was a time of unprecedented job upheaval, with unemployment statistics not seen since the Great Depression.

Quality was the one thing everybody could agree on—but not quality circles. Instead, the latter part of the decade ushered in the beginning of a nationwide evolution toward a consistent, serious process by which quality would become an integral part of the way everybody did their job every day—not just an after-the-fact measurement. The quality programs in IBM-Rochester, Federal Express, and AT&T-UCS are excellent examples of "walking the talk" of quality. (These are all Malcolm Baldrige Award winners, and their stories are available by contacting them directly. Part of winners' responsibility is to spread the word, give tours, and explain their process.)

This evolution was big news. The Malcolm Baldrige Award received national press. Companies trained their people in quality methods. They developed their employees through performance management. They celebrated them through company picnics and publicity. They communicated with them through corporate communications. They listened to them through corporate-sponsored feedback surveys and meetings. They reorganized them to function in all manner of work teams.

In the 1990s, the evolution that began as a move from productivity to quality has become a movement on a much broader scale. Quality was never meant to be a trade-off for productivity. Some organizations are beginning to find that the two can work together under a broad umbrella where people can be aligned with organizational strategies and objectives. This approach is being augmented by the emergence of customer value (the successor to customer satisfaction), cycle time, market share, employee satisfaction, operational measures, and finally, profit and loss as a measure worthy of focus by all members of the organization. But how can management engage employees so that they feel they really have some emotional, intellectual, and financial "skin" in the game?

It was in the late 1980s that I began to hear about Jack Stack at Springfield Remanufacturing Company (SRC), which I discussed briefly at the beginning of Chapter One.

Stack doesn't claim to have been the first manager to use open-book management (OBM). A Halliburton Oil operation in Oklahoma opened their books to all employees in the 1970s as a part of proving the credibility of their all-employee bonus plan. Herman Miller and Lincoln Electric have been practicing their version of OBM for years. But SRC is the poster company for the movement, and the primary supplier of the methodology to other firms through their spin-off company, "The Great Game of Business."

SRC is the poster company for open-book management.

What Still Had To Be Done

Prior to the 1990s, management had known intuitively for a while that it makes good, common sense to reward people for performance, but few managers had the data to know if it makes good business (that is, financial) sense. To find out whether performance-based reward plans could make a bottom-line difference, organizations first had to get over some hurdles.

First, management had to behave as if they understood that people are, in fact, smart and therefore a valued asset and that those valued assets could do more than dress up an annual report. They had to believe that employees want to be proud of their company and contribute to its success.

Second, management had to figure out ways to measure what nonsales people contribute to organizational success. The natural inclination of organizations is to think in terms of the *individual;* it made sense, therefore, to try to improve people's individual performance. However, unlike sales, individual performance is extraordinarily difficult, if not impossible, to measure. (Most of my earlier work in improving the performance of individuals and small groups was based on the behavioral teachings of Aubrey Daniels, which is based on the work of B. F. Skinner. Today I find those teachings useful, but I have had to make them far more pragmatic to influence organizational success. More about that in Chapter Five.)

Third, the combination of educating employees about the business, making them accountable for the company's performance, and offering them a reward plan had to become the way companies worked with employees.

Applying What Had Been Learned

If measurement of individual performance was not feasible, then it made sense to measure *small work groups* or *departments*. My Maritz team of specialists installed and operated about seventy plans in manufacturing and service companies throughout the country, where we could measure a small team's performance, usually productivity, quality, attendance, and safety and then reward those team members based on the measurements. Because the performance and resulting rewards were based on small work groups, the employees had a short "line of sight" to the measures and felt they could influence those measures directly.

This strategy of measuring and rewarding all small work groups as teams tended to die of its own weight. In most companies there were many teams, often from one hundred to eight hundred, each with three to five measures and unique reward schedules, making the measuring process cumbersome. In addition, the strategy was complex to administer, and the organization's ability to prove a return on its investment was difficult. Middle management and first-line supervisors often felt threatened. They felt they had lost control.

As my coauthor Carla O'dell and I suggested in *People, Performance, and Pay* (1987), the late 1980s were rife with plans to change the way organizations worked with their employees. Organizations were trying to involve their people in business results through profit sharing plans and recognition programs, with no idea of their effectiveness. Profit sharing was primarily a funding mechanism for retirement plans, and the reward was so distant that it had little effect on people's performance. Few companies other than OBM companies were making any attempt to educate employees about financial measures and how employees could affect those measures.

Recognition programs attempted to single out star employees, hoping that others would be inspired to follow their lead. Many of these recognition plans probably did a lot more harm than good. They did for me. For reasons that were never clear to me, I was named employee of the year in my third year on the job at GE, a recognition not appreciated by my fellow toilers. My reward was dinner with the general manager and his spouse at their country club. It was a painful two and one-half hours. They talked about stocks, bonds, cash transfers, country clubs, and tee times. I didn't play golf. I didn't own a share of stock. (It wasn't that I didn't know what to do with my money but that I didn't have any.) I was just glad that I hadn't won second place, because I might have had to endure two dinners with the general manager. The reward and the subsequent unpleasant reaction from my fellow employees certainly didn't encourage me try to duplicate my feats—whatever they had been.

The company had its corporate heart in the right place, but the execution was awful. On a day-to-day basis, they didn't treat me or any other rank-and-file employees as trusted and valued members of the organization, so my selection felt hollow. The employee of the year/quarter/month programs were vain attempts to show employees that the company cared about our contributions. We were still treated as interchangeable, if organic, machines. Unfortunately, some companies still act that way.

Even in the enlightened eighties, there weren't many options for people who wanted to earn more. Merit increases were slightly more than the cost of living, and bonuses for the rank and file rarely happened. About the only way to make more money was to be promoted, but that got harder to do as organizations began to flatten out and people started moving sideways instead of up.

Getting a Handle on What Was Really Happening

There were some real success stories about plans that shared company gains with employees. There were also stories about organizations that spent a lot of money for plans and then went broke. While doing the research for *People, Performance, and Pay*, my coauthor, Carla O'Dell and I heard these stories about real successes and equally as real failures. It was all anecdotal information, however.

To get hard data so we could understand the impact of the most important type of these plans—group incentives—on performance, Elizabeth Hawk (who worked for Monsanto, now Sibson & Company) and I formed the Consortium for Alternative Reward Strategies Research (CARS) in 1990 and published *Capitalizing on Human Assets* (*CoHA*) in 1992. *CoHA* was the first national research project in the area of group incentives. We asked, What works? What doesn't work? and Why? The study was process oriented. We wrote the results for people who were practitioners but who didn't know where to start. We also wrote it for consultants so they could have something on which to base their good advice.

In understanding the results of our study, the central question became, What is performance? We wrestled with that definition because we could not draw a correlation between a company's financial performance and its reward plans. It wasn't that the plans didn't affect financial performance. The problem was that financial performance is often profoundly affected by things other than the efforts of the people within the organization. Changes in interest rates, market conditions, national recessions, acquisitions, and new laws all can adversely affect financial performance, even with extraordinary work and cooperation by the employees. But companies can't get away with using "outside influences" as a cop-out. Companies still have to live and die by whether or not they make money.

Another problem is that most accounting systems just basically keep the books. They do a good job of that, but they are not particularly useful management tools. They can't be depended on to effectively link operational performance to the profit and loss statement. Because operational measurements are so often used as a basis for rewards, justifying the cost of the awards is often a function of being able to determine the dollar value of the operational performance improvement.

Maybe at some point it will be possible to link operational and financial performance more directly. Certainly the work being done by Harvard's Robert S. Kaplan and H. Thomas Johnson (1987) and others is attempting to make corporate accounting systems more of a management tool, but there is still a long way to go. Educating all employees about financial measures as practiced by OBM organizations will be critical to making the linkage.

A majority of the companies studied in **Capitalizing on Human Assets** *did show a dollar value for the improved performance.*

Although we couldn't link rewards with financial performance for the entire population of companies we studied, a majority of these companies did show a dollar value for the improved performance. Companies with reward plans said they saw them as business strategies for improving organizational performance rather than as traditional compensation plans. The plans were reported to work as well in service as in manufacturing, in union as well as nonunion organizations. Most of the companies surveyed said they installed reward plans to *lead* as well as to *support* cultural change. We also found that those companies that treated operational performance as a business strategy that involves, communicates, facilitates feedback, aligns, and rewards could often identify what they got for their money. The question of linkage was one that few before us had asked. We found that what companies paid out in rewards gave them a net return on their investment that was greater than their usual investments. Operational plans (using measures like productivity and quality) reportedly showed a return of nearly 200 percent on their payout. At that point, we determined that organizational rewards can make good business sense. Our intuition had been correct.

From Applied Research to Pragmatic Application

Companies with group incentive reward plans said they saw them as business strategies for improving organizational performance.

CoHA described the rewards process from group incentive plan objectives through plan reassessment. Our second study, *Organizational Performance and Rewards: 663 Experiences in Making the Link* (McAdams and Hawk, 1994), expanded the database and provided information in a topically organized, user-friendly way. This book is the next step. It presents the reinforcement model of the total reward mechanism. Reward plans are often described as ways to *change behavior* and *motivate employees*. While I will discuss these goals in some depth later, they are clearly not the whole story. Changing behavior suggests working harder and faster in one's defined job. It suggests doing things right the first time, for the right reasons. It suggests that consequences drive behavior.

I argue that it is equally important to open up the system, that is, to educate employees in how the business works and what the financial and operation numbers really mean. It is also important to allow and engage people to cooperate in making a difference, to move decision making down to the right level, to create an organization that puts accountability and responsibility on those who do the work, and to reward them as a result of their organizational unit's performance, just as companies have seen fit to reward top management.

I have worked with participatory management, educated workforces, quality, ad hoc, and self-directed work teams since the sixties. Some of these interventions have worked, but without a sharing of organizational performance gains, they do not live up to their potential. Learning the details of SRC's experience was gratifying for me, because it was a real American success story and it reinforced my experience and research. The reward systems described in this book accelerate the performance improvement process and share the rewards with everyone responsible for their success.

Conclusion

In a recent issue, *Business Week* declared SRC a "management mecca," along with AT&T-Universal Card, Motorola, Johnsonville Foods, Saturn, Disney World, Rubbermaid, and USAA (Bryner, 1995). Although each company has a unique contribution to make to the education of management, there is a common theme in their stories: people are as important to success as any other aspect of a company's business. For most of the companies mentioned here, people are their competitive advantage.

Much to my surprise and delight, a public statement was made of a change in attitude about employees by my old employer, General Electric. Jack Welch, chairman and CEO, and Paolo Fresco, vice chairman and executive officer, wrote in 1993, "No matter how many ideas we try, it all comes back to people—their ideas, their motivation, their passion to win" (General Electric 1992 Annual Report, p. 5). In 1994 they wrote, "We are betting everything on our people—empowering them, giving them the resources and getting out of their way—and the numbers tell us that this focus has not only pointed us in the right direction but is providing us with a momentum that is accelerating" (General Electric 1993 Annual Report, p. 2). And in 1995, "We now have a Company that is faster, more confident and higher-spirited than at any time in its history— a Company of people who believe in themselves, in each other, and in their infinite capacity to improve everything" (General Electric 1994 Annual Report, p. 5). This is another example of discovering the employee.

Whether it is the open-book management of SRC, the empowerment of Johnsonville and Saturn employees, the customer focus of AT&T-Universal Card and USAA, the product innovation of Rubbermaid, the engaging management style of Disney, or the cross-functional and open communications of GE, these approaches work only by aligning the strategic objectives of the organization and those of the people—all the people. My experience is that reward systems make a huge difference in improving performance and in the change process. They put some organizational and employee emotional and financial "skin" in the game, creating a competitive advantage.

CHAPTER 3

Objectives and Measurements

The purpose of this chapter is to describe how to establish a *focus* for everyone in your organization by identifying your company's business objectives and measures for assessing their fulfillment as the basis for reward plans.

Everything begins with an organization's objectives. Some of these can be measured by the progress of a project, some as a number; both indicate a result. Some objectives are really statements of intent, such as making all employees contributing stakeholders.

Management's challenge is to prepare and allow people to make a contribution and to share the rewards of performance improvement.

One of the most effective ways an organization can pursue its strategic objectives is to develop a spirit that everyone has a stake in the organization's success by building a sense of responsibility, accountability, and ownership (financially, emotionally, or both). In *Open-Book Management* (1995, p. xvii), John Case writes, "Since the economic future of every blessed individual on a company's payroll depends on whether the company succeeds in the marketplace, everyone who works there is 'in business' all the time, whether they know it or not." Organizations want loyalty, participation, involvement, dedication, hard work, and contributions from their employees, in addition to their just showing up. In return, organizations try to give employees security, appropriate working environments, and opportunities to grow and prosper. But that's not enough today. Management must *prepare* the troops to be able to make a contribution. They have to *allow* employees to make a difference. They must *share* with employees the rewards of the performance improvement.

What You Will Find in This Chapter

This chapter addresses how organizations state what they are all about and how their planning and objective setting processes lay the foundation for reward plans. It discusses:

- Useful missions and visions—and stakeholders

- Business planning and strategic objectives

- Characterizations of people strategies

- How to discover what the "real measures" of success are behind the profit and loss statement (P&L)

- An example of a company's list of business objectives and broad measures for reward plans

Vision, Mission, and Stakeholders

Mission statements often read like organizational versions of the Boy Scout code.

Most companies have vision and mission statements that are intended to be clear declarations of what the company is all about—its values, purpose, and intentions. To the average employee, these statements too often read like organizational versions of the Boy Scout code—"thrifty, brave, clean, and reverent—and cost competitive"—not such a bad idea, if organizations would live up to it.

The degree to which a vision and mission are fulfilled depends, in part, on two things: (1) how well management implements processes to ensure that day-to-day operations reflect the vision and mission, and (2) how much employees actually experience, rather than are just aware of, those processes. The first condition is a function of planning, discipline, accountability, communications, and what is reinforced in the organization. The second condition affects trust and is often ignored. Trust is often viewed as something other than a business issue. I don't mean to sound cynical, but from the rank-and-file employee's view, vision and mission can create trust and provide a central theme of an organization only if clear, tangible supportive processes are in place and operating. That's more than management training, the most common effort to connect vision, mission, and practice.

Management training is how most organizations address the promise of the vision and mission. It focuses on making managers

FIGURE 3.1. *Organizational processes must support a company's vision and mission statement.*

SOURCE: *DILBERT reprinted by permission of United Feature Syndicate, Inc.*

coaches who are employee sensitive, reinforcing, consultative, and supportive of the individual's development. While such training is valuable, it falls too often on ears made deaf by the manager's punishing and directive behavior. It is also difficult to apply without organizational processes, including open communications, education, and reward plans, which are in support of the vision and mission and management training. A Dilbert cartoon captures this situation nicely (see Figure 3.1).

This is not a book about vision and mission statements, but they are your starting point. If your organization already has vision and mission statements, they probably declare as goals something between being all things to all people and "Customers have money, and we want it!" If your organization is without a statement, consider the following:

We have four stakeholders in our company:

1. *Financial stakeholders:* our *stockholders,* who invest in our company and expect a return on their investment

2. *Product and service stakeholders:* our *customers,* who provide a lifetime of revenue potential and expect high value in our products and services compared to others in the marketplace

3. *Community stakeholders:* our *neighbors,* who expect us to operate in a sociably responsible manner

4. *Career stakeholders:* our *employees,* who invest their time, energy, skill, and creativity and who expect to be respected, full

members of the team, with the opportunity to increase their contribution to the team's success and to share in the gains of that
success

Our mission is to ensure that we meet the needs of *all* our stakeholders [adapted from Scanlon Associates, 1993].

In this era of focus on quality, some companies are also including
their suppliers as stakeholders. Suppliers expect to be treated as
business partners in serving the end customer by providing products and services of high value, and they expect to be compensated
in a fair and equitable manner.

This kind of statement provides a context and a framework that
give a business personality, energy, and responsibility. In each category of stakeholder, there are more specific objectives to be accomplished through a process of planning and action.

Although it varies by company, the amount of time and energy
that organizations spend focusing on improving the lot of their
financial stakeholders—usually with short-term financial measurements—seems inordinate. The voice of customers as stakeholders has only recently been rediscovered, and organizations are
wrestling with how to mine that opportunity. To widely varying
degrees, consideration of community stakeholders ranges from
minimal legal environmental conformance to being very generous
participants in the community, contributing to its health and welfare. Organizations spend an enormous amount of money on career
stakeholders, but they pay little attention to the return on that cost
or how it can affect the other three stakeholders.

Business Planning and the Measurement of Performance

In most organizations, top management determines the objectives
that will affect each type of stakeholder, develops strategies and tactics, and cascades them down into the organization. At each suc-
ceeding management level, managers address the objectives they
feel they can influence; they develop their own action plans and
tactics and cascade them down to the next level. And so it goes.
This approach is called a lot of things, but most commonly it is
referred to as management by objectives (MBO).

The deeper the process goes, the harder it is to carry out. The sheer number of objectives, strategies, and tactics can overwhelm even a moderately sized organization. In one strict MBO organization of two thousand employees, there were fifteen objectives with fifty-four strategies and an untold number of tactics at the company-wide level. By the time the process made it down through three levels of management, the numbers ballooned to eighty-four objectives with 260 strategies—and so on. This process simply becomes too cumbersome. The natural reaction is to go through the process, put the plans in a drawer, and see how the company did at the end of the year. (A good indication that this is happening is hearing the phrase, "The power in the plan is the planning process itself.")

Traditional performance evaluation processes attempt to connect individual employees to the cascading objectives—a less than satisfactory process. Even if the objectives, strategies, and tactics could be driven down to the level of the individual employee, measurement and the ensuing accountability would become very difficult. The result is that the employee evaluation, which is supposed to be objective, becomes a subjective process. Even if it is possible to measure individual employee performance, to quantify each employee's contribution against specific objectives, the value of that contribution doesn't flow back up the chain of command very well. Performance improvement gains are not easily captured in a reverse cascade *up* the organization. Maybe someday organizations will get a handle on this problem through managerial accounting or activity-based cost management, but currently it is not a widespread practice.

The overarching issue, however, is that this planning process rests on the "management thinks, employees do," top-down methodology. Emerging approaches to planning and follow-through recognize that organizations work not only top-down but also bottom-up and side-to-side. These approaches require that management determine the strategic objectives and, often, the gaps between where the company is currently and where they want it to be. The gaps are then turned over to the employees to close—with an ever-present awareness of the voice of the customer. The Hoshin planning process, for example, relies heavily on TQM methodology to close these gaps (Bechtell, 1995).

Most MBO systems rest on the "management thinks, employees do," top-down methodology.

***Most of what compa-
nies spend on employ-
ees is comparable to
spending millions on
a generator and only
using it to run emer-
gency lights.***

All companies need a planning and follow-through process. *The connection between planning and performance can be profoundly improved when employees are treated and rewarded as valued contributing stakeholders.* Right now, most of what companies spend on employees is comparable to spending millions on a generator and only using it to run emergency lights.

People Strategy and Follow-Through

People strategies can be characterized as:

1. Getting the right people and keeping them (attracting and retaining)
2. Making people more effective in their specific jobs (or broadly defined roles) and as people to be developed to meet the organization's needs
3. Improving the organization's business performance

The first and second needs are generally addressed by a "people strategy" section of a strategic plan. Organizations spend about 90 to 95 percent of their labor dollar getting and keeping the right people and trying to make them more effective as individuals. The specific reinforcement plans for these strategies are known as *individual compensation and capability plans.* Measurement of improvement in these two objectives is rarely boiled down to a few numbers. The third objective—improving the organization's performance—can be measured objectively and is just becoming a role for the rank and file. It is generally considered the responsibility of management, to be carried out by employees.

Attracting and Retaining Employees

The attract-and-retain objective is a complex one. Attracting the right people—identifying the organization's needs, recruiting and evaluating candidates, hiring the appropriate ones, offering them enough pay (but not too much), and starting them off properly—affects how successful a company is going to be. Retention of the rank and file, however, has been primarily a cost-control strategy. Organizations try to retain employees at minimum cost. In normal times, deliberative administration of base compensation focuses on limiting the growth of fixed labor costs while maintaining the appropriate turnover rate and getting the new people the company needs. This approach is fundamentally maintenance oriented, either by design or by evolution.

In more difficult times, such as in the past few years, labor cost control becomes cost reduction through salary freezes and layoffs. Such moves can be of great benefit to financial stakeholders in the short term, and devastating to career stakeholders in both the short and long term. Many of these actions can be justified. The attract-and-retain objectives are overwhelmed by "do or die" business performance objectives. The only stakeholders who win in this process are the financial stakeholders. The other stakeholders take it in the chops.

Labor cost control through layoffs benefits the financial stakeholder in the short run, but can devastate employees in the short and long runs.

Clearly, the forms of compensation plans—such as individual incentives, employee ownership, skill and competency development, and some merit increases—can influence individual performance. There is little evidence that beefing up these plans will affect overall business performance. It simply is not their purpose.

Making People More Effective

Making people more effective is both an individual and a collective developmental issue. Individual incentives, promotions, and merit increases (all base compensation plans) can have some effect, but the real hope is in thinking about employees as people rather than as the job they do. Be they competency- or skill-based, capability plans focus on developing the individual's ability to do the job and to make a contribution to the organization. They are currently just taking hold in the United States. The arguments favoring the necessity of aligning core organizational competencies with the competencies of every employee are compelling. The process has been developed; the deployment is a considerable challenge, requiring total management involvement over the long haul. Again, it is the individual employee who is directly affected. This practice is too new for us to know its effect on financial stakeholders.

In both the first and second broad people strategies, the effect on the product and service stakeholder—the customer—depends on how much the voice of the customer is considered in designing and implementing the individual compensation and capability plans. Without a voice, this critical group of stakeholders may not experience the effect of a plan. As we begin to understand the connection between employee satisfaction and customer satisfaction, however, employee satisfaction gains, largely influenced by improved compensation plans, may lead to better service to customers.

Improving Business Performance

Recognition and group-based reward plans can satisfy all four stakeholders.

Satisfying financial stakeholders by improving business performance has been management's job. Command-and-control organizations seem to believe that only management can really address this objective. The development of recognition and group-based reward plans can be a way to satisfy all four stakeholders, assuming that the plans are designed with them in mind. Organizations currently spend relatively little time and money in this area, but it provides the greatest untapped opportunity for growth.

Beginning the Process

The announcement of objectives by management is mildly interesting to employees. Announcing a reward plan to reinforce those objectives *really* gets attention. It telegraphs what is important and where the company is willing to invest its money. A reward system has a different agenda than that of the total business planning process. So, with the business plan as background information, it is often helpful to start with a blank sheet of paper.

Making a List

The first step in developing a total reward plan is to get the leaders of your company or organizational unit to sit down together and draw up a list of the critical issues in your business. You can begin by asking them, "How do you know if this organization is successful or not?" Too simplistic or naive? Not in my experience.

Business objectives tend to look pretty much the same in all companies, but the measures are different. Objectives related to profit, return on net assets, productivity, quality, customer satisfaction, new product introduction, and so forth apply to most organizations, at least in the private sector. Here's a brief list of objectives excerpted from a much longer list from a midwestern company. I'll use it as an illustration throughout the book. The list represents the critical objectives for their success.

Example Business Objectives:

Improve financial performance
Improve productivity
Reduce cycle time
Improve quality
Reduce turnover
Create a flexible workforce
Reduce benefit cost
Develop a contingent workforce for telemarketing department

Determining Measures of Success

If you have an extensive planning process, the odds are you already have objectives for each of your organization's units and that they are cascaded down to some lower organizational level. What are often not included in the planning process are the measures of success: how is performance measured? How do we know we are successful? Developing measures for each objective, strategy, and tactic is a critical step in the planning process, because as I noted earlier, what gets measured gets managed.

For too long, organizations have relied on the P&L as a main indicator of success. Even top management, who have the greatest accountability to financial stakeholders, will admit that the P&L is heavily influenced by factors outside their control. The further one moves down the organizational hierarchy, the more remote and less meaningful the P&L becomes as a motivator. The longer the line of sight to it, the fewer people there are who believe it is an appropriate measure for them. This is less of a problem if employees are financially literate. The lower the literacy, the longer the line of sight.

When I was at GE and going from operation to operation trying to figure out how to improve performance, I discovered the "center drawer" rule of success. I would walk into a manager's office that was piled high with green and white computer paper in fat blue binders and say, "How's it going?" Instead of going to those mounds of data for the answer, the manager would inevitably go to the center desk drawer. He would then pull out an envelope or scrap of paper with four or five numbers scribbled on it and say, "Pretty good."

Most managers know that a few measures consistently determine whether or not they are successful. The planning process and a lot of experience help determine those measures. Sometimes they are appropriate tools for reinforcing performance, and sometimes they are not. Nevertheless, these measures are what management believes to be really important. So, if you can get your management to sit down together, eventually they will come up with their own "center desk drawer" list of what they consider to be the organization's measures of success.

What broad measures will tell them whether they are successful? You will probably get several answers for each objective. Most measures are of business performance. It can be difficult to measure the first two people strategies, that is, to attract, retain, develop, and improve individual performance. Turnover is one potential measure when it is broken down into positive (promotions, transfers, and involuntary termination) and negative (voluntary termination) elements. Employee satisfaction is another. Progress toward these objectives is primarily measured, however, by projects and processes that address workforce flexibility, availability of qualified people for promotion, installation, and operation of a competency-based system, and so forth.

Business performance measures are very specific and abundant. They can be broken down into three groupings: lead, operational, and lag. All are important, and one size does not fit all parts of the organization. Here is an abbreviated list of primary performance measures in the three categories:

Lead: These measures are predictive of success, generally over a long period. Examples are market share, customer satisfaction or value, employee satisfaction (and possibly turnover), new product development, and research and development project cycle time. Some organizations would include sales as a lead measure.

Operational: These are the day-to-day measures most familiar to the rank-and-file employee and their immediate management. Some of these measures are linked directly to the financial statements, some have an indirect influence. Examples are productivity, quality, customer satisfaction or value (it can serve as a

Most managers know that a few measures consistently determine whether or not they are successful.

lead and operational measure), attendance, turnover, cycle time, safety, cost reduction, and project completion.

Lag: Lag measures are the most common and are supported by the accounting system. They include profit, return ratios (return on equity, sales, investment, and so on), economic value added, stock price, dividends, cash value added, cash flow return on investment, and total shareholder return.

Broad Measures and the Reinforcement Model

Objectives and measurements tend to break down into the two sides of the reinforcement model. Interventions that address attraction, retention, development, individual performance improvement, and workforce flexibility are best addressed by compensation and capability plans, which are on the individual side of the model. Business performance results (the lead, operational, and lag measures just listed) are best addressed by the group-based plans on the right side of the model. Recognition works both sides, for it reinforces all processes.

This is not to say that the two sides are mutually exclusive. Obviously, a project team plan could improve turnover, and individual sales commissions could improve business performance. But the most direct alignment of objectives and reinforcement and the best use of an organization's time and money are prescribed by the reinforcement model. (See Figure 1.1 on page 7.)

It is important for your management team to agree on how to measure success and at what level of the organization each measure makes sense to them. At some point, you will probably need to measure lower down in the organization, or break down a measure into more specific ones for different groups. But for now, you need to keep the conversation at this higher and broader level.

My experience is that top management can be very pragmatic. They can appreciate this exercise, and some organizations do it regularly. The leading indicators for one major financial institution are employee satisfaction, customer satisfaction, quality of assets, productivity, and market penetration. Each objective is weighted differently and each objective has a measure. When management asks, "How's it going?" these indicators give them the answer. They are the basis for all employee incentive plans, both management and nonmanagement.

A typical matrix of objectives and measures would resemble the following example, which builds on the list I presented earlier:

Business Objective	Broad Measure
Improve financial performance	Profit or return calculation
Improve productivity	Output divided by input
Reduce cycle time	Days from order to payment
Improve quality	Cost of poor quality
Reduce turnover	Percent of voluntary resignations per total employment
Create a flexible workforce	Skill-based pay installation project milestones
Reduce benefit cost	Benefits as a percentage of total payroll costs
Develop a contingent workforce for telemarketing department	Hire, train, and begin operations with new work

Once you have gone through this whole process with top management, you will have objective statements of what the organization is trying to accomplish. Some of these objectives will be inappropriate to use as a basis for any reward plan. Some of them will be best addressed by individual compensation or capability plans, so they will have a better chance of getting the management support they deserve. Others will be best addressed by recognition and group-based plans, because they lay the foundation for directly aligning what you want to accomplish with what you reinforce.

Conclusion

Developing reward plans often forces all levels of management to come to a consensus on the few critical business objectives and their measures. General business planning sessions, even when they include discussions of the same objectives and measures, tend not to have the brevity and clarity demanded by a reward plan, which requires that all consider the effect on each of the four stakeholders. Developing reward plans requires organizational units to consider what specific measures will reflect their contribution to one at a higher level. The process also requires consensus on the primary messages to the workforce about what's important, how they know how they are doing, and the degree of commitment the organization is willing to make in dollars and cents—in addition to talk and plans.

Few interventions can reinforce the vision and mission and enhance trust like a reward plan designed with the best interests of all four stakeholders in mind.

CHAPTER 4

Assessing Your Current Situation

Now that you are armed with management's blessing and a fist full of actionable business objectives and broad measures, it's time to look at the reward plans that are already at work in your organization and decide what to do with them—keep them, modify them, or pitch them.

You will also want to find out what employees really think about how the organization works. If reward plans are to have a positive effect on the culture of an organization, it is important to know what's currently not so positive. Identification of obstacles to success—real or perceived—in the minds of employees can have some effect on the plan design.

What You Will Find in This Chapter

The scope of this chapter is actually larger than the assessment of an organization's existing reward plans. The chapter will show you:

- How to characterize your organization's present culture using the Four Cultures Model

- How to assess your reward plans using the Reward System Effectiveness Model, including direction aligned with business objectives and desired culture

- How to assess the power of awareness, value, and performance sensitivity

- The importance of employee feedback about "how things

really run around here" and some ideas about what to include in employee research

The assessment process presented in this chapter is based on the *Reward System Effectiveness Model* (see Figure 4.1), which draws on the work of a variety of academics in the organizational effectiveness and human resource fields (Lawler, 1984; Kerr, 1987; Beatty, 1991; Kanungo and Hartwick, 1987). The model was developed by a team of researchers at Maritz Inc. in 1993 as the basis for assessing existing reward plans.

"Direction" focuses on where the organization is going, as defined by its business objectives and the culture that management desires. We have discussed the methodology of determining the primary business objectives and broad measures in Chapter Three. Looking at existing reward plans in light of the objectives they reinforce is perhaps the most critical element of the effectiveness model. Without alignment with objectives, reward plans do not necessarily reinforce what makes the organization successful. The "desired culture" component accomplishes about the same thing with culture rather than objectives.

"Power" addresses how dynamic the reward plans are in meeting their objectives.

"Awareness" can range from passive and expected (base pay) to being top-of-mind (participating on a project team plan). For example, there may be little or no awareness that a company subsidizes an employee cafeteria.

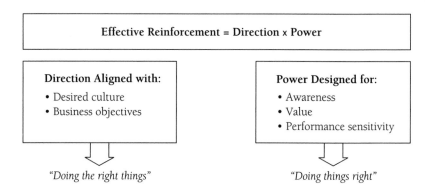

FIGURE 4.1. *The Reward System Effectiveness Model.*

"Value" is the reward plan's contribution to the organization, financial or otherwise. It is also the value to the individual, considering what she had to do differently to earn it. Finally, the "performance sensitivity" element relates the degree of accomplishment to the size of the reward.

An effective reward system relies on the evaluative elements presented in the model and on the degree to which each of those elements is present, properly incorporated, and implemented in the total reward opportunity. It would be easy to say that all of the elements should be cranked up like the components of a sound system, but the best balance of elements depends on the organization's objectives for each plan.

The element of *awareness* is one example of an element whose importance is a function of the organization's objectives for a plan. If people are not very much aware of a reward plan, how can they know what to do to earn a reward? If the reward plan objective is to secretly distribute funds to surprised and delighted employees in the hope that they will feel valued and continue to do good work (and stay with the organization), then you are on the right track. Low awareness in the general employee population is fine in that case. (I discuss this element in more detail later in the chapter.)

The Direction Component: Business Objectives and Desired Culture

The second step in influencing the effectiveness of your reward systems is to determine the nature of the organization's existing culture and then to decide what sort of culture you would like to have.

Characterizing Your Present Culture

Getting management to agree on a desired culture and determining the existing culture may look like a complex challenge. The *Four Cultures Model* (see Figure 4.2) introduced by Narendra Sethia and Mary Ann von Glinow (1985) can greatly simplify the process. I have slightly modified their model to reflect the demands of pragmatic application.

The Four Cultures Model is a matrix that characterizes organizational units as one of four types based on two core values. These

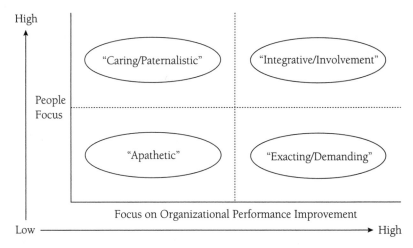

FIGURE 4.2. *The Four Cultures Model.*

SOURCE: *Adapted from Sethia and von Glinow, 1985, pp. 400–420.*

values are *people focus* and *performance improvement focus.* (Please note that this second core value is not "performance" but "performance improvement." Some high-performing companies, often in emerging markets or with patents of fast-selling products, are just running to keep up. Performance improvement is not high on their list of priorities. Therefore, a high-performing company can be low on the performance improvement focus core value scale.)

Apathetic Cultures   Apathetic cultures, located in the lower left quadrant of the model, do not emphasize people *or* performance improvement. In these organizations, seniority rules and procedure is extremely important. "We've always done it that way," is a common reason for any action. You might think these organizations are dysfunctional, but that's not necessarily true. Managers in these organizations are extremely bound by procedure because they've been reinforced to provide continuity. That way they can guarantee output, whether it's widgets or guidelines, and protect themselves from any criticism.

People who are attracted to apathetic organizations think there is high job security there. Such people tend to be risk-averse and noncompetitive. Not surprisingly, promotions in apathetic organizations are slow and automatic, evaluations are rare, "playing by the rules" is important, and politics and deal making are common.

The general public often feels that government agencies at all levels of our public structure fall into the apathetic quadrant. Just as it is unfair, as well as inaccurate, to characterize all government organizations as apathetic, it would be inappropriate to place any company in any one quadrant. But almost every organization has its apathetic unit. At one of the GE plants where I worked, it was the security department. Run like an army without a mission, security simply did not care. We used to joke that if we wanted to steal a new copier, security would hold open the door for us. When I was in sales, the apathetic department was the financial unit responsible for expense accounts. It is frustrating and demoralizing to those in exacting/demanding or integrative/high involvement organizational units to be dependent upon apathetic ones to get their work done.

Every organization has its apathetic unit.

Caring/Paternalistic Cultures   A core value of caring/paternalistic cultures is a focus on people, with significantly less concern for performance improvement than the organizations on the right side of the Four Cultures Model. As with apathetic organizations, people are attracted to caring/paternalistic organizations by what they believe to be high job security, but the comparison stops there. Caring/paternalistic organizations show concern for their employees, who tend to receive relatively high—or certainly competitive— pay and good benefits. In these organizations, people feel trusted, and they generally believe they are treated fairly. Employee satisfaction is very important; caring/paternalistic organizations can be seen leading the way in meeting employee needs for day care, flextime, special personal services, and so forth. Tenure, position (senior deputy executive director reporting to the senior executive director), "fitting in," effort and activity (not necessarily results), and promotion from within are valued.

Caring/paternalistic organizations are surprisingly hierarchical and are often characterized as having an iron fist in a velvet glove. A good friend described his experience: "I made a decision that was right for the company and for the customer, but was considered outside of tradition. They came down on me like a ton of bricks. It was as if I had injured a family unit, rather than a business one. I'm president of the company now and, in looking back, I think their feelings were hurt more than anything else."

Caring/paternalistic organizations are often characterized as having an iron fist in a velvet glove.

Organizations with this culture have been most effective in mature, capital intensive companies where systemwide integration is critical, change is slow, and competition is minimal. Many utilities are classic examples of caring/paternalistic organizations. Do they care about their people? You bet. Do they pay them well, and do they have good benefits? Absolutely. Do they communicate with them? Yes. But they also tend to be highly structured. They protect themselves, thinking and rethinking every decision. Change is often forced by outside influences—like deregulation.

Exacting/Demanding Cultures   Organizations with exacting/demanding cultures have reward plans that emphasize the organizations' core value: a concern for organizational performance improvement—usually financial.

Exacting/demanding organizations have been most effective in quickly growing businesses with fast-changing markets—businesses in which the emphasis is on sales and bottom-line performance. These organizations are sometimes referred to as "eat what you kill" companies. Stockbrokers, law firms, and some consulting practices are good examples. They focus on efficiency, competition, individual performance, and job position. They are often learning organizations, constantly working to change and adapt to maintain their competitive edge.

Many exacting/demanding companies tend to be "up or out" organizations. They usually pay well, but the pay is based solely on performance. If you don't perform, you're gone, and that's how these companies survive and prosper. How long would a telemarketing firm last if it were a caring/paternalistic organization? Not long.

Some of the most successful companies fit this model, and they are exciting and challenging places to work. They are constantly challenging themselves to improve. They cannot be characterized as heartless or uncaring—just highly competitive. If they have leading-edge benefit plans—such as a special services desk to handle personal tasks like dropping off or picking up dry-cleaning—you can be sure the intention is to increase employees' productivity, not to be altruistic.

Lincoln Electric is the classic example of an exacting/demanding organization. Hugely successful as a leading manufacturer of welding equipment in the United States, every factory employee earns on piece rate (what they produce) with no sick days or vacation paid by the company. Individual bonuses are a function of the profit, adjusted by each employee's performance review, often by peers. The review is based on production, quality, ideas, and team-work. Their lifetime employment guarantee is workable because of their piece rate system (with its 70,000 piece rate standards), peer pressure, and the extensive screening of new employees. Individual performance is exactly measured and is demanded for employment.

Integrative/High Involvement Cultures   The integrative/high involvement organization emphasizes both core values—people *and* performance. These companies are innovative. They foster cooperation, risk taking, and group performance improvement. They nurture their people, yet they are constantly concerned about improving performance. These are the true learning organizations. They accomplish their goals by involving people. They communicate, accept considerable feedback, and are egalitarian. This doesn't mean they are any less competitive or focused than other organizational cultures, but they tend to believe that a team-oriented environment is the most effective way to utilize the human asset.

The most contemporary examples of integrative/high involvement organizations are detailed in Stack's (1994) and Case's (1995) books on open-book management. Of the primary precepts of this approach, employee involvement is the critical element. The other precepts are sharing all the information, creating financial literacy in all the people, and giving everyone a stake in the game through a group incentive plan and/or stock ownership. This prepares employees to be informed as they become involved and gives them a financial reason for doing so. But it is involvement of all the career stakeholders—the employees—that makes the difference. Their knowledge, decisions, contributions, commitments, and accountability as an integrative/high involvement workforce are a demonstration of what can happen when companies trust and invest in their human assets.

Using the Model   To determine your organization's overall culture, look at each of its suborganizational units in terms of the four cultures just described, decide where it fits, and place a dot in the appropriate quadrant of the matrix. No company of any size will fit into just one quadrant on the matrix. Every organization is made up of many smaller organizations, each of which has its own individual culture or gradient of a culture. But you will end up with a cluster of dots that probably hits all of the quadrants while tending to gravitate toward one of the cultures. Figure 4.3 is an example of what a completed matrix might look like.

Decisions about where on the matrix to place a particular unit can be based on management interviews (known as "management SWAG" or "s'wild-ass guess") or on a formal organizational assessment. For those who prefer the formal organizational assessment approach, it is done with a series of surveys, management interviews, and focus groups. Questions are asked ranging from how managerial jobs are defined to how managers are viewed to how much risk taking is encouraged by the rank and file.

Generally, about twenty to thirty questions are asked. The answer to each question can be slotted into a culture category. For example, the question, "How is performance appraisal viewed?" may be answered and slotted as follows:

"As a development tool" (caring/paternalistic)

"As an evaluation tool" (exacting/demanding)

"As both a development and evaluation tool" (integrative/high involvement)

"What's performance evaluation?" (apathetic)

People may argue about how some of the feedback should be slotted (for example, is it exacting or integrative?), but when you

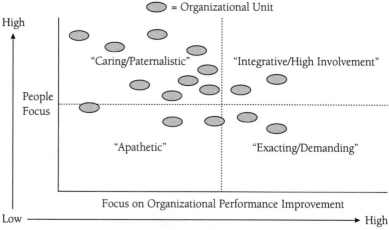

FIGURE 4.3. *Completed Four Cultures Model—Existing Culture.*

do it for all organizational units, you will have an accurate characterization of your existing culture.

An example of how unit cultures differ might be as follows: the sales and marketing departments might fall in the exacting/demanding quadrant, maintenance and finance in the apathetic quadrant, customer service and engineering in the integrative/high involvement quadrant, and all other units in the caring/paternalistic quadrant. The more you break down your organization into its component parts and determine their unique cultures, the more accurately you will be able to characterize your current total organizational culture.

Desired Culture   Management generally agrees on what it wants the desired culture to be. It may vary by organizational unit, but there is a general sense of what is most appropriate for the business. I find a discussion about desired culture is best held after the work has been done to determine the existing culture in the context of the Four Cultures Model. There will be a good deal of surprise and discussion of the outcome, as there usually is with the results of employee feedback, but it is an extremely useful process

.

Organizational Culture and Reward Systems   In order for an organization to shape its culture, must its reward plans—which send strong messages about what is important—support the desired culture? At the moment, they probably reflect your existing culture. If your reward plans are based on management discretion and subjective evaluations, then the caring/paternalistic culture is being reinforced. That's fine, if that's what you want. But if you want an integrative/high involvement culture, your plans are not working in concert with your desires. (I'm always surprised by how many *caring/paternalistic* or *exacting/demanding* organizations say they want to become more *integrative/high involvement.*)

How many companies preach teamwork without a single reward plan that reinforces working as a team?

The most common example of such a discrepancy is a company that preaches teamwork but does not have a single reward plan that reinforces people for working together toward a common objective. The organization may contribute a portion of profits into a 401(k) plan, but this is seen as an entitlement that comes with being an employee. This is an illustration of the difference between talking the talk and walking the talk.

Changing Culture Through Management Direction   In recent years, a lot of "solid" companies have gone through wrenching changes. These changes are a result of trying to compete in a changing market with the same old paradigms of doing business. In most cases (IBM, DEC, McDonnell Douglas, and The Travelers are a few of the most obvious examples), these companies needed to improve their performance, and they almost waited too long before they started to change things.

The approach in these organizations was for management to intervene, restructure, reengineer, refocus, and reform in desperate but necessary moves. The story of how each company is doing it would require a book on each, but in most cases, the method will work—and the employees will pay the price. Most of the companies started with a caring/paternalistic culture. The changes made were seen by the employees as Draconian, violating everything that, in the employees' minds, made the companies great. But management didn't have any choice. It was too late to begin the process of becoming an integrative/high involvement company, which could have had the same effect—improved performance—without the human toll, if management had paid attention and taken action much earlier. The line, "it's tough to drain the swamp when you're up to your tail in alligators" is a wise old adage.

Business Objectives

In Chapter Three, I discussed the importance of determining and measuring the organization's business objectives. It should be a pretty simple matter to determine the degree of alignment between your existing reward plans and the business objectives of the organization. If your objective is profit, how many of your employees are covered by a reward plan that reinforces improving profits? How about customer satisfaction? Or cost reduction? Or productivity?

Alignment is relatively straightforward. Reward plans should reinforce those things that will support your desired culture and your business objectives.

The Power Component: Awareness, Value, and Performance Sensitivity

The second element of effective compensation/reward plans is *power*. For a reward system to be powerful, it must create a high degree of *awareness* among employees, be *valued* by employees and the organization, and possess a structure that is *sensitive to performance levels.*

Awareness

Awareness (top-of-mind) is the degree to which a reward plan is present in the minds of employees. A reward plan must capture and sustain people's attention. Obviously, a performance reward plan with low awareness is not as effective as one with high awareness.

Awareness depends on how much communication and promotion is done on a plan's behalf, as well as the amount of focus given by immediate management. It also depends on how well employees understand the plan. (People avoid what they don't understand.) Employee behavior is a gauge of awareness. If people are reinforced for working on special teams, pay more attention to details, or focus on what's best for the customer because of a plan, then their awareness is high.

The amount of management support has a direct bearing on awareness. The CARS research on the impact of group incentives on performance (discussed in Chapter Two) demonstrated that management support and involvement are critical factors in any plan's success. That support is most effective when it is integrated with the day-to-day workings of the managerial process, particularly at the first-line supervisory level. A plan that is aligned with the organization's objectives should be another tool to help management meet their goals. The more useful a plan is as a management tool, the greater will be the natural awareness of it throughout the organization. Of course, with awareness of all parties comes accountability, and the real opportunity for everyone to collaborate.

An employee assistance program (EAP) is a good example of an important benefit that is of great value to employees as well as to the health of the organization. (An EAP is a benefit in which employees can receive confidential counseling for personal issues, at no cost to them. The initiation can be at the request of a supervisor, or the employee can act alone.) The key to an EAP's success, however, is how aware people—particularly supervisors—are of the program and what it can do. Industry spends billions of dollars on EAPs, yet generally relies on a few posters in the hall and one short training session for first-line supervisors (often not repeated for new supervisors) for awareness. When EAPs are underused, they are cost inefficient (most are flat fee, regardless of usage) and a lost opportunity for employees and the organization.

Awareness is also a function of the type and size of the award. The most common award, money, has to come in ever-increasing amounts to keep the attention of employees, particularly the higher you go in the organization. Other types of awards, often of far less financial value, such as catalogue merchandise, travel, dinners, concert tickets, or days off with pay, have a much higher awareness and recognition component than money.

Value to the Employee

Powerful rewards are those perceived by the recipient to have value in either financial or psychic terms. Financial value is expressed as a percentage of base pay or a flat dollar amount. Rewards with psychic value meet intrinsic needs and reinforce self-esteem and peer acceptance. They have lasting value and high recognition content. They can be just about anything that fills a basic social or psychological need: time off, educational opportunities, merchandise (trophies of performance), travel, feedback, or training.

Chapter Ten includes a discussion of the need for organizations to expand their use of a variety of awards to enhance the effectiveness of the reward plan. This need for variety can be boiled down to employees' perceptions of value. Some are looking for more money—the more the better. The amount is paramount if it is carrying the lion's share of the *power* component. For example, if a plan has little *awareness* and minimal *performance sensitivity,* the cash award has to be big enough to cause people to create their own awareness and figure out how to earn despite the system. A profit sharing plan that pays out once a year, has little communication or involvement, and is an "all or nothing" design needs a very large award to have any effect on how people perform. Group incentive plans with a good deal of communication, involvement, management support, and feedback mechanisms very often show significant performance gains even with modest awards (3 to 5 percent of base pay).

Project team incentive plans, which use award points that can be accumulated for merchandise, regularly outperform plans that use amounts of cash that are larger than the worth of the merchandise. The noncash award provides a greater *perceived* value to the employee than the equivalent amount of cash, in part due to the psychic trophy value of these unique items.

Value to the Organization

To the organization, value means results. Results are measured in financial terms—the payout and administrative costs, the dollar value of the performance gains, and the return on payout (relationship of gain to payout). Perhaps equally important are the subjective contributions of the plan that cannot be accurately measured in dollar terms. These contributions are satisfaction of customers, teamwork, management/rank-and-file communications, education on business principles, common focus on objectives, and process improvement.

Performance Sensitivity

Effective reward plans are also sensitive, that is, connected to performance levels. Performance sensitivity has two elements: *contingency* (do this and get that) and *discrimination* (the better you do, the more you earn). In our CARS research, Elizabeth Hawk and I called performance sensitivity the "performance-reward link." The connection can be as extreme as an "all or nothing" design that pays out only when very high goals are reached, which is not very effective. More commonly, however, a plan rewards performance by providing higher rewards for escalating levels of performance, according to a preannounced awards schedule.

> *Sensitivity in recognition plans means matching the reward to the employee's contribution, then reinforcing the right employees.*

A recognition plan is a good example of performance sensitivity without a preannounced awards schedule. The very nature of the after-the-fact approach is to surprise and delight the selected employee. Sensitivity in recognition plans means calibrating the reward to the accomplishment and contribution of the employee, then reinforcing the right employees. Again, the purpose of the effectiveness model is to determine effectiveness of the plan according to the plan's objectives. If the objective is something other than performance, the performance sensitivity is a neutral element. Benefits, along with most other entitlements, are good examples.

Assessing Your Reward Plans

Now it's time to assess your existing reward plans. Do they support the desired direction in terms of culture and objectives? Are they top-of-mind, performance sensitive, and valuable? How much do they cost? Do they get results? An assessment can be as simple as looking at each reward plan through the filter of these questions to get a snapshot of your reward plans. A computer analysis, however, is ultimately worth the effort.

How Many Plans Do You Have?

You will probably be surprised at the sheer number of compensation and reward plans you will find when you go looking for them. Of course, some are fundamental, like base salary with its accompanying merit increases, cost-of-living adjustments, and benefit plans. There are also rewards for things like attendance, safety, and quality.

Beyond the obvious awards, there is another layer that is likely to show up during your search. Some people will say that their title or the size of their cubicle or where they park their car is a reward. These benefits may not be seen as awards by the company, but they are, nevertheless, reinforcing to employees.

Rewards can also extend to such things as having a private office, a special business card, a leased car, a car phone, or a compensation plan that pays 30 percent of base salary for improving return on net assets. They can include the opportunity to earn a trip to Hawaii, or to choose a large-screen TV from a catalogue, or to eat in a subsidized cafeteria. Almost anything that people see as reinforcing should be included as part of your organization's current reward portfolio.

I've not found a sizable company that has been able to say accurately how many reward plans they have or how much they spend on those plans. No matter what number management chooses, the real figure is usually significantly higher. The large midwestern company I use as an example has a number of locations. Its management initially said they had six reward plans. It turned out they had thirty-four plans, not including things like plants in the office and a subsidized cafeteria. There were plans in which people were getting tangible rewards for everything from improving cycle time to just showing up. The company was spending far more than it thought it was; it did not know what it was getting in return; it had a number of plans with conflicting objectives for the same employees; and it had seriously underestimated the variety of messages sent by all the reward plans.

How does that happen? Every organization has people like Fred, manager of customer service. Fred desperately needs to keep his people answering telephone calls within three rings and with good cheer. He creates all kinds of little reward plans and somehow finds the money to fund them in order to get the job done. That shows a lot of ingenuity on Fred's part.

The problem comes when there are twenty Freds out there doing the same thing. Most people who design such plans do it with little attention to the other plans that are in place. These homegrown plans tend to fall into a trap in which rewards are based on subjective rather than objective criteria—generally at the manager's discretion. Also, the plan often stays long after the need has gone.

Reward plans often stay long after the need has gone.

With all that in mind, you can see why doing a thorough inventory of the plans you now have in place is critical to this process. If you don't know where you are, it's pretty tough to get where you want to go. You would think that you could go to the human resource department to get this information, but they usually don't keep track of all these plans. They can only get you information on base pay, merit increases, cost-of-living adjustment, bonuses, benefits, and company-sponsored perks.

Individuals are often responsible for company-wide suggestion, quality, and recognition plans, all of which can carry rewards. The hard part comes in finding all the other plans in each operation.

Analyzing the Results of Your Inventory

The depth to which you delve into everything that is reinforcing depends on how serious you are about shaping your organization's culture. If you are concerned about the hierarchical nature (command and control) of the organization and want to create a greater sense of egalitarianism, it would be a good idea to extend your research into the more subtle reinforcing symbols. Private parking places (for both executives and their secretaries and associates), executive dining rooms, and company-installed and -maintained plants in private offices are some of the most common perks that send the "management versus worker" message. If such a message is not adversarial, it at least communicates that management is special—and nonmanagement is not. These perks are not provided to make the company more competitive in the labor market. In fact, they strike a discordant note after a rousing speech to all employees about how everyone must work together as a team.

I've found that asking each manager to complete a matrix for those plans he or she controls or funds can ferret out the information in a reasonable time. The following items have proved helpful when used as headings on such a matrix:

Plan name

Objectives

Design

Organization unit(s) covered

Number of people covered

Percent earning

Average or median award value for those earning

Total cost

Type of award

Table 4.1 contains a completed assessment from the midwestern company I referred to earlier. Let's assume that the matrix includes all of the plans in the organization. The company is a caring/paternalistic organization (note the entitlements of CoLA, 401(k), merit increases, and the management discretion-driven Super Heroes employee-of-the-month plan). The organization's desired culture, however, is integrative/high involvement. "Teamwork" is the theme of every corporate communication.

The company's business objectives are profit, productivity, cycle time, and new-product development. Base pay is paid out every two weeks, a Super Hero is recognized monthly, and all the rest are

TABLE 4.1. *Inventory of Reward Plans at a Midwest Company.*

PLAN NAME	OBJECTIVES	DESIGN AND ORGANIZATIONAL LEVEL MEASURED	# OF PEOPLE COVERED	% EARNINGS	AVERAGE OR MEDIAN AWARD VALUE (FOR THOSE WHO EARN)	TOTAL COST AND TYPE OF AWARD
Salary	Attract and retain	• Defined by job • Individuals	4,000	100%	$27,000	• $110 million • Cash
CoLA	Attract and retain	• Same % of base pay for all • All non-exempt as a group	2,000	100%	$800	• $1.6 million • Cash
Merit Increases	Attract and retain Improve individual performance	• Based on performance management; management discretion • Exempt as individuals	2,000	95%	$1,750	• $3.3 million • Cash
401(K)	Retain	• 50% of all profits over threshold • All employees as a group	4,000	100%	$1,250	• $5 million • Cash
Super Heros	Role models; retain	• Management nomination • Individuals	3,990	1%	$100	• $4,000 • Merchandise
Total (without benefits)						• $119,904,000

annual. Communication is limited to performance reviews, mailing out revisions of the reward plans whenever they occur, and the company newsletter article on the yearly payouts for the 401(k) and CoLA. Super Heroes are announced each month in the newsletter, and their pictures are mounted in the "Hall of Fame." The design of each plan is pretty standard, except the 401(k) contribution, which is based on a percentage of net profits over the amount necessary to provide a targeted return on equity—something I'm sure every employee understands.

How effective are these plans? Considering what the organization wants, not very. Following is an assessment of the plans in terms of the effectiveness model:

Direction
Desired culture: integrative/high involvement. Only the 401(k) plan might be capable of supporting the company's desire to become an integrative/high involvement organization, since it is a reward for group performance. However, the complex and remote nature of the measure, not to mention the fact that the award is deferred until termination or retirement, lessens the impact. That deferral reduces its potential to be supportive of an integrative/high involvement culture. The rest of the company's plans are focused on individuals, not teamwork.

Business objectives: profit, productivity, cycle time, and new product development. Again, with the exception of the remote 401(k) plan, none of the plans is based on any of the company's specific business objectives.

Power
Awareness: Base pay has passive awareness, but it will not have a great effect on how people perform. The Super Heroes plan gets the most attention, with 1 percent of the people being recognized. The rest of the plans have a high entitlement content and draw attention only once a year.

Value to the employees: Employees share $9.9 million in addition to salary, an average of $1,225 in CoLA and merit increases during the most recent year; $1,250 is put in a deferred retirement account. Forty people get a $100 merchandise award each year.

Value to the organization: The only link to performance gain is the profit-based 401(k). I doubt that anyone would say that there is any connection between the creation of profit and this rather benign plan.

Performance sensitivity: Salary is job-based and priced on the competitive labor market. CoLA is sensitive only to the cost-of-living index. Merit increases continually struggle to be individually performance sensitive, but with a pool of funds and subjective measures of individual performance, it becomes a distribution method rather than a performance-sensitive plan. 401(k) is funded on a performance-sensitive basis of profit, but it is dulled by the remote, complex formula and the deferral of the award into a retirement account. The Super Heroes plan is a subjective selection process, and most of its sensitivity lies in those who don't get selected.

I would characterize these plans as a $9.9 million investment in a "field of dreams"—spend and maybe they will improve.

Clearly, each plan has its positive side. Base pay is necessary to attract and retain employees. It was not designed to improve organizational performance and should not be held accountable for doing so. Merit increases and CoLA essentially are adjustment to base pay to keep up with inflation, a necessary process if you want to hold onto your people. (*Some* merit increase plans are tied to effective performance management plans and can do a creditable job in developing and directing people in their jobs or roles.) Retirement or 401(k) plans are primarily retention devices, funded by profit. (These plans are transferable as the employee changes jobs, but there is no guarantee that the new company will have a 401(k) plan.) Employee-of-the-month plans are attempts to communicate that the company values its employees. All are focused on only one objective: to attract and retain employees.

Once you have completed the assessment process, it will become apparent which plans should be retained, which can be made to work with modifications, and which should be scrapped. Every organization reinforces employees in a number of ways. As organizations get bigger or more complex or more empowered, these reinforcement plans multiply.

Such unfocused proliferation of plans can inadvertently be counter to the purpose of creating synergy among plans. Synergy is necessary if organizations are to improve performance in a cost-effective manner. Too many of us think in silos—that is, we think of merit increase plans without considering the organization's mission. We design recognition plans in a vacuum, as if the group incentive plan didn't exist. One plan reinforces supervisors for budget control, while another rewards rank-and-file employees for new ideas that could require going over budget—and neither plan may relate to the ongoing communications campaign for improving customer service. Silo thinking is an inefficient, expensive, and even counterproductive way for an organization to capitalize on its human assets.

What Do Your Employees Really Think?

Establishing the culture you want requires making sure you know what that culture is and analyzing existing reward plans to find out what's reinforced in a company. Finally, employees tell us what really happens. Can you skip this part? Sure, if your intent is to simply control costs or redistribute a pool of funds. If you want to remove the barriers to real employee involvement in affecting performance, this step is crucial. It also gets top management's attention.

Employee feedback can be gathered through a combination of surveys and focus groups. Focus groups generally establish the questions to ask in the survey.

The primary areas of investigation are pretty common, and there are consulting firms standing in line to do this work for you. At one time, consultants tried to sell companies a "readiness" assessment for a reward plan. The assumption was that a company might not be ready to install in a cost-effective manner the plans it designed to meet its organizational objectives. Certainly, a few firms are not ready—and if they aren't, it is most likely a temporary situation that reduces the likelihood of success.

An assessment of employee opinion is intended to generate a list of the barriers, or speed bumps, to organizational success. You can address these obstacles in a plan's design and implementation. Here are some general areas in which to gather information:

Trust

- Do employees believe what the company says?

- Does the believability change based on the source of the information (such as an organizational level or function)?

- Does the company follow through when it says something will happen?

- To what degree does the company live up to its own vision and mission?

Information Sharing

- How well do employees understand the company's vision and mission? The business objectives of the company? Of the business unit? Of the department? Of the work group?

- Do the employees have enough information to do their jobs? To make a contribution outside of their jobs?

- How well do employees understand the competitive situation? Changes in the market? Names of competitors? The company's competitive advantage?

- How well do employees understand the measures of the objectives? What affects the measures? How important they are?

Customers

- Who are the external customers? Internal customers?

- How do they measure the quality of the company's service?

- How are they satisfied?

- How important is their satisfaction to the company?

- How does the employee's unit, department, or division behave in light of the needs of the customers?

Existing Compensation, Reward, and Recognition Plans

- What do employees get paid for? Is the reinforcement enough for what is being asked in return? Too much?

- Do the plans work? Do they affect how employees do their jobs?

- Are they fair?

- Do they encourage corporate citizenship?

Performance Improvement

- What needs to be improved? Why?

- What gets in the way of improvement? Procedures? First-line supervisors? Middle management? Top management? Other departments or work groups?

- Can improvement happen? How?

Listening

- Who listens to employees? Does anything happen as a result?

- What happens to ideas? Are they well received? Does anything happen?

Reinforcement

(These questions can be an approach to finding out "What's important around here?")

- What would happen to employees who did these things (ranging from definitely negative consequences to definitely positive consequences)? Would they:
    Improve customer satisfaction (resolve complaints, go out of their way to satisfy, step out of their job, and so on)?
    Reduce costs and improve processes?
    Add value to products or services?
    Prevent problems by planning ahead?
    Develop themselves by improving their skills and competencies?
    Use quality tools?
    Learn about the financial health and workings of the company?
    Get along with others? Coach others? Listen to others?
    Work on task forces?
    Be loyal?
    Take work home?
    Look busy?
    Play politics? Say what management wants to hear?
    Participate in community service?
    Stay within budget?

Gathering and analyzing these data is a profession in itself. Two techniques I've seen that have been particularly helpful are:

Allowing employees to give a range of answers and, when possible, ask or derive importance

The "say/do" approach, or asking employees to rate on a scale what the organization says and what it does on each question (which is enlightening for determining the amount of trust in the work force)

Feedback from such inquiries identifies the areas in information sharing, communications, education, feedback, employee involvement, and reinforcement that will have to be addressed, to varying degrees, to refurbish the total earning opportunity.

Conclusion

Assessment is often considered an overwhelming project, and it certainly can be. But it is as critical a step as any in the entire process of improving performance through people. Understanding what is and needs to be reinforced in an organization provides clear guidelines for whatever redesign of reward plans is necessary.

This process of assessment also uncovers the obstacles to success—be they lack of trust, poor communications, unreasonable expectations, or a dysfunctional culture in a few organizational units—that can be part of new or refurbished plans. Such obstacles can reduce the effectiveness of a new plan. They can be overcome if you know what and where they are.

At a minimum, such a process gives you an actionable road map of what you have now, what's needed, and the speed bumps you have to smooth out as you consider revamping your reward plans.

PART TWO

INDIVIDUAL COMPENSATION

So much has been written and taught about individual compensation over the past fifty years that it would be inappropriate to rehash all the methodologies, logic, law, and variations that have created the "profession" of compensation. Compensation is maintained, reviewed, and adjusted almost every year for everyone in the organization.

For middle management, professionals, first-line supervisors, and the rank and file, there is little argument about the role of individual compensation in employee motivation. (Executive compensation is almost a profession in itself, and the subject of many a controversy.) Individual compensation's role is to get people to work, keep them from leaving, hopefully improve their individual performance, and in some plans, to reinforce the addition of skills and competencies. The role of individual compensation is a critical and vital one, but it is often misunderstood. The objective of the next two chapters is to briefly describe the behavioral modification basics of individual motivation, arguments against it, and my own view on how to make it work for you. I will also cover my view of the elements of individual compensation, their objectives, and some thoughts on making sure that you know what you're getting for your money.

Behavior and the Individual

It is fashionable (and wise) these days for organizations to say that employees are a valued asset and should be treated as such. Organizations naturally focus on the individual employee and her or his behavior. Most individual reinforcement plans are on the left side of the reinforcement model, and they fulfill the employer side of the employee-employer agreement. They focus on reinforcing the behavior of individuals which, it is hoped, will lead to improved performance for the organization.

What You Will Find in This Chapter

Behavior modification is one of the fundamental elements of improving individual performance. There are some opposing views. This chapter looks at these concerns through the eyes of a practitioner who only cares what works in the business world over the short and long term. It includes discussion on:

- The importance of performance management

- The behavioral model, and base pay adjustments (merit increases) in the context of the model

- An opposing view of behavioral modification and what aspects of that view can be used in organizations

The Importance of Performance Management

There are good, solid business reasons for rewarding people variously as individuals, teams, and organizations. Improving organizational performance through people is a balancing act between focusing on individuals and groups as small as a work group to groups as large as the entire organization. The available books on improving individual performance—from business self-help books on motivation, discovery, esteem, awareness, team participation, communication, appearance, and leadership to technical books on training, skill development, job design, job evaluation, and performance management to individual compensation books on job-market pricing, merit pay, skill- and competency-based pay, and the so-called "pay for performance"—could fill a library. While no real data are available, I would guess that 90 percent of what has been published is about improving individual performance.

For years, organizations have believed that the way to improve organizational performance is to get every individual to do a better job. Somehow, the improved individual performance would accumulate and make its way into the profit and loss statement. Little data are available to prove that this actually happens, but the logic that individual performance improvement is critical is compelling.

The most common term for this effort is *performance management*. This is an individual-based process that usually takes place between an employee and his direct manager. It involves setting expectations, observing behavior, determining performance, coaching, and providing feedback—all of which results in a review discussion—the performance review. This process is being expanded to include 360-degree reviews, which get additional performance input from other employees, generally funneled through the immediate manager. The idea is that 360-degree reviews expand the scope and (it is hoped) improve the accuracy of the performance feedback. Millions of dollars are spent on performance management training for both the manager and the employee. It is a critical process and one that derives its success from ongoing communications among all the parties.

In a study of 437 companies, all sizes of companies and industries reported on their use of performance management (Hewitt Associates, 1994). An analysis was done of their financial performance, which was compared to that of companies that did not use performance management. In some cases, performance was determined before and after performance management was installed. In almost all of the cases, "companies with performance management programs have higher profits, better cash flow, stronger stock market performance, and a greater stock value than companies without performance management" (p. 1). That was true both generally and within industry groups. Productivity was also better in companies that used performance management. This is pretty compelling evidence that if people are treated as valued assets to be developed, it pays off for the organization.

The connection between performance management and pay is quite another issue, however. In the study, there was no common practice in linking merit increases to performance management, although 95 percent of companies made some connection (Hewitt, 1994, p. 14). Performance management is often tagged with the "pay for performance" label, and in my opinion that has screwed up the process. What was actually a coaching process designed for people development has been codified, legislated, and organized into one that distributes a pool of funds. I discuss the problems with merit increases in the next chapter, but I believe that the addition of rewards to performance management has spoiled an important process. By taking the focus off the coaching and developmental aspect and putting it into a justification for a small percentage increase to base pay, organizations have taken line managers off the hook. The measurement of managerial effectiveness in performance management has become meeting the time line to get the individual performance reviews and evaluations in so that the increases can be put into the computer for the new pay period.

By taking the focus off coaching we take management off the hook.

I always ask members of my audiences to raise their hands if they believe their performance management process is the basis for base pay adjustments. Most do. When asked to raise their hands if they think the process works pretty well, few do. I am struck by how dissatisfied people are with the performance management/merit increase connection. This is not scientific research, but it is compelling. Behavioral modification is at the heart of individual performance reviews and reinforcement.

The Behavioral Model

B. F. Skinner is generally acknowledged as the father of behavioral modification. A following of gifted academicians have spent their careers refining this science. It is a difficult discipline with complex ideas that require increasing specificity of language with each successive area of investigation. Behavioral modification theory, expectancy theory, and goal-setting theory have been the basis for many a book and consulting practice. In my own work, I have been influenced primarily by Tom Connellan, Aubrey Daniels, Dick Beatty, Charles Fay, Ed Lawler, and particularly Walter Nord, names that students of these disciplines will recognize.

The application of Skinner's research to performance management—to getting individuals to do what we want them to do, to behave in a certain way—can be illustrated by the model provided in Figure 5.1. The model is a template and checklist for ensuring that rewards used to change behavior, direction, awareness, and accountability work in a complete system of reinforcement. The process includes clear communications about what is needed and why, the measurement of results, positive consequences, constant performance and employee feedback, and assessment of the cost versus benefits to all.

Application of the model requires pragmatism. As a pragmatic practitioner, I respect the science of behavioral modification, but I don't allow myself to become bogged down by it. I am well aware that this is an area in which disagreements on technical issues abound. The objective of this discussion is to provide a point of view on human behavior modification that is being used by most organizations. I hope the average line and staff manager will better understand what they are doing with the company's existing reward

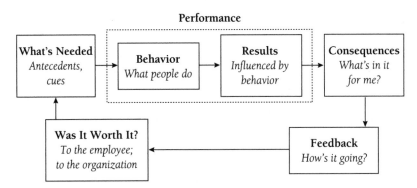

FIGURE 5.1. *The Behavioral Model.*
SOURCE: *Adapted from Connellan, 1978.*

plans and can design and implement new, improved plans. I have spoken in various forums throughout my career extolling the importance of the behavioral modification approach to performance improvement. There are drawbacks to it, however. While I still believe these concepts are important to understand, I have come to think that the focus should be on results and not on trying to control behavior. The reasons I think so will become clearer in this chapter.

A Win-Win Proposition

Skinner did most of his work with rats and pigeons rather than with people. I believe that applying the lessons of the behavioral model to business will work only if you follow a critical and fundamental rule: the requested behavior and subsequent results must be in the best interests of both the employee and the organization. It has to be a win-win proposition.

Let's say that a company and its employees are somewhat comfortable with their employment agreement (whether union or nonunion). The employees are in the door. Now, how do you get them to do what you want them to do? You put the employees in place, you give them what they need to do the work according to the parameters that are defined in their job descriptions, and you expect them to produce. Getting them to do their jobs *better* is a function of job content, environment, relationships in all directions, their intrinsic satisfaction with the work, and the extrinsic consequences—rewards—for improvement.

Figure 5.2 illustrates what people need to fulfill their job demands. They need physical and mental ability, and they may need training. They also need resources: tools, appropriate working conditions, sufficient budget, and technical support. Their behavior is also influenced by how other employees behave.

There are usually a few employees who don't need anything more to be satisfied in their work (assuming that they are paid adequately). The best example I can think of is my mother. Now retired, she worked for forty years as a registered nurse. She never made enough money to warrant the energy and time and caring that she put into her job. The only way to explain why she stuck with it for so long was that she was working for a higher goal, some intrinsic reward that she only realized when she could really help

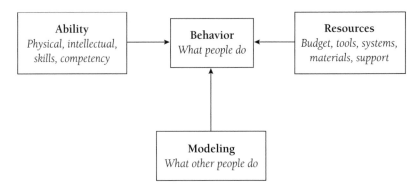

FIGURE 5.2. *What People Need To Fulfill Their Job Demands.*

people. Her complaints were almost always limited to her inability, due to lack of time or resources, to provide the care she wanted to.

There are lots of people like that: social workers, teachers, R&D scientists, ministers, and believe it or not, some politicians. They find satisfaction and inspiration in their work, despite the fact that they may not make enough money or have enough resources to do the job the way they would like to do it. Unfortunately, that's not enough for the majority of the population to be willing to improve their performance. Therefore, organizations often try to create environments in which they can encourage behavior that is productive for the individual as well as the company.

What's Needed

What's Needed
Antecedents, cues

The first step in the model is to signal people about what is needed and, consequently, what you want them to do, by using *antecedents* or *cues*. This step precedes a behavior. Antecedents can be job descriptions, goals, measurements, training, policies, education, verbal directions, and so forth. Management usually thinks it is possible to get people to do what management wants them to do by simply telling them to do it. That doesn't always work.

Any manager who has asked for employees to perform differently—and asked—and asked—with little result, will understand this. I was continually frustrated with project reports dribbling in from two to six months after their completion. "How many times have I told you to get the reports to me within thirty days after completion?" I asked my management team. One of the best of them, Marsha, promptly replied, "I don't know, eleven?" She was right—and not being rude, I should say. If they haven't done it the first eleven times I asked them to, why did I think it was going to happen on the twelfth?

Simply telling people what to do isn't enough. Nevertheless, antecedents signal to people what you want them to do, and they can provide necessary direction and focus, even if on their own they may not prompt the desired behavior.

And Why

I believe there is a direct correlation between a person's job satisfaction and their sense of understanding the bigger intent of the organization. The newly hired clerk who is told how to do filing but never told about the business, its objectives, and how he fits into the picture is simply not going to be as effective as the clerk who is told all this. Explaining what you want people to do and showing them how their efforts fit into the organizational framework helps them to be good, productive, and contributing stakeholders. It meets their need to be associated with a successful company and be proud of it.

New-employee orientation is the perfect time to do this. So much of the time, organizations focus orientation on what employees can and cannot do (start and stop times, breaks, smoking areas, rules and regulations, and job specifics), as if they were children starting the first grade. How can employees then be expected to feel like adults—contributing stakeholders responsible for improving the business?

On a day-to-day, project-to-project, objective-to-objective basis, knowledge of what is needed must provide direction, education, and context for the employee. It answers both how and why.

Results

Results are how the effect of behavior is measured and the degree to which it impacts the work group or organization. Measurement can be as simple as whether or not people come to work, as complex as the value of the service they provide, and just about everything else in between.

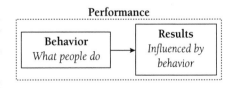

Behavior and results (measurement) taken together can be considered *performance*. Performance is what people do, and what happens as a result of what they do. (The degree to which business results are a function of employee behavior and the organization's reward plans is an important issue. They will be dealt with throughout the next few chapters.)

Consequences

Skinner argued that behavior is a function of its consequences. People will increase or decrease the frequency of behaviors according to the type of reinforcers applied. From the viewpoint of the pragmatic practitioner, one element of improving performance boils down to giving employees a good answer to the question, "What's in it for me?" (That's WIIFM, if you're fond of acronyms.)

There are many kinds of reinforcement, but one of the most powerful ones is intrinsic: "I feel better because I do this." The consequence for my mother, a nurse, was just that.

There are three kinds of consequences at work in any organization: *positive reinforcement* (increases the frequency of behavior), *punishment,* and *extinction* (both decrease the frequency of behavior). Technically, a reinforcer is defined by its effect on behavior. So, if behavior increases, the reinforcer must be positive. If behavior decreases, the reinforcer must be punishment or extinction. Discussion is easier, however, if we view reinforcement as a type of reinforcer driving the behavior as described in the behavior model.

> **Consequences**
> *What's in it for me?*

Extinction   Extinction is when there is no response to behavior. Nothing happens when people behave differently, reduce or improve their performance. Extinction is the most common consequence, particularly in hierarchical, directive organizations. Without contingent consequences, performance tends to deteriorate until something happens. Extinction has certainly been the biggest single problem in improving performance in a good portion of the civil services. Their regulated, seniority-based reinforcement process is based on the highly questionable assumption that competitive pay for fulfilling a job description assures acceptable performance.

If the objective is to reduce the frequency of an unwanted behavior, extinction can be an effective tool in certain situations. Ignoring a child's acting out for attention, as an example, can reduce the instances of that behavior. I've not found many positive applications of extinction in business situations because it is difficult to pull off effectively.

Punishment   Punishment is also a frequently used technique to control behavior. It is deliberate and is used to discourage specific behaviors. Punishment is generally connected with discipline. The organizational game has clear rules, such as attendance, grooming, safety, honesty, and so forth, that when broken, the organization has procedures to deliver punishment for. Successful organizations rarely exist in a constant environment of punishment, except for prisons, and there is some question about their success. Clearly, there are appropriate ways to use punishment but not as a performance improvement tool.

Going back to my project report experience: I threatened my managers with the punishment of writing the reports themselves in order to meet the deadlines. That would cause them to get their engineers to get their reports in on time. Punishment can change behavior pretty quickly. That quick change is probably one of the reasons its use is so prevalent in organizations. Managers like it because it reinforces their control. It can be delivered quickly, and it gets a fast response; that gives a manager a real sense of being in charge. But managing by punishment (or the threat of it) is like blowing up a balloon that has a hole in it. You have to blow and blow to keep the balloon at the same level. It's a lot of hard work for manager and employee alike.

Managing through negative reinforcement requires a strict definition of what's needed. The result is conformance. If you don't nail down everything you want, such as a specific quality of work, you've got a problem. That's what I fell into. The managers had the reports on my desk within the thirty days. They weren't complete or very good, but they were there, on time. I wasn't about to begin another series of threatened punishments to improve quality, and I had learned my lesson. The immediate compliance or behavior change resulting from the threat or delivery of punishment leads people to think that managing by fear gets a lot done. Organizations that manage through punishment, although they can be productive and in some cases very profitable, are generally not fun or particularly healthy places to work. They also waste lots of time trying to catch people doing something wrong.

Positive Reinforcement, or R+   The behaviorists teach that if the frequency of a behavior increases, the reinforcer is positive. Of the three types of consequences, positive reinforcement is the most effective and

> *Management by punishment is like trying to blow up a balloon with a hole in it. You have to do a lot of blowing to keep it full.*

> *When managing through punishment or fear, nail down everything you want or you've got a problem.*

efficient way to improve performance. Positive reinforcement can take two forms: adding something positive or removing something negative as a consequence of improving performance. The addition of something positive could be giving team members points toward catalogue merchandise for meeting a cost-reduction goal. Removing a negative might be excusing a work team from having to punch a time clock if they have a perfect record for not being tardy.

To be positively reinforcing, a consequence must be positive and immediate. The reinforcer must give people something they want. It must do so within a time frame that ties it to the accomplishment. Certainty is critical, depending on the type of reward plan you are creating. For consistent and cost-justified plans, employees must be certain of positive reinforcement as a consequence of the behavior or result. That is accomplished when the reinforcer is based on a preannounced formula or schedule. Recognition plans and spot bonuses often do not have positive reinforcers as certain consequences of behavior or results. Surprise is an important element of recognition plans.

What's positive is in the eye of the recipient. A reinforcer is positive when the individual sees it as a good thing and worth the effort or behavior change required to earn it. But human nature seems to dictate that if you try to predict what will be positive to an individual, you won't be right all the time. It's sort of the Peter Principle of awards. There are people who don't even like a simple "thank you" because it brings unwanted attention to them, and there are people who would rather have a simple and kind word of encouragement than a bonus.

Immediacy is the other critical element of a positive consequence. It means the reward must come reasonably soon after the behavior or end of the measurement period. For example, if you are measuring performance on a month-to-month basis, people need to know within a few days after month's end how they are doing. Then they need to be rewarded or at least told that they are on the right track. That's why reward plans that defer into pension plans have relatively little effect on behavior or the measurement of that behavior. The reward is too far off.

Certainty is equally important in a performance-based reward plan designed to consistently improve performance in a measurable (and, hopefully, a cost-justifiable way). The certainty element says simply, "Do this, get that." The concept is pretty simple: These are the measures—productivity, quality, attendance, and profit at specific levels—and this is what you can earn.

A lack of certainty exists in the merit increase or discretionary bonus plan that is dependent upon management discretion for distribution among employees. Everyone knows about the plan and maybe the basis on which the increase or bonus pool is created. There is the general expectation that most will receive something, but how much is unknown. When managers have the right to use discretion in distributing payments to people, the whole process is significantly less effective. The biggest complaint about these plans is that "merit" is in the eyes of the manager and his or her subjective evaluation. There is little certainty in what one has to do to earn.

The lack of measurable objectives is a killer to certainty. For example, a pool of money created through a profit sharing plan is to be distributed among employees. However, instead of distributing the money according to a preannounced formula that explains exactly what each employee will receive, management decides who gets what based on their judgment. There is no certainty in the eyes of the employees, and people are not motivated to change their behavior because they can't be sure of the consequence.

Management discretion leaves employees wondering whom they are serving. Employees should be serving the external or internal customer, not the boss. But when rewards are given out based on management discretion, employees are in fact serving an inside customer, the person who controls the money. The more management discretion there is in the distribution of awards, the more confusion there is in the minds of employees as to who their customer really is.

Management discretion leaves employees wondering whom they are serving.

The above "management discretion rap" gets the most consistent reaction from the audiences in my seminars and speeches on performance improvement issues. Nonmanagement employees nod their heads in agreement and can't wait to give me examples of their experiences. Managers, on the other hand, nod thoughtfully and formulate their arguments on why discretion is a good thing. After all, they use their discretion every day in business decisions and have used it (or been subject to it) in reward distribution their entire career. There can be little question that some managers use excellent judgment in the distribution of discretionary funds. Unfortunately, too many don't have the information on performance or enough funds to make appropriate decisions. In addition, too many just cop out and base the decision on what the person got last year.

When I'm faced with an organization that has a strong discretionary culture and history, I don't fight the battle, at least for the top tier of management. Upper management generally has a reasonable track record in the distribution of rewards for those who report to them directly—those who are also managers. Upper management with day-to-day contact with their direct reports probably have a good idea of the value and contributions of their managers. And they usually have a sizable pot of money to distribute to those who are already on the high end of the earning curve.

Moving down into the middle- and first-line management ranks, professionals, and the rank and file, organizations have a lousy track record in rewarding for individual performance. I argue that organizations should use performance management for capability development. Objective measurement should be used to determine rewards. Failing that, use cost-of-living or labor market adjustments.

"But what about our outstanding performers?" is the most frequently asked question. Reinforcement of these critical players must be positive and immediate but not necessarily certain. I suggest using significant adjustments in base pay, promotions, special assignments, and spot bonuses in recognition of outstanding performance—at management discretion and based on their judgment. These unscheduled positive reinforcers are arguably the most powerful of all, but for the few. They are difficult to use effectively for all employees.

Feedback

Feedback
How's it going?

Now that I have finished describing the top tier of the behavioral model, I move on to the next step in the process: feedback or assessing "how it's going."

By this point, employees have behaved in a certain way and have been measured and reinforced. Of course, measurement and positive reinforcement are feedback in their own right. Perhaps it would be helpful at this stage to think of feedback as two-way *communication*.

Feedback basically falls into two categories: performance feedback to employees and management, and employee feedback to management.

Performance feedback is a continuous process of letting everyone know how they are doing as individuals and the organization's performance against the objectives. Regular personal coaching and review sessions are the essence of performance management. Charts, newsletters, meetings, videos, and focused performance communications all tell employees what is being accomplished by the organization and what still needs to be done. Also, they provide reminders about the details of the measurements and objectives.

A good example of working without good feedback is Tom Connellan's story about bowling with a curtain between you and the pins, with just enough room under the curtain for the ball to get through. After rolling the bowling ball, someone at the pins yells, "Great job! You have three more for a spare." If you can't see the pins, it's tough to know where to roll. Performance feedback must be clear, exact, and frequent.

Employee feedback to management is equally important, if not as frequent, as performance feedback. There should be a steady stream of input from employees to management about the performance measures—about what can be done to improve upon them, what they don't understand, their perceptions of fairness, and the obstacles to improvement. This is much more than an "open door" policy—something that sounds great and is rarely used by the rank and file. Employee feedback must be solicited through surveys, focus groups, and meetings with immediate and upper management. If the organization does not make it a formalized process, employee feedback just won't happen.

Was It Worth It?

The final part of this loop of continuous reinforcement is evaluation: Was it worth it? The answer to this question is in the eye of the beholder. The traditional compensation community often answers the question solely on the basis of the size of the payout. Success is somehow related to the cost of the plan, with the interesting logic that if the plan paid out a lot, it must have worked.

For the recipients, large payouts will always be well received. Cynics would say that employees always want more, particularly if they don't have to do anything different to get it. In this case, the performance improvement process has broken down. The connection between the behavior and the measurement has been broken, and the plan is simply a way to distribute funds. That's how entitlements begin. Believe it or not, people are suspicious of getting something for nothing. They wait for the other shoe to drop. When

> **Was It Worth It?**
> *To the employee;*
> *to the organization*

they keep getting rewarded for doing what they have always done, the whole plan becomes a right, an entitlement.

When the behavior-measurement-reward connection is solid, the employee evaluation becomes, "I worked harder, smarter, with others, thought out-of-the-box, contributed my ideas, met my objectives, accomplished the organization's goals, and so on, and this is my reward. Was it worth it?" This is a critical question, to be asked on an ongoing basis.

The measure of a plan's success cannot be the size of the award. The measure must be the value gained for the time, money, and energy spent. Like most things in business, this valuation of performance improvement is as much art as science. Value depends on the type of measurement and the amount of positive change that is due to the plan.

If outstanding performers continue to be outstanding and voluntary turnover is low, the positive and immediate (but not certain) reinforcement plan may be worth it to both the performers and the organization. In a group incentive, for example, it is difficult to put a dollar value on 4 percent improvement in customer satisfaction, but it is important to do so. Another difficult question is: how much of the 4 percent improvement is due to the plan? And was it worth the $200,000 in awards plus the management effort? If the measurement accurately reflects the business objective of improving customer satisfaction, and if the design team got management's approval to invest $200,000 for 4 percent, the evaluation should be pretty straightforward.

Ask yourself this question: "What did the organization get in return for its reward plans?" Without a sense of the value added by the plan, it is difficult to determine if it was worth it.

At this point, the behavioral model recycles, beginning again with the antecedents and a slightly revised message of what's needed. Low or high payouts, improvement in certain measurements and little in others, specific feedback from employees, more clearly identified improvement opportunities—all are new antecedents for the next iteration of the model.

An Opposing View of Behavioral Modification

One of the most vocal critics of extrinsic reinforcement plans is Alfie Kohn. He has taken the position that if a consequence is an extrinsic reward, it is actually counterproductive. Kohn argues that extrinsic rewards decrease employees' intrinsic motivation and thus their performance, and that they do nothing more than reinforce temporary compliance with rules and regulations. His position is clear from the title of his book, *Punished by Rewards: The Trouble with Gold Stars, Incentive Plans, A's, Praise, and Other Bribes* (1993).

Kohn creates an extreme position, charging that people have accepted Skinner as the saint of positive consequences, without carefully examining the research. The research, he claims, proves that tangible awards are almost everything we don't want them to be: demotivating, punishing, and relationship rupturing. He argues that corporate America and the education community have trotted blindly down a path that does not work and, in fact, cannot work. Kohn agrees that rewards certainly change behavior, but he argues that the change is for all the wrong reasons. People should *want* to change and improve. Rewards, by their very nature, negatively affect employee motivation and self-esteem.

Arguments for and against behaviorism have been going on for more than forty years, mostly in the academic community. Kohn's position, as you may expect, plays particularly well with the college crowd and not so well with the experienced business crowd. His message counters what most businesses, whether they realize it or not, practice. Because his book is fun to read, and because it purports a counterintuitive position, it's gotten a lot of press, including reviews in the *Harvard Business Review* and *The New York Times,* and an hour's worth of attention on "Talk of the Nation" on National Public Radio.

My Argument with Kohn

I do not intend for this to be a treatise on why I believe Kohn's extreme position is mistaken; rather, I mean to say that I think he has simply gone too far. By calling a spade a shovel ("all rewards are bad") he has clouded the real issue—the ineffectiveness of controlling and micromanaging individuals.

> *By calling a spade a shovel he has clouded the real issue.*

One of the effects of this highly publicized and simplistic position is that "tough-minded managers" (who might say, "These days, just having a job is incentive enough") and those who believe that performance is *all* about environment, good organizational design, and excellent job-person matches, wave Kohn's book and news reports at their management and say, "See, research shows incentives don't work." There are also those who are so stuck in the behavioral position that they cough, sputter, and harumph in disbelief that there could be anyone in this day and age who would believe such a thing. Neither position is helpful. Kohn's work provides an opportunity to do some critical thinking.

In his book, Kohn repeatedly uses the phrases "the research shows" and "studies prove." These are backed up by more than six hundred references, the majority of which are on educating children, often those who are learning-disabled. Sifting through the rest of the references that negate the value of extrinsic rewards, I found that most are focused on academia's view of executive pay and individually based merit increases. Almost nothing negative is referenced about the group side of the reinforcement model. There are, however, several positive references.

Kohn does not argue whether or not his secondary research can or should be applied to adults in business. He argues that extrinsic rewards are bad regardless of the application and that no amount of fine tuning of the reward plan's design will make them a good thing.

My argument with Kohn is that he focuses only on the problems associated with rewarding behavior—the accomplishment of *tasks* rather than on improved performance and results. A managerial focus on tasks can lead to micromanagement, exactly what Taylor argued for in 1911 and what is still too often practiced today. My experience is that an environment that rewards basic job tasks and specific behavior is a micromanaged environment—one that makes all the decisions and intellectual contributions the responsibility of management, and all the *doing* the responsibility of nonmanagement employees. Trying to control the behavior of individuals, which brings with it all the images of manipulation, is simply not in sync with today's workforce or with the need of today's organizations to be flexible and creative. I agree with Kohn that rewarding individuals for accomplishing daily tasks does look like rewarding a dog for rolling over.

The Three C's of Continuous Improvement

Kohn's answer to the need for continuous improvement is the three C's: *collaboration* (allowing people to work together in an environment of teamwork), *content* (making the job interesting), and *choice* (providing more freedom in work through empowerment). With the three C's and fair, competitive base salaries, according to Kohn, all would be well. Rewards would never be used because they wouldn't be needed.

Tom Peters often uses a cartoon of two mathematicians staring at a blackboard filled with complex formulas. The caption reads, "Ah, if it were only that simple!" Any organization that could match people with the needs of the business, make the jobs so engaging that people would love them, and educate people so that being empowered would consistently contribute to the good of all—in a perfect world, with visionary and consultative leaders in management positions—would probably be hugely successful. Of course, the competitive marketplace would have to stand still long enough for it to get this perfect act together. It would also be an organization that had mastered the art and science of reinforcing behavior through consequences.

Removing rewards does not create a three-C world.

Other than the obvious naiveté of such a vision, the reason that a work force functioning solely in a three-C environment is unlikely because of a fourth and fifth C—*change and competitiveness* in the marketplace. The demands of the organization's four stakeholders are so great, the marketplace is so competitive, and yes, the expectations of employees are so conditioned that operating without rewards would spell doom for most organizations. By the way, removing rewards does not create a three-C world.

Research equally as compelling as Kohn's has been done on adults in business (the CARS research is one recent example). It has shown that properly designed and executed reward plans improve teamwork, performance, and motivation, reduce turnover, and encourage risk taking. The reinforcement model, on balance, addresses all five C's in a positive and supportive manner. Of course, not all reward plans work, and many a manager has used rewards to control and manipulate. That is *misuse* and not *prevalent* use.

Individual Focus and Micromanagement

The focus on the individual employee has spawned a good deal of micromanagement, in which control becomes the mantra of the "tough-minded" boss, whose favorite management technique is to count the number of times you use the word "the" in a memo or to become involved in whether or not the $3 bridge toll is included in the $23 New York City cab expense. These micromanagers telegraph (often unintentionally) that they don't trust their employees and that control is everything. Capability, recognition, and group-based incentive plans in addition to base pay and benefits are viewed as fluff and as sunk cost.

I had a boss like that once. He was upset about the number of times "this" and "that" were used in communications (both internal and with clients). This kind of micromanagement was no small matter. More than three hundred writers worked for the company, writing everything from a jingle for a sales campaign to understandable copy on complex group incentive plans. This type of controlling management is not well received by a bunch of creative writers. Fortunately, we were blessed with a man named Charlie who had the ability to diffuse almost any potentially difficult situation. Charged with carrying out the boss's command, he sent out the following memo:

> To all who write:
>
> This memo is about the use of this as a pronoun in presentations and communications.
>
> This is frowned upon by this guy that we have in a very senior position here. This is not meant to absolutely prohibit this, but rather to point out that this is a lazy and confusing use of the language. If this is not clear, use this as a daily reminder not to use this.
>
> Or that, for that matter.

No one was upset, and the message got through. It is too bad that all organizations do not have a translator/diffuser like Charlie available to handle micromanagement edicts.

Individual focus does not have to mean micromanagement. Fair wages can be calibrated to a job's content or a person's value. Clear performance objectives can be set that are mutually agreed upon by the employee and direct manager. A development plan can be created to increase or sharpen competencies. All of these are ways for management and employees to work together for everyone's benefit within the framework of an individual reinforcement system.

What Can Be Used from the Behavioral Modification and Kohn Camps?

If we move away from absolutism on either side, there are some useful principles we can follow. The left side of the reinforcement model—individual compensation—deals with fair pay for value received from employees. This pay is increased from time to time to stay competitive in the labor market. Capability plans also deal with developmental opportunities by focusing on matching people to an organizational role in which the employee will have the level of content (one of the C's) she wishes and the organization needs.

Management style and organizational culture tend to determine choice (another C). Though motivation is laudable, it can be destructive if the employee does not have the experience and competencies to use that energy appropriately. Everyone needs direction and to be told what is needed. To paraphrase a colleague of mine from times past, psychologist George Blomgren, "Motivation without direction and capability is energized incompetence." People need to be reminded that they are on the right road and told how well they are doing. Measurement and results, along with feedback, are as critical as any of the other components of the behavioral model for directing motivated people.

Motivation without direction and capability is energized incompetence.

In addition to management style and culture, reward plans are the most powerful change agents to reinforce collaboration (the third of Kohn's C's). Group incentive plans, project team incentive plans, and recognition plans are all designed to improve performance through collaboration—and to celebrate it. The fourth and fifth C, change and competitiveness in business, comes primarily from the group side of the reinforcement model. Improving business performance is an all-encompassing objective. Trying to apply the behavioral model to group incentives, project team incentive plans, and even recognition plans, requires less focus on behavior and more on results. Focusing on relating individual behavior to specific business improvement objectives clearly leads to micromanagement and does not reinforce the more important cultural focus on teamwork. Rather, the focus needs to be on what is accomplished, on providing processes like quality and suggestion plans to engage employees in making a contribution, on expecting and encouraging employees to step out of their job boxes and think like businesspeople and contributing stakeholders, and finally, on rewarding employees based on what is accomplished—if for no other reason than to be fair.

Aligning people with the organization's objectives is a balancing act between attracting, retaining, developing, and improving the performance of individuals through individual compensation and capability plans and improving business performance through group-based reward plans. Alignment requires the proper application of the behavioral teachings and incorporation of choice, content, and collaboration in order to be responsive to change and to be competitive.

Conclusion

The key to individual performance improvement is to focus on personal development and engaging and rewarding employees to work with others to advance organizational objectives. Organizations clearly have to perform maintenance on the basic way they pay people and manage that process to make it more effective. If behavioral modification is operationalized as micromanagement, it will be inappropriate and ineffective in improving performance over the long run. If the teachings of behavioral modification can be used to understand how to make reward plans more effective and meet the marketplace's competitive challenge, organizations have a real opportunity to capitalize on their human assets for everyone's benefit.

CHAPTER 6

Individual Compensation and Capability

Individual compensation is the essence of the employee-employer social contract. The employer says, "You work for me, and I'll pay you." The business objectives supported by compensation are operational necessities, two of which are to get and keep the people you want. Another objective is to improve the performance of those individuals. Success in meeting these objectives is a function of the organization's ability to communicate with and prepare people for their jobs, to observe and measure their performance, and to reward them for improvement.

INDIVIDUAL	
Compensation	Capability
Attract and retain; improve individual performance	*Develop individuals; align with organizational needs*

Capability plans focus on the ability of individuals to do a job or fulfill a role. The focus is on the person rather than the job. Most people wouldn't go to work if they didn't get paid. That's obvious. What they get paid and how that level of pay is determined might not be so obvious. Compensation experts (supported by the American Compensation Association) have created a practical art—not science—of compensatory theory, management processes, and administration that enables organizations to establish individual compensation and capability plans.

What You Will Find in This Chapter

For those of you without a human resources background, this chapter will help you understand how individual compensation works. It will clarify the role of each of these reward plans in your organization and briefly review each kind of plan, and its objectives, and to provide some observations about its effectiveness.

When I was a line manager, the only time I had even a passing interest in talking about human resources and compensation was when it directly affected my income or the incomes of people who worked for me. I didn't understand the importance of reward plans as tools for improving performance. This chapter would have been very helpful to me in my manager/leader role. In it, I review the basics of individual compensation and capability plans only to the degree necessary for a line manager to understand how to use them more effectively. I do so by discussing:

- Individual compensation and capability plans

- Base pay, which is the largest part of compensation, and the variety of ways to adjust it: general and range adjustments, step-rate adjustments, merit increases (and their connection to performance management), and promotions

- Compensation plans that pay out lump sums that do not add to base pay: individual incentives (commissions) and variable entitlements (a newly coined term)

- Employee ownership stock plans and benefits (mentioned only for completeness, because I want to comment on their role, or lack of it, as reward plans)

- Capability development plans, including competency-based and skill-based versions

The chapter will not deal with how compensation for jobs is determined to be competitive or how to develop a fair and competitive base pay program. These subjects are thoroughly covered by other works, by associations, and by compensation consultants.

Compensation

Base Pay

The fundamental tenet of employment is that employees be paid a competitive wage—known as *base pay*. Base pay traditionally has been designed and implemented to attract and retain people. Once agreed upon, base pay is an entitlement. It is expected from the organization by the employee, and it should be. It is not a gift from the organization, and it should be properly aligned with the job and the person who performs the job.

Individual performance is rarely linked with changes in entitlements. There is no evidence that doubling an employee's pay will double (or even improve) her performance, even if that performance could be measured. Everyone would like an increase in base pay and would like to expect increases if performance improves. But all such increases add to the labor load carried by the P&L. Base pay represents a significant percentage of the total cost of people, which in turn can represent a sizable share of an organization's operating costs. Increasing employees' pay has become an expensive maintenance process and a cost of doing business. Pay is increased with the hope that performance will improve.

An organization's compensation philosophy establishes how it will use pay to compete. It can set base pay over, at, or below the market, for a variety of reasons. Base pay that is ahead of (leads) the competitive labor market may attract better people and keep them longer. Base pay that is set at the market level allows an organization to attract and retain employees on a purely competitive level. Base pay that is below (lags behind) the labor market can make an organization's products and services more cost competitive, particularly when combined with an incentive plan, the cost of which varies with organizational performance.

Companies are very proactive in keeping base pay at the competitive level set by the compensation philosophy. They practice preventive maintenance. Human resource/compensation departments regularly test the labor market for competitive rates and practices. Job families fall into base pay ranges (ranges of base pay within which employees can earn more as time goes on). Adjusting the range itself does not necessarily change base pay; it just changes the parameters (minimum, midpoint, or competitive rate, and maximum amounts) of how the job should be paid. (Figure 6.1 illustrates a typical base pay range for a family of jobs.) Too few managers understand that conforming to the market's competitive pay is a complex and detailed process. Not all jobs can be directly compared with other jobs in the local or national competitive labor market.

The managers in many organizations, specifically in middle management, think the traditional base pay ranges for job families are too restrictive. Moving employees into new roles for their personal development is made more difficult than it should be when managers must conform to strict job families and their commensurate pay ranges. It also puts human resource departments in an adver-

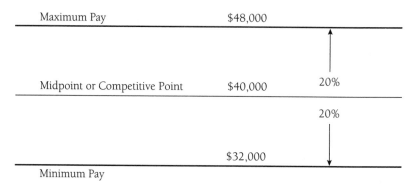

Maximum Pay	$48,000	
		20%
Midpoint or Competitive Point	$40,000	
		20%
	$32,000	

Minimum Pay

FIGURE 6.1. *A Typical Base Pay Range for a Family of Jobs.*

sarial role, as they try to maintain the integrity of the system. *Broad-banding* is being introduced as a way of increasing the flexibility of the compensation management process. It consolidates a large number of relatively narrow pay ranges into much fewer broad bands with relatively wide salary ranges. Instead of the ±10 to 20 percent range in Figure 6.1, a broad band could be as high as ±30 to 50 percent. For example, a narrow range with a midpoint competitive base pay of $40,000 may have a maximum of $48,000 (+20 percent) and a minimum of $32,000 (-20 percent). A broad band would include a number of narrow ranges and all the job families in those ranges for a $20,000 minimum to a $60,000 maximum. In some cases, organizations have taken as many as forty narrow ranges and created only five broad bands. This removes an obstacle to moving people from one role to another or from one job to another. It also allows for greater flexibility in adjusting base pay in support of personal development in new assignments. The responsibility for labor cost management moves to line management rather than the human resources department.

Adjusting Base Pay

Every upward adjustment of base pay increases the organization's people costs. Unlike one-time expenses, increases in base pay add costs for as long as the people affected are with the company. Increases in base pay cause corresponding adjustments to the cost of benefits. Both negatively affect profitability. Over a fifteen-year period, an annual 4 percent increase in base pay and its corresponding increase in benefit costs can increase the organization's people costs up to 100 percent, while a 4 percent lump sum (not added to base pay) increases the cost only about 60 percent (Schuster and Zingheim, 1992). (This is an unrealistic situation because downsizing and turnover tend to moderate labor costs. I am simply illustrating the effect on costs of adjusting base pay versus giving lump sums.)

Our business society is in a trap of believing that base pay will always go up, an idea that is constantly being reinforced. Both employers and employees have come to expect it. Organizations budget for it in their financial planning, and employees budget for it in their personal spending. The idea is so ingrained in our collective minds that justifying the traditional increases is becoming more and more difficult and often downright bizarre. But it is a sad day when we pay for simply passing the fog test. Here's the test: put a mirror under the employee's nose. If it fogs up, we pay.

Base pay is adjusted in a variety of ways: general (cost-of-living) adjustments, range adjustments, step-rate increases, merit increases, and promotions. Individual incentives, variable entitlements, and benefits add to the compensation package.

It is a sad day when we use the fog test for base pay adjustments: put a mirror under the employee's nose. If it fogs up, we pay.

General Adjustments A general adjustment to base pay usually means increasing the base pay of everyone in the organization. The amount is often based on the annual increase in the cost of living—hence the name *cost-of-living adjustments* (CoLAs). CoLAs are intended to keep people's incomes in line with inflation. Normally, CoLAs are given once a year. They are a common feature of union contracts for production and craft employees. They are somewhat less common for nonexempt employees (that is, those whose jobs are classified by the government as not being exempt from the rules of the Fair Labor Standards Act, which requires premium pay for overtime—in other words, those who are entitled to overtime pay). Some organizations give CoLAs for exempt employees, but it is rare.

CoLAs do not necessarily correspond directly to inflation, but there is usually some correlation. CoLAs are not related to individual performance but are related to the performance of the economy.

Range Adjustments Salary surveys are regularly conducted by compensation consultants and/or industry groups to determine what companies are paying for specific jobs locally, regionally, and nationally. When necessary, in order to remain competitive, an

Compensation

Attract and retain; improve individual performance

- Base pay
- General (CoLA) adjustments
- Range adjustments
- Step-rate increases
- Merit increases
- Promotions
- Individual incentives or commissions
- Variable entitlements
- Employee stock or ownership plans
- Benefits

organization's entire salary structure can move up. Such adjustments are often called *range adjustments*. They rarely guarantee that everyone will get an increase. Those at the bottom of the range may get a base pay adjustment if the range adjustment causes them to fall below the minimum.

If the survey finds that specific jobs or job families are falling behind the market (as is the case with local area network (LAN) administrators as I write this book), *market adjustments* are made to attract and retain these valuable people.

Step-Rate Increases   Step-rate increases are regular increases that are guaranteed on a time schedule. For example, at the end of six months the employee gets a fifty cents an hour increase by meeting the basic job requirements. The process continues until the midpoint or even maximum rate for the job is attained. The adjustment is an entitlement. It's part of the deal, and not such a bad one for the employee or for the organization, particularly when individual performance differences cannot be observed or measured. Failure to perform stops the increase. This plan is clear and predictable for both parties.

Merit Increases   In Chapter Five, I discussed performance management as a critical personal development process between an employee and his or her manager. I also suggested that the process goes sour when adjustments to base pay are introduced. Companies that have connected performance management and salary increases have done so in an attempt to move away from automatic adjustments. The original intent of these *merit increases* was to "pay for performance," that is, individual performance. However, management has had a tough time determining objective measurements and has gravitated to the delivery of the consequences—the merit increase—with little attention to the rest of the performance management coaching process.

Employees are usually discontented with their companies' performance management programs because in the employees' minds, such programs are identified with the merit increase alone. I know of few merit increase plans that are considered effective by both the organization and the employees.

Perhaps the best way to look at the merit increase process is to discuss it in the light of its theoretical foundation, the Behavioral Model, which I discussed in Chapter Five. The model, repeated

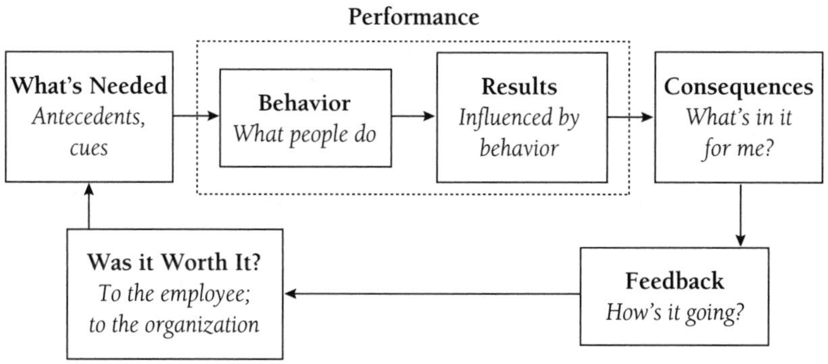

Performance

FIGURE 6.2. *The Behavioral Model.*

Source: Adapted from Connellan, 1978.

here in Figure 6.2, illustrates the basic steps in influencing and rewarding an individual's performance.

What's Needed   To fulfill the model's *what's needed* requirement, a well-functioning merit increase plan provides clear objectives for the individual. Such objectives, along with timing and measurement specifications, can be determined through a thoughtful discussion between the employee and the manager, usually culminating in a written agreement between the two parties.

Results   Trouble arises, however, with the measurement of *results* by objective evaluation of performance—the observation of specific behaviors and the evaluation of their effects. This can feel a lot like the dreaded micromanagement, and few employees feel they can be objectively measured.

Consequences   To be considered positively reinforcing (R+), the *consequences* of behavior (in this case, the merit increase) must be positive and immediate (and often certain).

1.   *R+ consequences are positive.* In other words, the consequences are positive to the recipient. Generally, it is the size of the merit increase that makes the difference. In the last five years, the average merit increase pool has been 3 to 6 percent of base pay, with individuals receiving from 0 to 10 percent or more based on their performance evaluation. When employees deduct what they think offsets inflation, the increase shrinks to a relatively small amount. (It is rare for companies to give both a CoLA and a merit increase to the same employee.)

It can be difficult to match an appropriate merit increase with individual performance when a manager is working from a fixed pool of money. The American Compensation Association says that about 3 percent of base pay will make a "meaningful difference" in levels of performance. That means that rating employees through a performance review process on a scale of 1 to 5, the difference in merit increase between a 3- and a 4-rated employee would be about 3 percent of base pay. However, there is never enough money in the merit increase pool to go around. The consequence is not particularly positive. Immediate management tends to carve out some extra for the one or two outstanding employees in a "rob Peter to pay Paul" scenario. It is rare for poor performers to get less than the inflation rate. Managers hate to give bad news, so most merit increases cluster around the average of the pool. Merit increases are parceled out over the next year, perhaps every week or two at payday, which reduces their impact.

When the merit increase pool is not allocated to individual managers but controlled at a broader level, there is a greater opportunity to couple a more appropriate increase with the performance rating. A manager with five outstanding employees out of five may be able to argue for enough money to properly reward each one. But someone somewhere always gets less. It is a zero sum game, and all too often, merit increases are about the same for everyone.

2.   *R+ consequences are immediate.* Immediacy is not one of the strong suits of a merit increase plan. Most organizations dictate that performance reviews are to be done on a yearly cycle. Some do it on the employee's anniversary of employment; some do it at the same time each year for everyone. The ability of a manager to remember during the January review what Fred did last February depends on the manager's memory and record-keeping ability. The lack of immediacy makes merit increases look like entitlements, unresponsive to progressive changes in individual performance.

3.   *R+ consequences are often certain.* If merit increases are to reinforce the consistent improvement for most employees, rather than a few, they require certainty. The work of most individuals cannot be measured objectively. The best that can be hoped for is a mutual evaluation of performance between the manager and employee. That evaluation can be expanded to include peer evaluation, which provides more comprehensive feedback than the sole opinion of one manager, but it is still subjective. Goodwill, constant communication, and regular evaluation of the fulfillment of agreements can be effective, but you have to work at it.

There is no certainty in the size of the merit award because it comes from a pool. At best, "do this and earn that" becomes "do this and I'll see how well you did versus the others in the pool, and I'll try to do what is fair considering the limitations of the money I have to work with"—not exactly certain, but about as good as it's going to get.

The standard premise is that the amount in the merit pay pool is based on the company's performance and on the competitive market. There is some truth to both of these statements, but only some. The company's performance drives the merit pool only when company performance is poor; companies may give no increases in a year like that, or minimal ones at best. When the company's performance is terrific, does the merit pool increase at the same rate? Rarely. So, employees do share the risk but little if any of the gain.

When the company performance is terrific, does the merit pool increase at the same rate? Rarely.

The competitive market is the real driver of the size of the merit increase pool. Its effect seems to be related to inflation and the health of the economy, but the relationship is not a direct one. No one really knows what it is based on. Everyone simply looks to everyone else to see how much they are going to increase base pay rather than base increases on any fundamental parameters of organizational performance. Most companies swear they do not consider inflation in determining their merit pay pools, but of all the economic factors considered, inflation is, over time, the closest correlating factor.

Feedback If the yearly review and merit increase session between manager and employee is the only feedback an employee gets during the year, that review is not enough to make sure the employee is on track. Managers who practice performance management as a coaching and developmental process have regular, periodic review sessions with each employee, and that makes a world of difference. Ongoing feedback is a critical developmental process for both the employee and the manager. At merit increase time, there should be no surprises.

Was It Worth It? Fred got the average increase (which is top secret, except that everyone knows it) from the merit pool. Four percent minus inflation (real or perceived) leaves 2 percent. At $30,000 per year, that's $600 additional real income *before taxes*. Fred gets paid twice a month, so his raise nets him, after inflation and taxes, about $17.50 every two weeks. At that rate, and assuming a range adjustment of 3 percent every other year, it would take Fred about fifteen years to go from the minimum to the maximum of his job range. Was the increase worth it to Fred? "I guess it's better than a poke in the eye with a dirty stick," as my manager said to me every year for several years—before I left.

Was it worth it to the company? There is a reasonable hope that a 4 percent compounded increase in payroll costs retained the people the company wanted to keep. And the intended goodwill in keeping people at least up with inflation is a possible outcome. The hope of getting a return on the investment, however, is unfounded. Merit increases were not intended to improve business performance but to adjust base pay in order to retain employees. Companies hope that there is enough money to reinforce the really good people and that managers have the nerve to withhold increases from those who should be in another line of work.

Merit increases were not intended to improve business performance but to adjust base pay to retain employees.

What To Do?

Some organizations are disconnecting merit increases from the performance evaluation process because entitlements don't work to improve performance. One option is to call a spade a spade. Give a general increase or CoLA to everyone who gets an acceptable review, and use other plans described in this book to improve performance. Performance management is a developmental process in which managers have the opportunity to guide those who report to them directly in becoming more effective. Trying to tie in raises from fixed pools works against the real objectives of performance management for individuals.

The risk of this approach is obvious. We have created an entitlement mentality about merit increases. Most organizations that do not give increases in a year receive a very negative backlash from employees, particularly when executive bonuses are paid in the same year. One option is to only give merit increases based on a pass-fail performance level. The problem of having only a fixed pool of funds remains, but setting a standard for receiving increases should mean more money for those who deserve it.

I've always been a fan of "zero-based budgeting" for merit increases. This is a bottom-up approach in which managers with direct reports request the amount they believe they need to adequately reinforce their employees. They would have to be given a good deal of information to do the job properly—the competitive market data, the estimated inflation rate, and the placement of employees within their salary ranges. These data, combined with the manager's judgment of how much each employee's expected performance should earn, would roll up from every manager to one number for the organizational unit. Top management could always change the total amount. The change would be the same for every manager's requested amount. The worry is that zero-based budgeting would create a request much higher than is realistic. When I did it for a group of five hundred employees, the total of the managers' requests came to 0.1 percentage point less than what I thought we would have budgeted in the traditional, top-down way.

At-Risk Pay   The most extreme version of at-risk pay is when you reduce base pay and give the employee opportunities to earn enough to bring the amount back up to the original pay level plus extra, based on performance against specific measures. This practice is common in the world of sales, where people often have a somewhat lower base salary but can earn considerably more by selling more. Generally, 80 percent of targeted pay is in salary, and 20 percent is based on performance (O'Dell and McAdams, 1987, p. 76).

The CARS research discussed in Chapter Two found very few companies that reduced base pay for nonsales employees in order to create an at-risk incentive plan (McAdams and Hawk, 1994, pp. 177–178). The companies that have installed such an at-risk plan have found that it put too much pressure on the accuracy of their measurement systems. And the companies, whether out of paternalism or sensitivity to employee reaction, made sure that employees were paid more than they were before. These organizations have ended up spending more money than they wanted to, and the credibility of at-risk plans has come into question.

In some cases, an at-risk plan is too much too soon. One manufacturer of truck frames was paying about 25 percent above the competitive labor market due to some unwise labor negotiations. In a do-or-die move, management got the union to agree to a 50 percent reduction in the hourly rate—from $18 to $9 per hour—with the opportunity to earn back the $9 plus another $4.50 based on productivity performance. It was too much too soon. The measurement system on which the earnback was based, which had been used for years but not for a reward plan, wasn't good enough. I'm not sure that many measurement systems are. I know that the ability to engage people in ways that can directly influence results depends on the three principles of open-book management: making all employees financially and operationally literate, sharing responsibility and accountability with all employees, and offering employees a reward plan that rewards for improving the organization's performance. That won't be done, at least in the near future, by core changes in the compensation plan. Instead, it will be done by some combination of capability plans, recognition, and group-based incentive plans. This is what it will take to reduce the growth of the cost of doing business.

A less extreme and less risky at-risk option is to leave existing base pay alone and moderate how merit increases add to base pay according to an employee's position in a salary range. One option now being tested is the "midpoint cap" approach, in which any payout is given as a lump sum rather than added to base pay when an employee reaches midpoint. This approach was considered radical in 1980 when it was proposed at a symposium, although I'm sure it had been proposed before.

The midpoint cap is based on the idea that the market position (the midpoint of an employee's salary range) is appropriate pay for fully competent work. It becomes the most the organization will pay in base for that job family. The minimum is what someone with entrance-level qualifications doing entrance-level work is paid.

In the midpoint cap approach, the objective is to get everyone to midpoint. This requires an active performance management process. Employees whose salaries are between minimum and midpoint are given a customized performance plan with time lines for getting to midpoint through performance and demonstration of ability. At each stage, base pay is adjusted according to a predetermined time schedule. The employee knows that by a specific date, if she performs at an agreed-upon level, she will be at midpoint. The actual amount of each step is a function of her performance, so poorer performance will slow the progress toward midpoint, while improved performance accelerates it. Budgeting for the adjustments must be done based on the number of employees under midpoint and the time line to reach midpoint. When an employee reaches midpoint, any further payouts do not add to base. Anyone at or above midpoint would be operating on a lump-sum-only plan.

Two questions must be asked about the midpoint cap approach: how do managers handle individual performance plans for employees under midpoint and what about the people above midpoint?

First, employees are the customers of managers, whose job it is to provide whatever employees need to get their jobs done and to develop the employees in the process. It therefore seems reasonable to develop a base pay adjustment schedule for those employees who are under midpoint (generally four to seven of a manager's ten direct reports) and to develop a cost budget around what it would cost to move all employees to midpoint within a certain time. I believe this can be a more proactive and objective approach to merit increases than what we have today.

Employees are the customers of managers.

As for the people above midpoint, remember that employees who are already at or above midpoint are essentially frozen in place at their base pay until natural market adjustments bring the midpoint to their salary level. There will be a negative reaction from employees who have been used to getting an annual increase. However, many "over-midpoint" increases are quite small anyway. Individuals over midpoint could receive a lump-sum payout, of course. Plans on the capability side of compensation or recognition and group-based reward plans can be used to motivate all employees and to increase their income.

The Lord Corporation, located in Erie, Pennsylvania, implemented a strategy akin to this approach. This seventy-year-old manufacturer and marketer of chemical and mechanical products has sales of over $250 million. It is moving its employees to market rate over time with regularly scheduled base pay adjustments, and it is freezing base pay for those who are at or above market. For those under market, qualification for the base pay adjustment is a simple "pass-fail" performance evaluation. The company has made a commitment to its employees: "You will be paid at market rate (midpoint) in bad times, and we will all share in the good times."

Regardless of position in their salary ranges, all Lord employees participate in a group incentive plan that pays out lump-sum awards based on organizational unit performance. There are no merit increases in any form for people over market. When the strategy was implemented, there was a negative reaction from those over market, particularly those considered outstanding performers. But that response has died down over time. Robert Fine, the human resource manager, believes that the change in the process of adjusting base pay controls the swelling of base labor costs and lays the groundwork for the group incentive plan.

Compensation is a complex subject. Fortunately, there are compensation experts, consultants, and practitioners who are making compensation work better and more cost effectively. Compensation administration that is well communicated and executed can have a profound effect on morale, spirit, and loyalty. Compensation has become a cost management tool, however, and has little ability to improve organizational performance.

Promotions   In most cases, promotions bring a base pay adjustment, as well as perks connected with the new position and its increased responsibilities. The worst possible promotion scenario is when an employee is promoted into a manager's job simply because it is the only way to get him more money. Of all the reasons *not* to promote someone, that's probably number one on the list. Promoting an outstanding individual contributor who has limited people skills and little interest in administrative procedures to a management position sets up both the organization *and* the individual for failure.

Cross-training and succession (career) planning provide ways to make appropriate promotions. These programs move people around in the organization, exposing them to many disciplines, and then giving them next-level responsibilities before they get promoted to the actual position. A rigorous application of succession and career planning deep in the organization can enable companies to develop the competencies they require without making the mistake of moving people into jobs they're not able to do. The farther down into the organization the planning is taken, the less likely it will be that people will be promoted just to get them more money.

One nontraditional promotion policy is to see whether a person can do a job before base pay is adjusted. In the traditional approach, the base pay adjustment is often rationalized by saying that the increased responsibilities naturally require more base pay. Of course, if the person fails in the job, something management can generally spot within a year, the organization is stuck with an employee who is being paid too much. Consider giving the newly promoted employee an immediate lump-sum payment rather than a salary adjustment for the first year. If the person pans out, increase base pay accordingly. A lump-sum payment equal to or even less than the base pay adjustment has a higher recognition value than an increase spread out over twelve months. If you're worried about the newly promoted person leaving after getting the bonus, you've picked the wrong person in the first place.

With organizations becoming flatter, the opportunities for promotion are declining. The time has passed when people assumed they would remain with one company for their whole career and move into their boss's job when the boss moved up the ladder, hence the need for other types of reward plans to meet the natural demand for development and increased pay.

Earnings That Are Not Adjustments to Base Pay

Individual Incentives and Commissions   Individual incentives, once very popular in U.S. manufacturing businesses, are becoming rare for non-sales employees. One version—the traditional piece rate for the nonexempt employee—generally is given in addition to a relatively low base pay. The incentive is paid as a lump sum, not as an adjustment to base pay, and is based on individual measures, such as how many checks he accurately processes per hour, how many widgets she makes in a day, and so on. What is required, of course, is measurement against a reliable baseline (the lowest point at which the incentive may be paid). The problem is that the measurements are sensitive to technological changes, to how much work there is to be done, to the experience and training of the employee, and to the stability of the production line. Measurement can become an administrative nightmare. In most organizations, this inability to measure individuals precludes piece rates or individual incentives.

Commissions are one version of individual incentives given to salespeople. And they clearly work—to a point. They work because it is possible to measure salespeople individually, and because the incentive can be calibrated to meet the needs of both the organization and the individual. They are not an adjustment to base pay. Even with individual incentives and commissions, people tend to find their comfort level—the point at which they have balanced their effort with their acceptable income.

Too many sales incentives have become entitlements, however. For this reason, there has been an explosion of noncash incentives (merchandise, travel, and so on) to break employees out of their comfort level and motivate them to improve performance. (I discuss noncash awards in Chapter Ten.)

Variable Entitlements   "Variable entitlements" is a term I coined to describe bonuses given out by managers based on their subjective evaluation of individual performance. I make a distinction between variable entitlements and "spot bonuses." Variable entitlements are cash or stock, generally given out once a year to professional or managerial employees, that amount to more than 1 to 2 percent of base pay. Spot bonuses, according to my definition, are much smaller cash or noncash awards given spontaneously by managers and peers for doing something good and as a way of saying thank you. (See the discussion of recognition plans in Chapter Seven for more on spot bonuses.)

Highly valued and generally misunderstood, variable entitlements are reinforcing to those who get them, resented by those who don't, and expected to get bigger each year by all who know about them. They are primarily given to reward performers, after the fact, for contributing to the success of the organization. They are actually distribution plans that provide a mechanism with which to distribute the funds to covered employees. Variable entitlements do little to make the pool of bonus funds grow. One difficulty with variable entitlements is that they can live up to their name, that is, they can become *entitlements,* expected each year, that *vary* in size at the discretion of management.

Variable entitlements are reinforcing to those who get them, resented by those who don't, and expected to get bigger each year by all who know about them.

Everyone gets a kick out of giving someone an award. It makes the giver feel good, and the giver knows that it makes the recipient feel good. For the giver, the feeling is a powerful one that often is confused with largess and control. Giving such bonuses reflects goodwill, and often paternalism, toward the people who made it all happen.

Variable entitlements are subjective and difficult to explain, particularly if they are influenced by a sense of management largess and control. People are delighted to get the bonus, but they want to know why and what they have to do next year to get another, preferably larger, one. If the bonus isn't as big as last year, people get mad.

The most common variable entitlement is the management discretion profit sharing bonus. Everyone knows it is generated from profit, often according to a preannounced formula. For example, 6 percent of pretax profits may be allocated for profit sharing. How and why employees get what they get may be a complete mystery, but they sure better get more next year. Of course, if the penetration rate (the percentage of people getting a variable entitlement bonus) is 30 to 40 percent, then the other 60 to 70 percent of the people are unhappy unless they have an incentive plan of their own. Variable entitlements add to the expected compensation package with little consistent connection to individual contribution because of the management discretion wild card.

The most insidious thing about discretion is the message it sends. If your manager controls your bonus, you are going to serve and delight her (if you've got half a brain). So, who is the customer? The manager. The needs of the real customer are clearly secondary to those of the manager. The more management discretion there is in the distribution of variable entitlements (or rewards of any kind), the more confusion there is in the minds of employees as to where their allegiance lies. Even an innocent financial "thank you" can backfire. In 1994, the chairman of a major company gave each of his tens of thousands of employees a year-end bonus of $400 and a day off for "doing a great job." The response was terrific, particularly in an employee survey done the following month, which was a fluke of timing. The researchers did not know about the bonus. In 1995, the bonus was modestly increased. The tradition has been set. People will expect it, and it will cost the financial stakeholders millions for no return. But killing that bonus will have a significant negative effect on morale. The more variable entitlements in an organization, the more a paternalistic and hierarchical culture is reinforced. As organizations move away from hierarchy and paternalism, they will have to use more appropriate plans.

> *If your manager controls your bonus, you are going to serve and delight her. She just became your customer.*

Employee Stock Ownership Plans Employee stock ownership plans (ESOPs) give employees ownership in the organization. The hope is that because the employees actually own a portion of the company, they will behave as owners. When this happens, the financial and career stakeholders are one and the same.

Many organizations with ESOPs are still managed in traditional ways. Employees can either buy or be granted publicly traded company stock. Options to buy stock at a future date at the current (and hopefully lower) price are also granted. These practices are far more common for management than for the rank and file. *Open-book management* (OBM) companies, which believe in improving the organization by improving its performance through the financial literacy, trust, engagement of all employees, and a customized reward system, are not managed in a traditional hierarchical, command-and-control way. Many believe—Jack Stack of SRC for one—that ESOPs are critical to the process of creating OBM companies. A number of OBM companies, such as divisions of larger companies or private, family-owned firms, cannot become ESOPs, however, and yet they are very successful.

It can be argued that employees are rewarded by the growth of their stock value, but ESOPs are more often than not a tax-advantaged way of leveraging capital for the organization. (Sometimes, becoming an ESOP is the quickest way of raising money to save a company from going under.) For this reason, I have included ESOPs in this discussion of compensation. But it could be argued that they don't belong here. Instituting an ESOP is a significant financial business decision rather than a reward for performance. New businesses, such as start-up software companies, often give or issue stock in lieu of higher salaries. The expectation of the company's growth creates that sense of ownership in stakeholders, hopefully increasing their contributions to mutual success.

Benefits   Benefits are an important part of the total compensation package. They are clearly an entitlement, and they should be, since they play a pivotal role in the employee-employer social contract. They carry such power that any discussion about benefits as a way to improve organizational performance is limited to seeing how cheaply the company can get by without reducing the value of benefits so much that the organization's ability to attract and retain people will be affected.

Organizations are beginning to question whether benefits provide them with a competitive advantage. Not long ago, a CEO of a large West Coast utility told me his company was considering returning the administration of all of its benefit plans to the finance department. For thirty years, they had been administered by the human resources staff. The reason for the move, he said, was that benefits no longer had the power to attract and retain people and had become merely a cost of doing business (much like plants and maintenance). He felt that the finance department was better prepared to deal with cost centers. The next step would be to outsource the entire benefits operation.

Certainly, progress has been made in making the benefit package more adaptable to individual needs. There is an argument that connecting benefits to performance, such as matching funds based on organizational profit performance to individual 401(k) savings plans, can make employees more motivated to improve organizational performance. I believe it motivates people to save more money because of the matching fund plan. That's healthy, but it has little effect on an organization's performance.

Flexible benefits allow employees to "spend" the money the company would have spent anyway on the kind of benefits that makes sense to them. These plans also allow employees to spend even more on additional benefits by deducting the additional cost from their paychecks.

Benefits are included in this discussion of compensation only for completeness. Do benefits attract and retain? If the employee doesn't have any now, the answer is yes. Otherwise, benefits are entitlements. They are not connected to individual performance, and they are a cost of doing business.

Capability and Pay

Organizations already pay for capability; they build it into an individual's qualifications to do a job or fulfill a role. "Pay for knowledge" is usually practiced in an organization's hiring process by offering higher base pay or special one-time bonuses for people with certain technical skills or experience with specialized business situations. It also exists in underwriting all or a portion of college expenses of employees as part of the benefits package. This discussion, however, is about developing employees as a part of the overall performance improvement process.

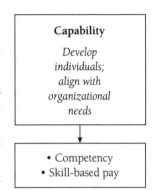

Capability plans offer ways to integrate personal development into the day-to-day fabric of employees' work lives. The connection to pay is not as clear. It depends on the plan. This portion of the reinforcement model is a mixed bag of processes, policy, management dedication, and reinforcement. The danger is that organizations will see the need to align individual capability with the organization's needs and will force pay into the process. There is a real risk of creating another inappropriate process like the performance management–merit increase process discussed earlier.

The most discussed labels in human resource circles today are *competency-based pay* and *skill-based pay*. Both focus on increasing the capability of individuals to meet the needs of the organization. Competency tends to be applied to exempt, professional, and managerial employees. (Competence is a defined state of being qualified, and competencies are specific areas of knowledge and abilities.)

Skill tends to be applied to nonexempt employees, focusing on proficiency or dexterity as applied to specific jobs. A focus on developing capability in the workforce is critical to an organization's future competitiveness.

Why Capability?

The growth of our intellectual capital will be a defining competitive advantage only if there is alignment between the individual's capabilities and those required by the organization.

The very nature of doing business has changed as our economy moves from manufacturing to service. But both sectors operate in the Information Age. Our employees contribute more and more through their knowledge, as well as their ability to work in a rapidly changing environment and to adapt to fluid work groups. The focus on employees has expanded from the job they can do to the larger role they can play in the organization and the contribution they can make. Technology now demands that our personal capabilities grow and adapt, both in our business and professional lives. The growth of our intellectual capital will be the defining competitive advantage of the truly successful organizations only if there is some alignment between the individual's capabilities and those required by the organization.

The need for employees with the appropriate capabilities is clear. The approach to getting them should be pragmatic, that is, not over-engineered; the approach should depend on the organization:

- Identifying the capabilities it needs

- Inventorying the capabilities it already has in its existing employee population

- Closing any gaps and establishing growth opportunities for employees

- Supporting employees who want to obtain more depth in existing capabilities and to add additional ones

- Determining whether employees have been successful in increasing their capabilities

That's a tall order but if it can be accomplished, organizations can support people development in a way that meets their employees' intrinsic needs to grow and to contribute, as well as the organization's need to be more successful by employing the right people with the right capabilities. It also provides an opportunity to move away from the ineffective individual performance review and to use all the positive elements of performance management.

Competency and Pay

Competencies can be generally categorized into two groups: role (what is needed to do a job or fulfill a function) and facilitation (what is needed to be more effective, such as communication, teamwork, and so on), but are not job- or function-specific. Role competencies for a financial manager might include knowledge of a variety of accounting techniques, cash flow management, and computing tools. Her facilitation competencies might include the ability to work in a team, make presentations, contribute ideas outside her normal role, and translate financial information to those not so financially literate. The combination of competencies each professional and managerial employee has or should have varies by individual and with the organization's needs. Developing both the needed competencies is no small task.

I believe competencies should become a basis for the development and coaching process of performance management. If we can effect a mutual agreement between an individual's performance and an overriding focus on the development of his competencies, we can better serve all of our stakeholders. But evaluating how successfully the individual demonstrates the appropriate competencies requires more information than a single direct manager can produce.

An approach that can contribute to the quality of performance and competency reviews is the *360-degree review.* In this feedback process, the employee is asked to identify a group of fellow employees (managers, direct reports, peers—anyone with whom they work) to regularly complete a survey about their performance and/or demonstrated capabilities. Combining this feedback with the manager's evaluation and the employee's personal opinion of his own performance improves the validity of the evaluation process significantly.

What is the purpose of the evaluation? Is it to determine an adjustment to base pay or a lump-sum bonus? Or is it a critical element in the performance management development process? Either will take a good deal of a direct manager's time. Either requires buying into the idea that employees are an asset, to be treated as customers and coached into greater effectiveness, and that evaluation is as important, or more so, than any other aspect of the manage-rial role. The capabilities development/evaluation process simply cannot be handed off to the human resources staff to administer. It must be the job of line management, along with good consulting advice from human resources. It is the job of upper management to value this process by insisting that successful competency-based performance management is a competency in itself, equally as important as any other in the managerial role. Again, it is a tall order but one that is critical to most organizations' future success.

"It is difficult to predict whether paying for competencies will have the long-term value as a way of paying for the person because current methods of establishing desired competencies and assess-ing an individual's competency are both time-consuming and rela-tively subjective. . . . On the other hand, competencies provide an excellent method of reorienting the organization around the newly emerging culture by encouraging a shared set of behaviors to accompany the decline in structure and management control" (Tucker, 1995, pp. 51–52). You betcha. Pay can be added to this process, but as a reinforcer, not as the primary focus. As one of the elements of an evaluation/performance review effort, competencies can shape an individual's ability to contribute in a positively rein-forcing way. It can affect the adjustment to base pay or simply pre-pare the individual for an expanded role or a different one altogether.

A "formula-ized" competency-reward linkage. A complex, over-engineered system. Just what we need.

Systems that "formula-ize" the competency-reward linkage would be counterproductive. That's just what we need: a complex, over-engineered system that tries to measure the imprecise very pre-cisely and reward equally precisely. We've done it throughout our salary administration history, and it would be folly to attempt to do it again under the banner of "competency-based pay." Rewards may be influenced by developing and demonstrating competency, but if they drive it, we've taken a step backward. I suggest we forget about competency-based pay as a type of reward plan and focus on iden-tifying and developing competencies in a way that will be accepted and utilized by line management. Whether or not you add any pay adjustments to the process is a decision you can make after the competency concept has settled in.

Compensation professionals are well on their way to developing the mechanics of making adjustments to base pay. A version of competency-based pay plans that organizations—particularly those with a large number of technical, often scientific, jobs—have used for years is known as *technical tracks* or *ladders*. We may quibble about the exact definition, but *technical tracks* do allow for a specific road map of base pay increases by demonstration of increased expertise. Increases in base pay are related to a person becoming more valuable to the organization, not to becoming a manager of people.

Technical tracks tend to be for exempt, professional employees only and to focus on the depth of expertise, the *role* competencies. The *facilitation* competencies are generally ignored. They are looked upon as an alternative to the traditional management track. Someone on a technical track can make more base pay than his or her direct manager. The power of this approach is that it puts a value on what a company needs: seasoned experts in particular roles.

Broadbanding is a part of making rewards supportive of competency development. Making the pay ranges much broader allows managers to move employees from role to role without fighting the narrow range system. Movement does not guarantee increases in pay but doesn't preclude it either.

Westinghouse's Energy Systems Business Unit (or ESBU—their commercial nuclear power operation) has introduced a competency-based performance management process that includes compensation adjustment. They have established a "competency index" as the measure of competencies demonstrated by an employee. That index, along with the employee's current base pay position in his or her salary range, determines the base pay adjustment.

A critical part of the process is the creation of an annual "zero-based" budget for each of the managers through a highly automated computer system. The system connects the competency indexes to what is needed in dollars to make the determined compensation adjustments. Top management adjusts the total request based on the company's overall financial performance. The adjusted amount is then prorated to all the managers' budgets. In this manner, base pay adjustments are directly tied to observed increases in competency levels—a major cultural shift. The responsibility and accountability for people development, evaluation, and determination of base pay adjustments have shifted from the human resources function to line management. The computer system provides all the information each manager needs to do the job.

When they have evaluated an employee's competencies, managers enter their results in the system and receive immediate feedback about internal equity (how an adjustment compares to others in the same situation) and the financial effect on their budgets. "It's a pragmatic system, engineered for automation," says Bob Holben, the ESBU's compensation manager, who designed and coordinated the process and implementation. "The managers like the automated aspects of the system, but they as well as the employees are uncomfortable about their current ability to accurately evaluate employee competency levels," Holben says. Rather than being discouraged by the concerns, Westinghouse's ESBU has redoubled its education and communication efforts to both management and employees. This approach is a major paradigm shift for a workforce steeped in entitlement, but it is critical to the success of the business.

I don't know many companies that are sophisticated or dedicated enough to the competency development approach to follow in Westinghouse's ESBU footsteps. Westinghouse emphasizes that their process is a management tool to support the development effort, not a formula-ized system. It is still rooted in the subjective, mutual employee-manager evaluation process. Although I have a general concern about a system that relies on automation and data sources, such a system can look scientific and empirical to the employee. Every effort should be made to explain the process in detail to everyone involved, so the system doesn't overwhelm the objective—development. In addition, the financial ramifications of a competency approach to employee development are not known, but the approach holds real promise if integrated with performance management, 360-degree feedback, and open communications.

Once we figure out the system, a competency acquisition process will be next on the list of challenges.

A final note about the use of a competency approach: if you are going to inventory, evaluate, respond to, and maybe even reward the development of competencies, you should be prepared to help employees acquire the needed competencies. I remember an employee's question about how he was supposed to acquire these highly valued competencies. The company answer: "Well, we've got a darn fine community college available and we'll pay for part of your schooling costs though the benefit plan." That is not going to cut it. Once we figure out the system, a competency acquisition process will be next on the list of challenges.

Skill-Based Pay

Skill-based pay generally applies to nonexempt employees. It provides compensation for the skills a person has or has acquired rather than for the job the person performs. Skill-based pay plans break down jobs into their components, or skill clusters, giving each component a value. When moving to skill-based pay, an inventory of skills is made for each employee. After the inventory, each employee knows what skills he has or needs in order to justify what he is making in base pay. Time is allowed for those who need to develop skills to justify their present base pay. If they don't, their pay drops to the appropriate skill-defined level. If the employee is underpaid for his present skills and his skills fall within the category, the company adjusts base pay accordingly.

After this initial phase, employees can add to their base pay by adding and then demonstrating skills according to a predefined schedule. This is the attribute of skill-based pay that is most appealing to employees—the clarity of the process. They know in advance what has to be done and the incremental earning opportunity. Figure 6.3 is a grid known as the *skill block matrix*. An example from the insurance business of how this grid can be used demonstrates skill-based pay at work. An entry-level job in a dental claims office requires that a new employee demonstrate ability in a specific skill cluster. For that, the employee would receive $20,000 a year. This entry-level position falls in the bottom left-hand corner of the skill block matrix. Over time, the employee might choose to add depth to his or her skills by learning to do initial screening. This skill would fall in the second block from the bottom of the left column of the matrix. The next level of depth might be to handle all basic claims, and so on, until the column is filled.

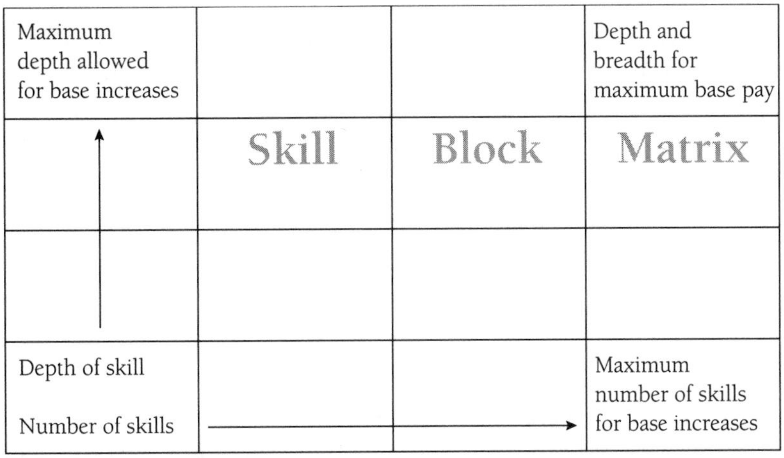

Maximum depth allowed for base increases			Depth and breadth for maximum base pay
↑	Skill	Block	Matrix
Depth of skill Number of skills	⟶	⟶	Maximum number of skills for base increases

FIGURE 6.3. *The Skill Block Matrix.*

The person might also acquire the skills necessary to handle additional types of claims. This would add greater breadth to the employee's skill base, and the particular skill would fall in the second block from the left in the bottom row of the matrix. As the employee continued to add to his skills, in depth and breadth, he would work his way to the top right-hand corner of the matrix and be earning a base pay of $30,000.

Some organizations require that people acquire depth before they add breadth. Some apply the concept to whole jobs. A hotel desk clerk, for example, can add housekeeping supervision, restaurant management, and back office management to his credit. Either way, the common requirements that must be met before the base pay adjustment kicks in are training, certification, and demonstration of the new skill.

The need for controls is obvious. Few organizations can afford to have employees as full-time students or pay for a rapid growth of base pay through uncontrolled skill or job acquisition. Defining the amount of time an employee has to wait before adding new skills or jobs, or controlling the number of skills or jobs that are available, based on the organization's needs, are ways to control the growth of skill-based pay costs. Skill-based pay had its genesis in manufacturing, where employees could expand their skills by, for example, learning to do maintenance on their machines (depth) or to run different kinds of machines (breadth).

Skill-based pay is a way to objectively increase base pay, as well as to increase the flexibility of the workforce through the development of people. But as Gerry Ledford of the Center for Organizational Effectiveness argues, organizations need to be "nimble" in their design and operation of skill-based pay (Ledford, 1995, pp. 46–54). Skill-based pay can become over-engineered and so complex that it dies under its own administrative weight. Even the simplest of plan designs, based on clear skill clusters and equally clear demonstration of mastery, must be adapted to different jobs within an organization. Developing skill-based pay for a group of one hundred employees spread among twenty different jobs, each with six to nine skill clusters, could be quite a project. Doing it for a thousand employees with a hundred jobs could be quite overwhelming.

The real cost, in addition to setting up the plan, is in the administration—training, certification, demonstration, observation, and crowd control. Plus, people may "top out" more quickly than in other plans. One option is to make the reward for skill acquisition a lump-sum bonus rather than a base pay adjustment. In this approach, traditional methods of base pay adjustments could be used, with the bonuses serving as one-time awards that must be re-earned by recertification. Skill-based pay does not pay for how well an employee does a job but rather for the number of skill sets he or she has and for the depth at which these can be used. For these reasons, I suggest going slowly. Select your applications carefully, and regularly assess the plan's effectiveness. There are few data to show the effect of skill-based pay on organizational performance, although in certain applications it is considered quite successful. I advise testing the process by piloting in small departments with well-defined skill sets before moving to an organization-wide implementation.

Conclusion

Individual compensation plans represent the portion of the total reward opportunity that is unseen. They are a cost of doing business. The expertise required to maintain this expensive system is increasingly important. Compensation must be made more cost efficient. Organizations cannot afford to allow their labor cost bases to grow faster than their profit margins.

I think organizations will continue to whittle away at the edges of individual compensation plans, with midpoint freezes, lump-sum bonuses, and reduction of entitlements. The ability to go to the heart of the matter—to reduce base pay levels and allow people to earn it back, and then some, based on how well the organization does—is a long way off.

Capability plans are another issue all together. I think we need to focus on using these plans to merge the language of personal performance and development from simply "This is how well you did your job this year" to "This is how we mutually agree you performed this year; here is the feedback on how you did on your role and facilitation competencies; and finally, this is how we can work together for you to develop your abilities—for your own development and for the organization's success." The language of capability can successfully focus on the people and their roles in organizations rather than on their jobs. Whether or not that language includes rewards will be a function of how well we develop a process that is line management supported and implemented and that focuses on performance and development rather than just pay. That's a real culture shift for most organizations—and a healthy one.

PART THREE

RECOGNITION, GROUP, AND PROJECT TEAM INCENTIVE PLANS

Just as individual compensation plans are too broadly defined as any plan that combines employees and pay, reward and recognition (R&R) plans are generally too narrowly thought of as "after-the-fact" recognition of individual jobs well done or a broad-based profit sharing plan. R&R plans are much broader and more dynamic than commonly supposed, for their objective is to *improve business performance.*

There are three types of R&R plans: *recognition plans, group incentive plans,* and *project team incentive plans.* All three types are most successful when they work together as a total strategy.

It is easier to attribute results to R&R plans than to individual compensation plans. Recognition plans influence results more than capability plans, group incentive plans more than recognition, and project team plans more than group incentives. By results I mean only those results that the R&R plans are developed to affect. There are side effects, of course. Recognition plans improve morale. Group incentive plans increase a sense of teamwork and synergy. Project teams give employees a sense that they can directly influence a result solely by their own efforts and contributions.

Recognition plans are pure investments in the performance improvement process in that the dollar value of a performance gain cannot be measured. What is recognized includes objectives, people, accomplish-

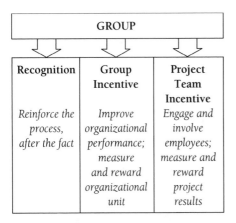

GROUP		
Recognition	Group Incentive	Project Team Incentive
Reinforce the process, after the fact	*Improve organizational performance; measure and reward organizational unit*	*Engage and involve employees; measure and reward project results*

ments, activities, and needs. Recognition plans are after-the-fact interventions rather than "do this, get that" interventions. Recognition plans are powerful ways to say thank you in a manner that is positively reinforcing and lifts the person's spirits, self-esteem, and probability of continuing on a positive path. In this light, they *reinforce the process* of performance improvement.

Recognition occurs after an event (a behavior, accomplishment, contribution, and so forth), which in itself can be reinforcing. It is highly likely that, given the opportunity, the event will happen again. For this reason, recognition is slightly more connected to results than are individual compensation plans.

When a team of employees, such as a cross-functional team formed to design a new reward plan, makes a contribution that cannot or should not be measured, the contribution is reinforced through recognition rather than through a formal project team incentive plan.

Group incentive plans measure the performance of an organizational unit and reward employees in that unit through a top-down process. They can measure the performance of a whole company, individual facility, division, department, or work group. They can also use different measures at different organizational levels. Because all (or at least most) of the employees within an organizational unit are rewarded for the performance improvement, it is reasonable to assume that most, but probably not all, of the improvement is due to the group incentive plan.

Project team incentive plans are grassroots efforts. Their focus and measures of performance can be chosen by the team itself (cost reduction is common) or be assigned by top management (such as integrating a new customer satisfaction assurance system). Team idea plans (or team suggestion plans) tend to focus on cost reduction and customer satisfaction. Continuous improvement or quality action team plans (or corrective action team plans) are products of the employee involvement element of the quality and continuous improvement movements. Ad hoc teams are formed under the direction of management in order to solve specific problems. Each team is rewarded based on its objectively measured and valued contribution. There is no question that the team is responsible for making the contribution. There is complete attribution. If, as noted earlier, the contribution of the team cannot be measured or valued, it should be reinforced instead by the recognition plan.

In addition, project team incentive plans can reinforce the connection between individuals and the measures of an organizational unit's group incentive plan. Project team incentive plans reduce the line of sight. When used in tandem with a group incentive plan, which may have measures that are remote to individual employees, project team incentive plans answer the question, "What can I do to make a difference?" These plans reward team members in two ways: based on the measurement and valuation of their project, and as members of their organizational unit.

These next few chapters focus entirely on the right side of the reinforcement model, where the rules are less clear than on the left side. Given that, the challenge to organizations is to recognize the power of people as assets capable of affecting overall organizational performance. Before accepting the challenge, companies need to understand that R&R plans have the unique ability to reinforce and accelerate other organizational interventions, such as quality programs, continuous improvement plans, new product development efforts, and the introduction of new technological systems. R&R plans are designed to benefit everyone—the company and the employees.

To appreciate the importance and power of this process, human resource and compensation departments are changing (and being forced to change) how they look at the world. They are generally the facilitators and administrators of these plans, but rarely the champions, who come from the ranks of top management.

Those top managers who have the greatest problems embracing R&R

as a solid way to affect business performance will say that they have gotten to their positions the "old-fashioned" way: they "earned" them. They have worked their way up the chain of command, focusing more and more on financial performance, working on satisfying more financial stakeholders, and being well compensated for their effort. By this stage in their careers, they have been conditioned to accept a long line of sight between actions taken in the short term and paybacks in the long term. They are often poorly equipped to craft R&R plans for their organizations because of their tendencies to project their own feelings and biases onto other people. ("I can affect profit at my level—surely you can too at your level.")

Ironically, the one bias that many executives often forget is their own personal experience with R&R. They sometimes like to recall their own careers as having been built on the purest altruism—with all the hard work and personal sacrifices made for the greater good of the business. An honest retrospective look generally reveals an escalating pattern of perks, incentives, bonuses, and other rewards. Considering the limited upward movement of most employees, it is even more important to appreciate the power of R&R when it links individual contribution and performance of the business. If it is good for the executive goose, isn't it really good for the rank-and-file gander as well?

R&R plans affect how people are treated, empowered, engaged, valued, directed, reinforced, energized, developed, informed, and trusted. Organizations tend to appreciate the contributions employees can make as individuals, but not their contributions as team members. The emergence of the employee as a career stakeholder to be served with the same vigor and effort as the other stakeholders can be difficult to swallow. But swallow we should, for everyone's benefit.

Recognition Plans

It is universally accepted that recognition is a powerful part of our personal and business lives. The most famous research on the matter is reported by Kenneth Kovach. In 1949, when supervisors and managers were asked about what they thought employees wanted most, they answered: wages, job security, and promotion/growth opportunities, in order of importance. When the employees were surveyed, they answered: full appreciation for work done, being involved, and sympathetic help on personal problems. Wages ranked fifth (Kovach, 1980, pp. 54–59). Similar findings have come from studies by the Families and Work Institute (1993) and Nelson (1994).

The need to have accomplishments recognized continues to grow as a driving force in organizations. When people feel unappreciated and are treated as if they must "check their brains at the door," they leave.

Recognition
Reinforce the process, after the fact

• Celebrate organizational objectives
• Reinforce activities and contributions
• Recognize extraordinary people
• Reinforce desired and demonstrated behavior
• Recognize service
• Recognize needs of employees

What You Will Find in This Chapter

Almost all organizations have some form of recognition plan in their operations. This chapter reviews the most common plans by:

- Discussing the appeal of recognition plans to management, their use and misuse

- Showing how they are rarely effective when they stand alone

- Understanding why competition belongs in the marketplace, not in the workplace's recognition plans

- Reviewing what recognition plans can do in an organization

- Reviewing how to design a recognition plan through the use of a recognition coordinator with enough budget to make a difference

The Appeal of Recognition Plans to Management

There is a perception in the management ranks that recognition plans are universally motivating and that the awards are "no cost–low cost." When asked to describe a really good plan, a manager's answer is often something like "a plan that recognizes our best performers." Stories are told by tough-minded managers of the tears in their eyes and in those of the person being singled out as a role model of what the company is all about.

Organizations love anecdotes about recognition plans. They are the emotional *proof* of the company's strategies, its approach, its plans. Organizations perpetuate their plans with little or no assessment of the role those plans play in reinforcement. Management uses its personal experience to justify the plans. This is how they understand the need people have to be appreciated for what they do.

Management uses its personal experience to justify recognition plans.

You remember when the boss went out of his way to write a note on your report about what a good job you had done, and how you felt when you read it, eight years ago. You remember when a fellow worker sincerely said what a good job you had done on a project last year. The feelings still run strong from the company meeting of all employees when the big sale was announced, and everyone felt they had contributed to the success. It felt good when the company marked your tenth anniversary with a service award. You realized how important the company is when you used the employee assistance plan, at no cost to you, to get some help on that serious personal problem.

For those of the employee population who have been singled out, recognition is a defining moment. The thrill of being wined, dined, listened to, photographed, rewarded with money or awards and plaques and publicity, and talked about by the president of the company can be right up there with the birth of a child, a graduation, a marriage, and a promotion. Those feelings should be celebrated and savored.

Not surprisingly, one of the better selling books of recent times is a paperback, *1001 Ways to Reward Your Employees,* by Bob Nelson (1994). It is a collection of anecdotes, presented in a style that suggests that they can be easily adapted to most organizations. It's fun to read, but like all such books it is not intended to tell you how to make the various options work in a coordinated fashion. Nor is it intended to tell you which methods are successful and which are not. The goal of the book is to supply readers with anecdotes and to call attention to the potential of recognition plans. And it has certainly done that.

A little recognition goes a long way. A lot of recognition goes further. The behaviorists say that reinforcement delivered as a surprise is the most powerful of consequences. They still need to be positive and immediate, but, with recognition plans, certainty is not required. Like quality, recognition is most effective when it becomes an integral part of an organization's day-to-day work life. Any salesperson will tell you that sincere customer appreciation is one of the best ways to get more business. Treating fellow workers and those who report to you as if they were your *customers* (as though our job is make *them* successful by doing whatever is necessary and reasonable) is an attitude that singles out companies as being great places to work. That attitude can be the foundation for all forms of performance improvement. More importantly, it is an essential element of teamwork and of the organizational flexibility that is needed to meet competitive challenges.

The Problem with Most Recognition Plans

Most recognition plans are built on anecdotes and out-of-date traditions rather than on research; most lack alignment with organizational objectives, underestimate the real cost to the organization, encourage counter-productive competition between employees, and inadvertently punish the unrecognized majority of employees.

Recognition is an act of acknowledgment. It is meant to be a reinforcing and positive process. It can be as simple as "thanks for doing a good job," as involving as being selected to work on a special developmental task force, or as memorable as a $25,000 award for developing a new product. Recognition is also being aware of what the organization and employees need.

Whether intended or not, recognition is an integral component of everything an organization does. Companies recognize the importance of an employee's skills through skill-based pay plans.

They recognize that certain positions are more important to the organization's success than others, and they show it in a variety of ways. They recognize the importance of a healthy workforce through the delivery of insurance, and of retirement through a pension plan. Just about everything an organization does recognizes an event, activity, or effort in some way.

A recognition plan is a formalized system that reinforces *the process of improving performance through people.* A helpful distinction from other types of plans is that recognition plans recognize events, activities, efforts, and contributions after the fact. There is no preannounced formula as there is in a group or project team incentive plan. Recognition simply acknowledges that an event has occurred and reinforces those who made it happen. The award vehicle may be a cash amount, or more often, a noncash or symbolic award. In almost every case, recognition is an investment in the improvement process, with no expected measurable gain.

Recognition plans do not always focus on the outstanding individual. They do not always use some form of noncash award. They are not limited to "catching someone doing something good." They are rarely "no cost–low cost," because of the time and energy they require to be effective. While employees do things that may improve performance, it is rarely due to the recognition plan, although they are likely to continue to improve because they have been recognized.

A Recognition Plan Should Not Stand Alone

The total reward opportunity in most companies is often compensation and an employee-of-the-month plan, which is a form of recognition. There is a problem when a recognition plan is the only reinforcement available other than compensation.

Recognition is most effective when given regularly in little chunks and integrated into the organization's overall process.

Recognition is most effective when given regularly in little chunks and integrated into the organization's overall process. If the CEO sees an employee of the month every month, she begins to think she is doing her bit to improve things through the workforce. The employee-of-the-month plan can take the place, in her mind, of a capability, group incentive, or project team incentive plan. I have seen more cynicism develop over poor recognition plans than almost anything else. When compensation is the only other plan, the recognition plan is scrutinized unfairly and expected to do things for both the organization and employees that it cannot do.

No Competition Allowed

Any time you select a few people for special recognition, you run the risk of creating winners and losers. If you select the "best of the best," the slogan doesn't offset the implication that work is a competitive race. Americans love competition, but competition in the workplace is counterproductive. (Alfie Kohn wrote an excellent book on this subject called *No Contest* [1992].) An organization's competition should be in the marketplace, not in the workplace. I want my customer satisfaction representative trying to outdo the representative from my competitor, not his peer sitting next to him. If an individual is competitive by nature and uses that competitiveness to do a better job, that's her decision. But corporately condoned competition through any reward plan detracts from the performance improvement that can be attained with teamwork. Leave competition in the sports field and the marketplace, where it belongs.

Competition should be in the marketplace, not in the workplace.

What Recognition Plans Can Do

The variations are enormous, but recognition plans can:

Celebrate organizational objectives

Recognize extraordinary people

Reinforce activities and contributions

Reinforce desired and demonstrated behavior

Recognize service

Recognize the needs of employees

Like most plans, these are only as good as their implementation and operation. The plan itself must be highly visible, and it must be flexible enough to meet changing needs. Because a plan's design can change so rapidly, it is important to have a wide range of recognition awards available, from "thanks" to a free lunch to cash to theater tickets to time off to points for catalogue merchandise. (I'll say more about that in Chapter Ten.)

Ill-advised generosity to employees on the part of the organization can backfire. In Chapter Six, I mentioned the major organization that awarded everybody $400 and a day off at the end of the year as a gift for having "worked hard." This symbolic gesture cost them more than $12,000,000 (not including the time off), and the company's performance was only mediocre. Granting the awards made the president feel good. It was his idea. It made employees feel good for a while. But what happens when they don't get the same award next year? Did it make good business sense? No. It would have made a lot more sense to use that $400 per person to fund a plan that supported the company's business objectives. Instead, the recognition gesture became a variable entitlement (a bonus that is expected each year, based on whatever management thinks employees should have) that has little value to the company.

Celebrate Organizational Objectives

If one of a company's objectives is to reach a certain level of customer satisfaction, reaching that level is cause for celebration, and the form the celebration takes should focus on the objective itself. Having a company picnic is one way to reinforce the customer satisfaction objective. All of the games and events can relate to some element of customer service: a ring toss with pegs identified as "on-time delivery" or a ball toss in which you hit the "product quality" target and dunk the volunteer manager.

Employee involvement in charity fund drives is the objective most commonly rewarded with recognition. The community stakeholder is well served when a company beats its fundraising goal with a high percentage of employee giving. The United Way thermometer can be seen in most companies' cafeterias. When the goal is met or exceeded, company-sponsored events recognize the accomplishment and reinforce how important it is. Every employee might be given coffee and donuts or a free breakfast. Individual givers of a certain level might receive a lapel pin marking their generosity.

Most quality efforts regularly recognize the objective of continuous quality improvement. Organizations have inundated people with "quality first" hats, coffee mugs, pen and pencil sets—all designed to remind employees of this particular company focus.

Recognize Extraordinary People

The most pervasive type of recognition plan in the country is of the employee-of-the-month ilk. These plans developed because they appeared to be the easiest. Managers or peers nominate the person they consider to have been outstanding during a particular period. They are usually reminded by the human resources department or the quality officer that it is time for another nominee. A management committee diligently goes through all the nominations, selects one or a few, and announces the results. The selected employees have their picture taken for the "wall of fame," receive a remembrance of the selection, and attend a luncheon in their honor. Top management sees all this and thinks it is really doing the job of motivating people.

Ask yourself why you would want to pick an employee of the month. Would it be to demonstrate that you care? To call attention to the person as a role model? To keep the person from leaving? Most of these plans do far more harm than good.

Employee of the whatever-it-is plans are time-based. There has to be a new outstanding person every month, quarter, or year, which forces organizations to go on reinforcement hunts as the end of each period approaches. Does it make sense that there really will be an outstanding performer every time? No. How do you measure outstanding performance anyway? It's hard to impossible. Consequently, you see plaques on hotel or supermarket walls with pictures of different "outstanding" employees every month. If you look at the little gold nameplates, you'll probably notice that names are seldom repeated. For some reason, each of these individuals suddenly became "outstanding" for one month, then presumably fell back into their nonoutstanding ways. After the first few selections, the process becomes a rotation selection, in which case it loses its credibility.

So, why does management think these plans are doing a great job? Just look at all of those outstanding people. CEOs and department heads will fight to keep employee-of-the month/quarter/year plans because they've seen the smiles of the winners. No question, the experience can be a very positive one for the person who wins. But what about the people who aren't "outstanding"? Since they aren't winners, they must be losers.

Ask yourself why you would want to pick an employee of the month.

That's the problem with competition imposed from the top down: since management discretion is inherent in choosing "outstanding" people, and managers are allowed to reach down into the organization and pluck out people for recognition and reward, who are employees going to try to please—their boss or the customers? The boss, of course. But it's not appropriate. These kinds of plans can also turn into rank-and-file lotteries rather than opportunities for employees to earn something.

A major complaint about employee-of-the-month plans comes from the supervisors who do the nominations. Sometimes they go to the effort of writing up the nomination and telling the employee she has been nominated, but then management selects someone else—sometimes a person less than outstanding in the employees' eyes—and the plan loses credibility.

Peers choosing peers doesn't work much better. It might be fine for the first six months, but in time the same people will probably be nominated over and over, and even if they are outstanding, the process isn't very motivating for everyone else.

Some organizations argue for these plans, claiming that outstanding people are good role models. If that's true, then the winners need to be *used* as role models. They should be able to tell their peers why they were nominated and what it means to be outstanding. If they can't explain it, then it's really counterproductive and can even be embarrassing. Some people just don't like to be singled out. If shy, retiring Jerry has done something that warrants being recognized, do not assume he likes *public* recognition. Organizations should exercise some good manners and ask before publicly recognizing people. So, if you must have an employee of the month/quarter/year, ask the winners if it's all right to communicate what they did so you can tell people what is important to the organization.

Outstanding performance doesn't occur on schedule.

It is possible to recognize extraordinary people in a positive way by removing the time constraint from these plans and recognizing people when they truly have acted in an unarguably outstanding way. There are extraordinary people in most organizations—for example, the linemen who worked seventy-two hours straight restoring power during a snowstorm and the package delivery person who crawled over the accidentally locked fence to get the time-sensitive laboratory samples to the plane on time. When employees do something far in excess of almost anyone's expectations, it is legitimate (with sensitivity to their personal wishes) to recognize them. Just don't do it on a rotation basis. Outstanding performance doesn't occur on schedule; you may have thirty in one year, or you may have none.

You can also look beyond the confines of people's jobs for outstanding performance. A welder on an assembly line who spends every weekend working with inner-city youth deserves to be recognized as outstanding. So does a secretary who spends two days a week running "meals on wheels" instead of taking her own lunch, and so does the manager who serves on the board of directors of a charity—at his own initiative, not at the company's request. These efforts support community stakeholders. Broadening the scope of recognition plans to cover extraordinary people who also happen to be employees is a powerful message of appreciation.

Without the rigor of having to select an "outstanding" person every month, it's easy to let an individual recognition plan go fallow. Don't. Constantly promote it. Remind all employees that the company values people who bring their humanity to bear on the company and the community, and that there is a process to recognize them.

Reinforce Activities and Contributions

Continuous improvement is a process that is difficult to measure in terms of specific results, especially when teams are involved. So, to ensure success, *continuous process improvement programs* are designed to recognize and reinforce activities that contribute to improvement.

Continuous process improvement programs are best characterized under the quality movement. The program is supervised by a management steering committee; quality management boards do the monitoring, and process action teams (or corrective action teams) become involved in improving the program. Employee involvement is critical to continuous process improvement, so employees must be continually recognized for the contributions they make.

The quality circle movement of the early 1980s failed because quality circles did not have the top-down discipline of the present-day continuous process improvement programs. Also, participants in quality circles were rarely rewarded for their contributions in a meaningful way. (Actually, the quality circle training manuals of the time touted the reward as "being allowed to present your ideas to top management." The strategy worked for a few organizations but not often enough to keep the effort alive.)

Someone who completes a training course may receive a plaque. Members of an ad hoc management team that complete a tough project might get time off, an engraved item specific to the project, or some other cash or noncash, tangible award.

The annual product fair held by some companies in which work teams set up booths and show their peers, their families, and management what they have been doing to improve quality can be a great celebration. Food, entertainment, and an integration of the family into the workplace have served to recognize everyone for their work.

The regular quality breakfast or banquet provides an opportunity to showcase the work of the teams that are to be recognized. No competition. No "quality team of the year." Just a celebration of the outstanding contributions employees have made. This occasion is also a perfect opportunity for management to share what is going on in the company and to reinforce the employees' role in improving performance.

These are all legitimate ways to recognize activities. There is a motivational quality to them because they remind the employees that the organization appreciates them and what they do. They are not "do this, get that" propositions. They're more like, "Thanks for doing that—and keep doing it." They are an investment in the process, just as celebrating objectives reinforces the process.

Reinforce Desired and Demonstrated Behaviors

Management is always talking about improving performance through changing behavior. When you pin them down by asking specifically what behaviors they want, they fall into generalities ("a good attitude" is one of my favorites) that are of little use. But talk about a specific situation and they can single out individuals who did just what the managers wanted. The employee demonstrated desired behaviors. You know it when you see it. And when you see it, you need to reinforce it right then. In this area recognition becomes a very personal thing. It requires good judgment, immediate action, genuineness, and the tools available for tangible recognition. The obvious is a solid "thank you," but sometimes you need more. And that is what spot awards are all about.

Spot Awards   Middle management and first-line supervisors are critical to the success of any business. They are given the operational responsibility for the organization's day-to-day work. But to give them the right to recognize a quality action team with awards valued at $400 without a series of management approvals? Somehow, that's risky. Most supervisors do not even have the right to buy an employee lunch in the cafeteria to say "thank you" for a job well done—regardless of whose budget it comes from. Organizations talk about empowering employees. How about empowering the people they have chosen to make the business run?

You do not need a formal plan for empowering all levels of management to tangibly recognize employees for doing a good job. You simply need to provide a process that makes it easy. One option is to allow managers to grant *spot awards* (which I introduced briefly in Chapter Six in contrast to variable entitlements).

Unlike variable entitlements, which generally are annually generated bonuses of significant value, spot rewards are frequent and of modest value—usually small cash or noncash awards that are given to individuals or teams simply for having done a good job. They are designed to reinforce desired and demonstrated behaviors of as many people as possible. The more often you say "thank you," the more motivated people will become. Maritz gives everybody a checkbook containing ten checks worth $5 each in award points. People can hand an employee or peer a $5 check with a note on it saying "thanks" for whatever they did. There might also be a requirement on the check that it be used for specific objectives, such as quality process improvements or customer service ideas or doing a little extra on developing that notion for the team idea plan. It doesn't feel right to hand someone a $5 bill, which would most likely be combined with other cash anyway and lose its recognition value. Checks worth $5 in award points can accumulate and be used to get something of value. Receiving these checks makes people feel good, and they are inclined to repeat the recognized behavior. That's one of the goals of recognition.

Spot awards are an ongoing process, so they provide the ability to thank people whenever it is appropriate. Does that mean you have to reinforce everybody for everything? Of course not. Spot awards are merely an enabling mechanism for a first-line supervisor or peer to say "thanks" and have it really mean something to the recipient.

Surprisingly enough, the problem with this type of plan is not runaway costs, as most people believe, but getting people to give out the spot awards. The idea of recognizing employees is so foreign to most supervisors that organizations have to organize breakfast or lunch meetings to promote a positively reinforcing environment. At these gatherings, supervisors tell how they use the spot awards and suggest ways that others can put them to use. Upper management can learn a good deal about a supervisor's style by how and why she uses spot awards.

Reinforce Project Teams   Project teams may be reinforced through project team incentive plans, which are formalized processes of rewarding employee involvement and the results of that involvement. These plans will be discussed in detail in Chapter Nine. The primary requirement of project team incentive plans is that performance must be *measurable and valued* (generally as a dollar gain or as a function of the measurement itself, for example, a 3 percent gain in customer satisfaction). Whether the team is focused on a cost reduction project, whether the project is a system change by customer service representatives to improve their service, or whether the team is a quality corrective action team that regularly responds to each quality problem in the system, the team and its project make a significant contribution to the organization. Cost reduction, for example, can be measured and valued. The individual or team that came up with the idea, developed the business plan for approval, and saved money for the organization deserves to be rewarded in accordance with their contribution. The customer service reps may have developed their system change and implemented it with an agreement that if customer satisfaction increased, they would receive an award based on an agreed-upon award schedule. But if a team *just did something* and it made a difference that could not be measured or valued, the team members are candidates for recognition.

Quality corrective action teams may operate as a part of a group incentive plan that rewards everyone in the organization on an internal measure of quality. Management may also be wise enough to recognize and celebrate the team members' day-to-day contributions in serving on the teams. The contributions of these types of teams probably shouldn't be measured and valued. To do so would miss the point of continuous improvement. But after-the-fact recognition and celebration of their work are terrific stimuli and ensure team members' ongoing participation.

So, the bottom line is: if you can't measure and value the contribution, recognize it. Recognize it formally, informally, on a schedule, as a surprise. But do it.

Peer Recognition   For peers to recognize peers by saying "thank you" is a lost art in American business and social life. As society becomes embedded in the world of voice mail, E-mail, and computer tools that help with planning and thinking, people become more isolated from one another. The "high tech, low touch" prediction has become a reality. In a time when teamwork is more important than ever before, service and staff organizations particularly have to find ways to encourage employees to interact with and express appreciation for each other.

An idea that has stood the test of time is a simple process for encouraging people to say "thanks." Everyone is given some 4×6 cards. The cards have no value in themselves. Whenever someone helps you with a project or responds to a request in a particularly helpful way, you send a card to the person with your thanks, specifying the reason. At the end of the month, the cards are put in a barrel and a public drawing is held. The first card to be drawn gets the grand prize—something significant. Merchandise or travel are good choices. Whatever it is, it should be impressive and well-publicized. Both names on the card are winners. Up to 25 percent of the rest of the cards are drawn for less significant prizes. (A value of $25 each is a good amount. That's a good rule for drawings: one big prize and lots of smaller ones.)

This process makes saying "thanks" fun, and it gives a corporate push to the spirit of teamwork. You don't do it every month but certainly every three to four months. Make it a surprise, not on a pre-announced timetable.

Recognize and Celebrate Service

Service awards have come a long way since the gold watch at retirement. They serve two purposes. The first is to tangibly celebrate milestones in an employee's tenure with the company. These milestones are usually in five-year increments (five, ten, fifteen, and twenty plus), with the service award increasing in value with each increment. Traditionally, the organization decided on a specific award for each milestone (a pen and pencil set, then a glass paper weight, then a desk clock, and so on, all with the company logo). I appreciate the thought, but I've never found the large, expensive cut-glass bowl, emblazoned with the logo of my company and "15

I've never found the large, expensive, cut-glass bowl, emblazoned with the logo of my company and "15 years," something I wanted to display on my dining room table.

years more," something I wanted to display on my dining room table. Today, organizations are trying to make the service award more personal and more to the employee's taste. They are offering a wide range of merchandise at each level. In addition, most organizations are given additional days of paid vacation days for longer service.

The second purpose of service awards is to publicly express the value the organization puts on longevity of service. New entrants into the workforce do not expect to stay for long, and there is some value in letting them know that the company celebrates continuity of service. The publicizing (with the employee's permission) of anniversaries in the company newsletter is often accompanied by a display of color photos in a length-of-service display in the company cafeteria. (A framed copy of the photo sent home with a letter from the CEO is a nice touch.)

Recognize and Meet the Needs of Employees

Providing services for employees makes the organization a special place to work, while reinforcing the process of performance improvement. The advent of flexible benefits can be a recognition of the unique needs of different employees. Most flex plans are touted as a way to reduce the cost of benefits to the company, but I would argue that communication of the value, financial and otherwise, of the plans, is equally important. A single person does not need the same level of insurance as a family of six. Flexible benefit plans allow the employee to redistribute funds (both those provided by the company and those deducted from her paycheck) to obtain the benefits most appropriate for her. At the same time, it breaks down benefits from one large chunk into smaller ones, each with its value in dollars and cents. That significantly increases the positive reinforcement potential of benefits.

Employee assistance programs (EAPs) recognize employees' needs to specifically address the stresses of modern working life (which can result in credit and substance abuse, relationship issues, and so forth), free of charge and completely confidentially. Companies are generally charged for these services not on the basis of usage but with a flat fee, so there is every reason to actively promote EAP to all employees. Like all recognition plans, EAPs must be constantly promoted. One of the real wastes of money is for EAPs not to be used to the fullest extent possible. Managers should reintroduce the plan to all employees each year and make it an integral part of all new-employee orientation.

Celebrating and recognizing the importance of wellness is quickly becoming an integral part of business life. Healthy food offerings in the cafeteria and vending machines are common. A yearly health fair may be held to provide basic blood pressure checks and other simple tests, health food education classes and displays, and an opportunity to give blood to the Red Cross. At Maritz, walking, jogging, and exercise events are held daily for all employees. Each participating employee keeps a record of his mileage or hours of class. At certain levels, sportswear is earned, ranging from caps and water coolers to full running suits. The plan is promoted monthly, and feature stories on those who have reached different levels of performance appear regularly in the newsletter.

Other plans are available at full or shared company expense in recognition of employee needs. A recent survey of one hundred major employers reported that nontraditional services are becoming more prevalent. Of these companies, 50 percent had on- or near-site banking, 40 percent had child-care resources or referrals, 40 percent had medical services, 25 percent had travel ticketing and discounts, 24 percent had convenience stores, 14 percent had dry-cleaning services, and 10 percent had hair salons or barber shops (Towers Perrin, 1995, pp. 18–19). Other services and benefits that might be provided include tuition sharing, shopping services, errand-running services, mailing and packaging of personal items, matching donations to charity and arts organizations, flextime, sabbaticals, vacation planning assistance, carpooling and special bus routes, free meals when working late, summer camps, emergency car services, stop-smoking seminars, and birthday cards and Mother's Day flowers.

Designing a Recognition Plan

There are far more than 1001 ways to recognize objectives, activities, individuals, teams, and employee needs. Like most reward plans, the possibilities are limited only by the creativity of the designers. The Reward System Effectiveness Model, discussed in Chapter Four, still applies but less stringently. After all, you are not going to spend as much money on recognition plans as on any other option. You do want to follow the strategic objectives, desired culture, awareness, value, and performance sensitivity elements closely, however. Designing a recognition plan and ignoring the effectiveness model may not cost you much money, but it can create some very bad feelings among employees.

Unlike most plans, recognition plans are also budget bound. Recognition plans rarely have a financial justification in themselves. They are investments in improving the environment and in reinforcing the process of improving performance through people.

How much is enough? The usual budget for the infamous employee-of-the-month program and other minor activities is from $10 to $30 per employee per year. Companies that understand the importance of recognition to their effort to improve performance spend from $100 to $300 per employee per year. What most companies do not realize is how much money is actually spent on those myriad recognition plans developed by first-line supervisors who must have them to meet their objectives. A recent assessment of a large bank discovered a total expenditure of $275 per employee, not the $40 budgeted. When supervisors and managers need a plan, they find the money.

Corporate control of recognition budgets is not the answer. Making it easy to get recognition design advice and standardized recognition awards is. By providing a centralized coordinator of all recognition plans, a company can get the best bang from its recognition buck. You do not want supervisors spending their time selecting awards from the dozens of premium suppliers that appear like paparazzi. Most important, you do not want them wasting time in the administration of these plans. A centralized coordinator ensures centralized billing, so supervisors know what they spend. The coordinator can make sure there is synergy between the variety of recognition plans, and he or she can work with the design and operations teams for the group incentive and/or employee involvement plans.

One of the value-added services that a recognition coordinator can provide is a wide range of awards. These are available from a variety of suppliers or from an all-purpose merchandise catalogue. Recognition points can be issued as awards in check form and accumulated for larger items.

So, other than what is obvious in each type of recognition plan, the design is a matter of style, promotion, and reinforcement of all the other activities and reward plans operating in the organization. The easiest thing to remember is that when you don't think measuring and valuing contributions make sense (or when you think that measurement just may not be worth the time and effort), recognize your employees through social, symbolic, financial, or non-cash awards.

Conclusion

Recognition plans are intended to reinforce the process of performance improvement by constantly reminding everyone how much the organization appreciates their efforts and contributions. The design of these plans is driven by their application, and there are as many creative variations as there are creative people. The plans should not create an internally competitive atmosphere. They are an investment and are rarely cost justified. They usually are heavily promoted and underfunded. Recognition plans can add the fun, excitement, and satisfaction a company needs in these times of competitive market stress. They make everything work a bit better.

Group Incentive Plans

Group incentive plans include a wide range of reward plans that align organizational objectives and employees. In the CARS research discussed in Chapter Two, they were called *organizational performance reward plans,* technically the most correct label of the myriad options, but somewhat unfamiliar to the average manager. They are also called measurement-based plans, team-based incentives, gainsharing, success sharing, goal sharing, safety incentives, winsharing, performance sharing, and profit sharing. The reasons for so many name variations for group incentive plans range from the desire to be technically precise to the desire to create a name for consultants to trademark for marketing purposes. Regardless of the name, all of these plans are variations on the same theme: they focus on an organizational unit, define its measures of success, and reward all or some of its employees for improved performance based on all or some of the measurements. The earnings (or payouts) from group incentive plans do not add to base pay.

> **Group Incentive**
>
> *Improve organizational performance; measure and reward organizational unit*

Group incentive plans are the most powerful of all the reward plans that aim to align employees with organizational objectives. They reinforce teams, whether as a cultural statement (as in the integrative/high involvement culture described in Chapter Four) or as an organizational unit (as in a team of employees from all functions organized around a specific product or service).

Payouts from group incentive plans do not add to base pay.

What You Will Find in This Chapter

This is the longest chapter in the book and the closest thing in it to a "how to." Its length is due to two elements. First, group incentive plans are customized to the organization's needs, so a number of options are discussed. Second, the final design must take into consideration a number of variables—measurement, participation, time frame, structure, and financial rationale, to name just a few. I describe the principles of and options for these elements, which often is like trying to describe which came first, the chicken or the egg. The design of group incentive plans is an iterative process that requires regular reassessment of where the team stands as a design team, checking the emerging design against the needs of the company's stakeholders—particularly the employees, and the financial stakeholders, represented by top management. It is truly a balancing act.

I begin the chapter by providing a definition of group incentive plans and of the terms I'll be using through the rest of the chapter. Then I will discuss:

- How to design a plan

- Top-management direction of the planning process, including determination of desired culture, objectives, broad measures, and weighting; funding and at-risk elements; and design teams

- Key points regarding measurement and its use in different organizational units

- Who should participate in group incentive plans

- Setting baselines and goals

- At-risk elements, the art of payouts, and determination of the plan period

- Calculating gain

- Creating the reward structure

- Line of sight and cycling

- TQM and incentives

Definitions

Here are a few definitions that will be useful as you read the rest of this chapter.

Group

A group is any organizational unit; it is any association of people that is seen as an organizational "set" when viewed from the top down. It could be the whole organization, a business unit, a facility (location), a department, or a work group. Groups can limit who participates according to the person's level in the organization—middle management only, rank and file only, production people only, and so forth—although it is the norm to consider everyone in the organizational unit a potential member. A work group can be a traditional first-line supervisor and her direct reports, or a self-directed work team.

Team

The second definition of "team" in the dictionary defines it as a group of people working together for a common purpose. (The first definition has to do with two or more oxen harnessed together. It's my hope that this definition has no place in this book.)

Generally, the first question people ask me on the lecture circuit is how to reinforce teams. They are generally referring to self-directed work teams. I believe they are really asking about how to pay for individual performance within a self-directed work team. I have addressed individual compensation in Chapter Six. If the question is about reinforcing them as a team, the answer is to handle them just like any other organizational unit that can be measured and valued. There's nothing unique about reinforcing the accomplishments of self-directed work teams. The goal of such teams is to create some commonality of focus, responsibilities, and tasks so that employees will be able to work together more effectively. The measurement of the outcome of such teams is usually not based on individual members' contributions but on what the members accomplish together.

There's nothing unique about reinforcing the accomplishments of self-directed work teams.

If your organization has continuous improvement, quality, or suggestion teams and they are rewarded on the basis of their contributions, they have the project team incentive plan (discussed in Chapter Nine) all to themselves.

Incentive

An incentive is any type of award (cash or noncash) that is contingent upon some measure of performance. It is not based on largess or any other nonperformance-based criteria (that would be a variable entitlement).

Line of Sight

Line of sight (LoS) is an employee's perceived ability to influence a measure upon which a reward is based.

Line of sight (LoS) is an employee's perceived ability to influence a measure upon which a reward is based. LoS is variously described as *long* (a single measure of profit for a large organization) or *short* (a measure of productivity for a small work group), and as you would expect, everything in between. LoS is affected by the level of the organization measured and rewarded, the type of measurements, and the frequency of payouts. I'll say more about this later.

Cycling

Cycling can reduce the organization's net gain in performance.

Cycling is the net effect of performance as it varies from group to group, period to period, measure to measure, or any combination of these elements. Cycling reduces the organization's net gain in performance if that performance falls below baseline in any one group, measure, or payout period. For example, one group's poor performance can counteract another's good performance; February's performance can be offset by March's downturn.

At-Risk

I discussed at-risk plans in Chapter Six, primarily as ways of reducing base pay and allowing employees to earn back what was taken away and more. The most common way employees earn back and more is through a group incentive plan. Reducing base pay is very rare and risky, but reducing the merit increase pool is less so. The fact that the popular definition of at-risk includes reducing or slowing down merit increases attests to the extent to which they have become an entitlement. Nevertheless, it is becoming a common practice as a partial funding mechanism for group incentive plans.

Group Incentive Plan Criteria

The reward structure describing the formula for earning in group incentive plans is preannounced. People are told before the plan starts what they can earn on each group performance measure. The formula also tells people *when* and *how* the plan will pay out.

Once the award is earned by the group, everyone included in the plan receives a payout. (The only exception is when an employee is on probation.) Group incentive plans do not limit awards to a few "winners" chosen by their supervisors. Plans that use management discretion to determine who is rewarded undermine performance improvement through teamwork. Group incentive plans rely on objective, measurable results. Differentiation among individual employees' performance is the purpose and responsibility of compensation, not group incentive plans.

Group incentive plans do not limit awards to a few "winners."

The CARS research was even more restrictive in its definition of group incentive plans. It excluded plans that covered only managers and those that required the earnings to be deferred into a retirement account. In this book, these two approaches are considered design options.

Development of a Group Incentive Plan: An Overview

The assessment of the organization's culture and existing reward plans has already been completed (see Chapters Three and Four). The results of these assessments will be used by both top management and the design team in the group incentive plan development process. Figure 8.1 illustrates the steps in this process.

The first step in the development process is for top management to decide what culture they want to foster in the company, based on their assessment of the organization's existing culture. (Top management can be the company CEO or the plant manager and her staff, but it should be the management level that has the authority to make the final decision on whether or not to install the plan.) Next, they determine which of the company's primary objectives can be influenced by the majority of the employees. Then they weight the objectives. The next step is to appoint a design team. Top management can provide the design team with direction on the specifics of the design—for instance, they might insist on certain measures of success for the objectives—but these and other decisions are best left to the design team. In fact, the less top management attempts to direct the design effort, the better.

The design team lives up to its name—it designs the plan. As a first step, it is wise for the design team to get some sense of management's understanding of plan funding. Most managers think of the group incentive plan as a way to distribute the funds created by some financial measurement. I'll refer to them as "distribution of

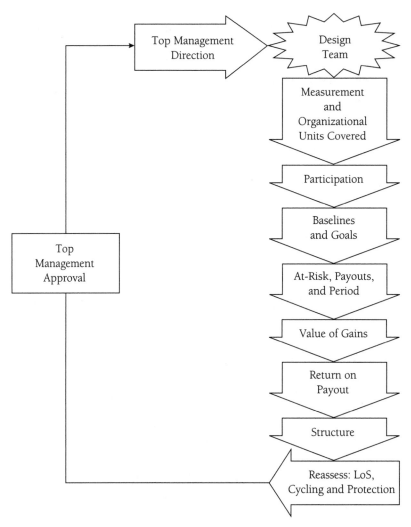

FIGURE 8.1. *The Group Incentive Plan Design Process.*

funds" plans. Another view, and one that makes plans more effective, is that plans create the funds through performance improvement, called "creation of funds" plans. Employees are to understand that by improving performance they are also earning their awards.

The steps in the design development process are as follows:

1. Determine the measures for each objective.
2. Determine the appropriate organizational units to be covered by each measure, based on what's possible and reasonable.

3. Agree on what part of the employee population should be included in the plan.
4. Set baselines and goals for each measure.
5. Decide if there is any "at-risk" for employees, what amount of reward is necessary to motivate employees to reach the goal of each measure, and how long the plan should run before reassessment occurs.
6. With the help of the finance department, place a dollar value on the performance gain at goal for each measure. For those measures for which a dollar value of the gain cannot be determined, express the goal achievement in the terms of the measure itself.
7. Calculate the probable return on payout (return on investment) at goal. If the return is not acceptable and reasonable, adjust the plan elements accordingly.
8. Create the reward (payout) structure.
9. Reconsider the plan in light of two key elements: Line of Sight (LoS), which is important for employees to be motivated, and protection from cycling, which is important for the organization's projected return on plan investment. Also consider the degree of protection necessary: what is the connection between organizational profit and plan payouts?
10. Agree with top management that the plan is justified to become a business strategy and worthy of top management's commitment and support.

As you read this chapter, you will discover that the design process is not always linear. Rather, it is like a mosaic. There is constantly a need to weigh different parts of the design against each other.

> ***The design process isn't always linear. It is like a mosaic.***

Top Management Direction

The first step for top management is to determine the desired organizational culture (see Chapter Four, especially Figure 4.2). The options are the caring/paternalistic, integrative/high involvement, and exacting/demanding cultures. (I doubt that anyone wants their organization to be apathetic.) Group incentive plans support and shape all three cultures, although they are most applicable to developing an integrative/high involvement one.

Top Management Direction

Objectives, Broad Measures, and Weighting

The next step is to determine which of the company's primary objectives can be influenced by employees. A sample list of my Midwestern Company's objectives, and their associated measures, is as follows:

Business Objective	Broad Measure
Improve financial performance	Profit or return calculation
Reduce cycle time	Days from order to payment
Improve productivity	Output divided by input
Improve quality	Cost of poor quality
Reduce turnover	Percentage of voluntary resignations of total employment
Create a flexible workforce	Skill-based pay installation project; project milestones
Reduce benefit costs	Benefits as a percentage of total payroll costs
Develop a contingent workforce for telemarketing department	Hire, train, and begin operations with new workforce by January 1

Not all of these objectives are appropriate for group incentive plans. Top management must agree on which objectives are appropriate. Group incentive plan measures should be closely connected to the measures of those business performance objectives that can be affected by the largest number of employees in the group. In the example, financial performance, productivity, cycle time, and quality are the most obvious choices. Turnover could be a measure for managers only, possibly in addition to the other four. The last three objectives (flexible workforce, reduced benefit costs, and a contingent workforce for telemarketing) are affected by a small group of people, often as projects (candidates for project team incentives) or as part of their normal responsibilities.

Top management should establish the broad parameters for the plan design. For instance, they may decide which organizational units are to be included—the whole company, a division or facility, and so forth. They may require that one or more specific measures be covered or addressed in the plan. For instance, they may be very specific about the measure of financial performance being returned on net assets or net income before taxes. Finally, top management could weight the relative value of each objective. (This could also be done by the design team.) The impact of weighting is in the message it sends ("This is what is important around here") and in its function as a distribution mechanism for awards (more about that later). Following is the Midwestern Company's list of appropriate objectives and their corresponding measures and weights:

Objective	*Broad Measure*	*Weighting*
Financial performance	Profit or return calculation	25 percent
Productivity	Output divided by input	25 percent
Cycle time	Days from order to payment	25 percent
Quality	Cost of poor quality	25 percent
		100 percent

Funding and At-Risk

The funding of a plan often determines the plan design, so if there are strong management directions on how it is to be funded, it is critical to get them now. The options are:

Distribution-of-funds: Profit or some other financial measure creates a pool of funds that is distributed to suborganizational units or individuals based on whatever criteria they wish. This is clearly a distribution-of-funds approach, which is typical of profit sharing plans. Nothing is distributed unless the pool of funds is created by profit. That gives top management a sense of security. It doesn't do much to improve the profits, however, because the LoS is generally so long for the rank and file. So, if you want to be safe, the distribution-of-funds approach is for you. Simply realize that the ability of employees to affect the results is significantly reduced.

If you want to be safe, the distribution-of-funds approach is for you. There's little hope for performance improvement, however.

Creation-of-funds: This group incentive plan is designed as a business strategy, with the usual upsides and downsides. The plan should generate gains, generally enough to cover costs, plus some. The real intent, however, is to align the reward plans with the business objectives and the desired culture. It will not be possi-

A creation-of-funds approach, for the most part, will create a more attractive return on investment.

ble to give all of the objectively measurable improvements a dollar value. The plan may require an investment (cost) or the risk of one in order to improve performance and reinforce the desired culture.

Creation-of-funds plans reduce performance improvement. Without the potential pain or risk, there is little hope or gain.

Organizations get what they pay for and that requires some risk. I suggest that group incentive plans be designed as creation-of-funds plans. They are more dynamic than the distribution type, and they get everyone in the game (management doesn't have to play as hard when they are protected). If management will not approve it, you can fall back to the funding that comes from a financial measurement like profit. It won't change the design much, and you will have learned a lot about how your measurements can be refined to more accurately reflect performance. For the rest of the chapter, I will assume a creation-of-funds approach. For most organizations, it will create a more attractive return on investment than the distribution-of-funds design.

The discussion of at-risk for employees may or may not be held at this stage of the process. As discussed in Chapter Six, at-risk is pay (either present—base pay—or future—merit increases or cost-of-living adjustments) that has been reduced, while the employee has been given opportunities to earn back what was given up, plus more. If one of the objectives of the plan is to curtail the employees' entitlement mentality (that merit increases are expected), management may direct the design team to consider reducing future merit increases. In the more extreme (and rare) situation, management may direct the design team to reduce base pay. In both cases, employees would be given opportunities to make up what had been taken away and to earn even more. These decisions have broad cultural implications, but such reductions can provide an additional source of funds for the plan itself. It also sends a very strong message that the organization has to have results for employees to make more money.

Top management generally provides the design team with only sketchy information about other aspects of the plan's parameters. They may suggest that the plan be self-funded, or that top management should be excluded from eligibility, or that different measures be used at different levels of the organization, but these specifications are rare. The more open top management can keep the parameters, the more creative the design team can be. One caution: the design team should make sure it knows top management's deal breakers—those terms that are completely unacceptable.

The Design Team

Plan design is a funny business. It is a bit like advertising; people think they could have easily come up with a good slogan *after* they've read one. CEOs like to fiddle with reward plan design. Unfortunately, they think the rest of the employees have the same understanding of the financial side of the business as they do. Given the opportunity to fiddle, the plans they design tend to look like a poor version of the executive compensation plan. Group incentive plans are expressly for nonexecutives. The successful ones bear little relationship to executive incentives, which tend to be solely driven by financial performance. Nonexecutive group incentive plans generally combine all types of measurements, financial and nonfinancial. So, CEOs should not try this at home. It is a job for professionals—for the design team.

Design Team Membership

Most group incentive plans are designed by a team of managers, usually six to eight from the middle ranks. Teams with both management and nonmanagement members are also common. Members are generally appointed to the project by top management. It takes about forty-five employee days over a fifteen-week period for a design team to come up with a group incentive plan proposal for top management. The time invested is less for service industries and more for manufacturing. When nonmanagement employees are a part of the design team, the required number of employee days doubles and the time frame increases slightly (McAdams and Hawk, 1994, pp. 121–123).

Why involve nonmanagers? For their point of view. The broader the input, the higher the quality and acceptability of the design will be. Most managers argue that the reason for involving nonmanagers is to gain the plan's ownership by the rank and file. However, representatives of the rank and file are included on the design team not merely to gain their ownership but to allow the plan's promoters to say honestly that the design process was more egalitarian than it would have been if the plan had been designed by a management-only design team. The CARS research shows that teamwork, communication, and feedback are better in plans that have been designed by teams that include nonmanagers.

Note: Sometimes people worry about including union employees on design teams. They may also be concerned that having nonmanagement employees serving on a design team might violate the National Labor Relations Board rules. If you're concerned about these issues, discuss them with your legal and labor relations department.

Some Rules for Getting the Job Done

How to run an effective design team process is another one of those subjects extensively covered elsewhere, particularly effectively by Glenn Parker. Following are a few rules for making design teams effective (adapted from Parker, 1990, 1994):

1. *Every design team needs a champion.* This person may or may not be a member of the design team, but you need someone who can handle the political intrigues that can scuttle a design process. Most champions are from top management, and in the best of all worlds, he or she would be involved and supportive throughout the design process. With no slight intended to the human resources and compensation departments, the champion should be from a line rather than a staff position.

2. *The design team leader is in for the long haul.* The leader of the design team needs to be an influential line or executive staff person whose focus is either strategic (creation-of-funds) or administrative (distribution-of-funds). Teams should not be headed by someone from the human resources or compensation department, but they should be represented. It is common for the leader of the design team to be the coordinator for the plan when it is implemented.

3. *Most of the stakeholders in the organization should be represented by the design team members.* At the same time, it's best to limit the design team to six to ten members. Anything beyond that can cause effectiveness and scheduling problems. The design team should always include someone from the finance department. You'll need her expertise. She will be asked to provide a lot of the financial rationale. (And at some point she will be asked to defend the plan, so you don't have to. Plans that involve money are always better received coming from finance people.)

Always include someone from the finance department. You'll need her expertise.

A representative from management information systems (MIS)— the computer folks—is also critical. If you're going to collect data to be fed back to people as measurements, it will be done through the organization's information system. Also, include someone from the organizational design or organizational effectiveness staff, if you have a person like that. Finally, key line managers are, well . . . key.

4.   *Find someone who is familiar with computer modeling programs who can provide technical support, and invite him or her to participate.* This person needs to have simple spreadsheet expertise. If you have any young, bright MBA bushy tails running around, they are perfect for this job. This person doesn't have to be an official member of the design team. Of course, if the MIS representative can do this work, so much the better.

5.   *Be open.* Never keep the design process secret. Members should feel free to tell fellow employees what they're up to, with the understanding that nothing is certain until top management approves the plan. That way you won't create false expectations or set the grapevine on fire.

6.   *Do you need an outside consultant?* It depends on how fast you want the process to go. A good consultant will enrich the process and save the design team from going down blind alleys or reinventing the wheel. A bad consultant will show up with a plan already designed. One of the most important roles an outsider can play is to maintain the continuity from design to implementation, something most organizations find difficult.

The Design Development Process

The first order of business is to make sure that everybody on the design team understands *why* they have been asked to develop a group incentive plan. If they think they will be developing a compensation plan designed to pay people more, you have started off on the wrong foot. Design team members need to understand that a group incentive plan is part of the organization's business strategy. It is an integral part of the management system to improve business performance. The rewards are a critical element in the mix, but they are not the objective.

Design team members also need to understand that the job of designing the plan doesn't stop when the plan is approved (although their participation on the design team may end). *The power of the plan is in the implementation, not the design.* It is therefore important for the design team members to keep implementation issues, as well as the plan's parameters, in the front of their minds. A separate implementation team may be created, with the team leader and any outsiders carried over for continuity.

The power of the plan is in the implementation, not the design.

Measurement and Organizational Units Covered

Measurement
and
Organizational
Units Covered

Discussing the measurements will be the richest of all the design team's discussions. Do the measures make sense? What influences them other than what employees do? Are they fair? Whose ox is gored if the design team recommends improvement in a particular measurement? I've found the discussion to be unpredictable and very valuable.

Kate McNally, an incentive specialist and a good friend, says, "It's all about measurement." She's right. Without clear measurement of success, group incentive plans will not work. Unfortunately, the difficulty of identifying measures is a great excuse for doing nothing at all. The line, "We really want and need to install a group incentive plan, but we just haven't refined our measures quite enough yet" seems to be a guarantee for endless delay. The pressure that a group incentive plan puts on the design team to get the measurement thing done is a good illustration of how both the design and installation of such a plan forces a company to do what it should have been doing in the first place.

Resources for Understanding Measurement

If there is any area that is researched, documented, and published for any application, it is measurement. For my money, the measurement guru in the United States is Carl Thor, former president of the American Quality and Productivity Center. He and William Christopher have published an overlooked anthology of articles on measurement, primarily dealing with measuring productivity—*Handbook for Productivity Measurement and Improvement* (1993). For a volume completely full of possible measures, covering everything from financial to marketing to purchasing, I also recommend Richard Sloma's *How to Measure Managerial Performance* (1980) as an invaluable tool.

The data are there.
You just have to dig
them out.

Your greatest resource for measurement, however, is your own management team and information systems. The problem is that most of the data in organizations' systems are used for things other than performance measurement—such as scheduling, budget keeping, directing, and running the business. If you can get consensus on the measures that accurately reflect top management's strategic objectives, the data are there. You just have to dig them out.

Key Points About Measurement

The following key points apply to group incentive plans:

1. *Choose more than one measurement per strategic objective.* Be expansive in considering different measurements. Just because top management has given you some guidelines doesn't mean you can't be creative. I've found top management to be open to new twists on their ideas about measurement criteria, if the design team's recommendation is backed up by a solid rationale. Measurement is a lead, operational, or lag indicator of how well the organizational unit is doing relative to its business objectives. "As measured by" doesn't have to be just one measure. Today, most plans use a number of measures (a "family of measures") as a balanced scorecard.

2. *Measure a lot and reward a few.* You should not and cannot grant rewards for every measure. Each objective probably has dozens of measures that apply—some more directly than others. Measurement without reward serves as communication and performance feedback. So, you can measure each and every organizational unit, but you will not reward on every measure. These submeasures communicate to the member of the organizational unit what contribution they are making to the measures on which rewards are based. Whether rewarded or not, they help to identify what else needs to be addressed.

Measurement without reward serves as communication and performance feedback.

3. *The more quickly the performance feedback is provided, the better.* You have to be able to track the measure in a meaningful time frame. Poor measurement systems can hold up performance feedback. If you are five weeks late in making a measurement and making a payout, it is too late to be effective.

4. *Share information.* You have to be willing to communicate to the rest of the organization all elements of the measurement. That's how employees know how they affect the organization's performance. Let's say your measurement is productivity in the insurance business and you measure productivity as dollars of controllable costs divided by insurance policy serviced. You've limited the employee's ability to make a difference if you are unwilling to tell people what accounting categories make up controllable costs and how much is spent in each.

5. *History helps.* Knowing the historical performance of the measure helps. Most payouts are based on performance improvements over time. Payouts based on management expectations (that is, seasoned judgment) of performance or a business plan are fine,

if they are reasonable and the goals are attainable. Check out any effects of seasonal or other outside influences (interest rates, supplier or customer changes, and so on) that would cause significant fluctuations in the measurement. Fluctuations will not eliminate the measurement from consideration, but it will have an effect on the plan design.

6. *Use the Watergate rule: follow the money.* Try to pick measures that will give the organization a financial gain to be documented by the finance department when the measurements improve. Not all measures will allow you to calculate a dollar value of the gain. Research shows that one of every three to five measures has a financial opportunity. The measures that cannot be assigned a dollar value are still critical to meeting business objectives, however, and can be used for group incentive plans. But try to find a few that everyone can agree will add a real value to the gain. (That doesn't mean you should only use lag—that is, financial—measures. In fact, operational measures generally provide the best opportunity for putting a dollar value to the gain.)

7. *Everyone is a player.* Try to choose measures that can be influenced by the largest number of employees—in or out of their traditional jobs. Beware of measures that can only be influenced by the actions of a few people. Perhaps you remember the quarter that Pan Am made a profit—when they sold the Pan Am building in New York. If you had been on a profit sharing plan at the time, you would have made some money. But the reward had nothing to do with the effectiveness of the organization.

8. *Do you really want* that *to improve?* The acid test of any measure is the question, "Do you want to reward people based on that measure?" (One hint: don't overreact. As you will learn later, the amount of money available for payouts for a particular measure may be determined by how important it is to the organization rather than its dollar value contribution. Greater awareness may be the real objective.) Just remember: watch out what you reinforce. You will get it.

Beware of measures that can only be influenced by the actions of a few people.

What Can Be Measured?

The first question is, "What *can* be measured?" The design team must determine what measures reflect the strategic objectives identified by top management. Top management has provided a list of objectives with broad measures connected to them. The design team must determine whether or not these are the measures they really want to use.

Management may have explained what they want to measure, but the design team may discover glitches that management didn't see. The most common glitches are:

- The measure is easily influenced by outside events (inflation, exchange rates, and so on).

- Measures for which the performance data aren't timely. Can you get the information on monthly performance on time, or will it be six weeks late?

- The measure is significant to an executive but not to the rank and file. Return on net assets, or RONA, is a good example.

- It takes a lot of education to make RONA meaningful to most employees. Even if they understand it, they probably won't feel they can influence it, except in smaller organizations or OBM firms with financially literate employees.

- One measure with a lot of components. Economic value added (EVA) comes to mind. It is one number, but it has so many components it becomes very hard for managers to explain and for employees to effect.

- Measures that suboptimize. If you measure an organizational unit smaller than the entire organization, certain measures can create a silo effect. They can reinforce performance that might be great for them but counterproductive for another unit. I once broke down an organization into shifts, measuring the productivity of each. One shift would leave all the rework for the next shift because rework reduced productivity. It suboptimized and had to be corrected.

So, find out what you can measure accurately and quickly at each level of the organization, from the top to work groups. The measure will probably change as it cascades down the organization. *This is more than a design exercise.* Remember: measurement rewarded or not at every level of the organization is the primary performance feedback system for performance.

Do You Want To Base Rewards on These Measures?

People slip into the "Oh my God, you mean this may be real?" syndrome when they realize measurements are connected to rewards.

The next step sometimes causes people to do strange things, so beware. So far, the design team has focused on objectives and measurements that are important to the organization. When you begin to get serious about rewarding for improvement against these measures, you're likely to see some real tap dancing. When there is no reward tied to the accomplishment of measurements, people like the exercise. When they realize management is actually going to reward people based on the measurements, they slip right into the "Oh my God, you mean this may be real?" syndrome.

It's a little like the old story of the preacher who was at the pulpit expounding on the importance of honesty and reverence and charity, and the more he preached, the more excited the congregation became. There were nods of agreement in the sanctuary and an occasional "Amen!" Until he got to the part about church members' preoccupation with Sunday night Bingo. It seems some folks were doing a little gambling on the side. At that point, the congregation rose to its feet and shouted, "Hold it right there, preacher. Now you've stopped preaching and started meddling!"

That's how people feel when you start to talk about rewarding for organizational performance improvement. The preaching was good, but now you're meddling. Suddenly, the legitimacy of the measures the team has worked so hard to design comes under a scrutiny that it has never been under before.

The key in measurement development is to determine when the rubber meets the road, without becoming roadkill.

The key here is to determine when the rubber meets the road, without becoming roadkill. If you're lucky, you will have enlightened management like the man who headed a 22,000-employee organization. He wasn't happy with his profit sharing plan because the line of sight was too long and nobody knew what they could do to affect the measurement. He thought the plan was a waste of money. (The data showed that he was right.)

He then decided to install a new group incentive plan for his managers instead of retaining the one based solely on profits. The new plan wouldn't have anything to do with "executive compensation"—stock options and all that. He believed that a group incentive plan would focus all the managers on the same objectives and measurements. Once that was accomplished, he wanted to expand the plan to include everyone in the organization.

I asked him how he knew when he was successful. He said he

had three indicators: customer satisfaction, productivity, and one other industry indicator.

"Those are the things that are critical to your success?" I asked.

"Yes."

"Fine, let's just reward on those."

"I can't do that," he said. "I don't know for sure that those three indicators are accurate predictors of profitability."

"You mean that hadn't been foremost in your mind before you considered making each one of those measures compensable?" I said (rhetorically).

Fortunately for me, he is a pragmatic—and polite—man. He leaned back in his chair and said, "It just isn't as important until you think about rewarding for it."

Characterizing Measures: Lead, Operating, and Lag

Measures are critical. They guide management in assessing how the organization is doing and in determining what it needs to do. The lead, operating, and lag categorizations of measurement were introduced in Chapter Three. Deciding which measures fall into the lead category is a subjective process that often depends on the nature of the business. The goal is to identify those lead measures that are considered predictive of success. Operating measures reflect the day-to-day operations of the business. Their link to the lag (or financial) measures runs from direct to tenuous, depending on the accounting system. Lag measures are traditional financial measures—the financial results of the operation. Someone once said that running a company solely on the basis of the financial statements is like steering a boat by looking at the wake. You can run into a number of hazards that way. Clearly, a balance of different measures makes the most sense in the majority of applications.

Running a company solely on the basis of the financial statements is like steering a boat by looking at the wake.

The following list reviews the three types of measures I've previously described:

Lead: These measures are predictive of success, generally over a long period. Examples are market share, customer satisfaction or value, employee satisfaction (and possibly turnover), new product development, and research and development project cycle items. Some organizations would include sales as a lead measure.

Operational: These are the day-to-day measures most familiar to the rank-and-file employee and to their immediate management. Some of these measures are linked directly to the financial statement; some have an indirect influence. Examples are productivity, quality, customer satisfaction or value (it can serve as a lead and operational measure), attendance, cycle time, safety, cost reduction, and project completion.

Lag: Lag measures are the most common and are supported by the account system. They include profit, return ratios (return on equity, sales, investment, and so on), economic value added, stock price, dividends, cash value added, cash flow return on investment, and total shareholder return.

The list in Table 8.1 shows the types of measures used by the plans studied in the CARS research. Many of the plans used measures from more than one category, so the total is more than 100 percent.

Typical business-plan measures have a long line of sight and are often viewed with some suspicion by employees. They have not tra-

TABLE 8.1. *Measures Used in Plans Studied by CARS.*

TYPE OF MEASURE	PERCENTAGE OF PLANS USING MEASURE
LEAD	
Quality (including customer satisfaction)	45%
OPERATIONAL	
Productivity	44%
Output/volume	31%
Cost reduction	23%
Safety	21%
Attendance	12%
Project milestones	8%
LAG	
Financial	47%

Source: McAdams and Hawk, 1994, p. 140.

ditionally affected how people are rewarded, and because of this they have had little effect on behavior and involvement of those people. Introducing measures on which rewards are to be given is quite another story. The new measures need to be pretty common and understandable to the employees. Creating new measures is expensive, and creating a historical performance record can be difficult. Don Barry of Chase Manhattan Bank likes to use a litmus test for measurement. He says to plan design teams, "You can propose a measure for a group incentive plan if you can bring in one year's worth of data in sixty minutes."

Type of Measure and Level of Organization

You can determine performance for each organizational unit for which there is a measure. The process is to start at the top of the organization and work down, determining measures that reflect your business objectives each step of the way. This doesn't mean you are going to reward for every measure. The process simply tells you what is possible. If you are not going to reward on measures at lower levels of the organization, those measures will be important as performance feedback and communication. As you will read later, I recommend measuring for reward purposes higher rather than lower in the organization, for a variety of reasons. I do not suggest, however, going beyond the level of location, unless there is no other option. I'll discuss this design issue later.

Organizations tend to use lag financial measures to measure performance at the corporate or division level, while lead and operational measures are usually used lower in the organization. That makes sense. The lower the performance is measured, the shorter the LoS will be, because employees will be able to see the impact of their efforts. Table 8.2 summarizes the types of measurements used by the 737 participants in the CARS research. For example, of those organizations that had a lead measure in their plan, 15 percent used the measure at the company-wide level, 31 percent used it at the division level, 47 percent at the facility level, 15 percent at the department level, 11 percent at the work group level, and 4 percent at the individual level.

My rule of thumb is that lag or financial measures keep management happy, while lead or operational measures engage employees. Of course, if you have a high degree of workforce financial

TABLE 8.2. *Types of Measures Used at Different Organizational Levels.*

LEVEL OF ORGANIZATION MEASURED	LEAD	OPERATIONAL					LAG
	QUALITY (INCLUDING CUSTOMER SATISFACTION)	PRODUCTIVITY	SAFETY	ATTENDANCE	COST REDUCTION	OUTPUT/ VOLUME	FINANCIAL
Company or corporate-wide	15%	9%	12%	19%	19%	11%	57%
Group, subsidiary, division	31%	30%	17%	21%	31%	29%	36%
Facility (physical location)	47%	53%	59%	24%	34%	36%	17%
Department	15%	14%	13%	19%	10%	12%	7%
Work group or small team	11%	10%	5%	8%	6%	13%	2%
Individual	4%	5%	8%	33%	NA	6%	NA

SOURCE: McAdams and Hawk, 1994, p. 144.

> **Financial literacy moves financial measures from lag to operational.**

literacy, as espoused by Jack Stack (1994) and John Case (1995), you've got the best of both worlds, because all measures will make sense to everyone. Financial literacy moves financial measures from lag to operational.

A warning: avoid starting your plan with only work group measures. The LoS is short, but the risk of cycling is great. In the beginning, try to keep most of the measures at location level, with one measure higher if you have to and one at a lower level if you feel you have a real LoS problem. (Keep reading. It will become clearer.)

You don't need to worry too much about this yet, but research shows that plans that have three to five measures report better nonfinancial results (teamwork, communications, and so forth) than plans with more. So, at some point you may need to pare down your list. Three to five measures seem to be enough to give organizations a comprehensive look at their business and to help them customize the plan to fit their needs. Plans with six or more measures probably have too many to communicate clearly and to provide effective employee focus. Too many measures are much less effective than too few.

Leading Measures

The following paragraphs discuss the measures most commonly used in group incentive plans and the most appropriate levels of organization at which to use those measures.

Customer Satisfaction   The voice of the customer rings out in the halls of most organizations' corporate headquarters. The management of customer value, as taught by Bradley Gale (1994), combines extensive corporate commitment, staff and systems work, external and internal measurement, and a rededication of all employees to serving the customer. Two gurus in this area, Bradley Gale and Leonard Berry (1991), along with a number of professional customer satisfaction agencies and research companies, can provide you with what you need to establish your organization as a leader in customer satisfaction. Little has been written, however, about the importance of rewarding employees for focusing on customer satisfaction.

Customer satisfaction has emerged as a common measurement for reward purposes. It is vital to understand what your customers think is important. Indicators of satisfaction have historically been a customer satisfaction index (CSI) (percentage of customers satisfied or very satisfied), complaints, customer focus groups or customer feedback, and third-party assessments. The most common measure for reward purposes is the CSI. It typically is generated from a questionnaire, telephone survey, or computer-query system. Organizations often calculate the percentage of people who report that they are satisfied or very satisfied as a percentage of the total, and that's the CSI. Then they tell employees that the measure is at, say, 78.6 percent, and if it can be moved to 80 percent, everybody will earn as a part of the group incentive plan.

It's obvious that in using this method, the LoS is pretty long. The ability to push and see something move is remote when you use something as general as a percentage of people who, based on a random survey, are satisfied or very satisfied.

Most advanced customer satisfaction research gets information from the customer frequently and attempts to determine the importance of each aspect of service. If a survey asks a customer about five elements of product and service, he may give high marks on four and a lousy mark on one. If the element that gets the lowest mark is the most important thing to the customer, you have pinpointed a very specific and often measurable opportunity for improvement.

Customer satisfaction surveys derive importance from a labyrinth of involved statistical analyses that say what the key drivers are, rather than simply asking customers what is important to them. Researchers are concerned that the customers will rank everything as important. Either way, getting information on what is important to customers is critical to determining what needs improvement. Figure 8.2 illustrates a way to visualize what drivers of satisfaction to work on and in what order. Both satisfaction and importance are rated from low to high, generally scaled in the same manner as the results of your customer satisfaction survey. If on-time delivery has a high importance rating and low satisfaction, it would go in the upper left-hand quadrant. Accurate invoicing: low importance and high satisfaction—bottom right-hand quadrant. Friendliness of telephone order entry representative: low importance and low satisfaction—bottom left-hand quadrant. Quality of product: high importance and high satisfaction—upper right-hand quadrant. You would place a dot for every driver in its appropriate quadrant.

The primary actions to be taken—and potential basis for a reward plan measure—would be on those drivers in the upper left-hand quadrant—high importance, low satisfaction. The secondary focus should be on those in the upper right-hand quadrant—high importance, high ratings, as much as a maintenance effort as anything.

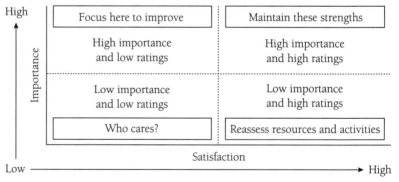

FIGURE 8.2. *Customer Satisfaction Driver Matrix: Importance Versus Satisfaction.*

The method of identifying the most important drivers with lowest satisfaction allows the reward plan to focus on the specific ones with the greatest potential impact on overall customer satisfaction. In the example, on-time delivery is the key driver.

Improvement can be focused on in a few ways. On the most simplistic level, you can take the measure of selected individual drivers and reward employees for improvement, with the greater rewards for the more important drivers in the upper left-hand cell of Figure 8.2. The opportunity is to reward employees for closing the gap between importance and satisfaction. A specific driver is likely to be able to be measured and clearly has a shorter LoS than the remote overall customer satisfaction index. Finally, in addition to a group incentive plan, you can allow people to start focusing on fixing the system in a way that will improve the high importance/low satisfaction drivers. This is a classic example of how an employee involvement reinforced by either a recognition or project team incentive plan can support group incentive plan objectives.

If drivers are inappropriate for some reason, or just not available, rewards could be based on a customer satisfaction index for each group of customers served. Customers can be grouped by type (such as order size or overall volume of business), by geography, by the product or service they have purchased, or some combination of these. Your ability to identify your customers in more specific but ever-decreasing numbers may cause you some problems in getting a valid sample, but you can rely on your market research supplier to work that out.

Level of organization to be covered: If you are able to identify the drivers that are of high importance and low satisfaction, everyone connected to the measured customer base can be rewarded for performance improvement.

Employee Satisfaction: Rewards for Management Only   Employee satisfaction should be rewarded only at the management level. (If people were going to be rewarded for saying how happy they are with their work, you can bet they'd be smiling when they filled out the survey.) Research has shown that employee satisfaction is a good measure for the effectiveness of management in leading and supporting their customers—the employees. Recently, some research has shown that employee satisfaction is correlated with customer satisfaction. A Marketing Science Institute report, *Service Quality Implementation: The Effects of Organization, Socialization, and Man-*

Research has shown that employee satisfaction is correlated with customer satisfaction.

agerial Actions on Customer-Contact Employee Behaviors, by Michael Hartline and O. C. Farrell (1993) on three nationwide hotel chains reported that employee satisfaction is the single strongest predictor of both service quality and value. The study used 2,343 surveys from 257 hotels. The report is the first evidence I've seen that supports what has been assumed for some time—that high employee satisfaction translates into serving the customer more effectively.

Far too many organizations reward managers on employee satisfaction based on an equivalent of the CSI—the percentage of employees satisfied or very satisfied. This causes the same problems in employee satisfaction as it does with customer satisfaction. To be useful and effective, employee satisfaction research must be as specific about the level of satisfaction and importance by driver. The same plan design described in the customer satisfaction section can be used to close the satisfaction-importance gaps. Turnover is another measure of employee satisfaction. It is measured by the percentage of the population that leaves the company voluntarily.

Level of organization to be covered: One of my favorite Dilbert cartoons has the boss say to an employee: "My bonus depends on how satisfied all the employees are. Since you are the biggest malcontent, I'm going to fire you and I'll make money." As the boss is walking away, he says to himself "I'm beginning to get the hang of this touchy-feely stuff."

Employee satisfaction is important enough that employees with people reporting to them should be measured—as a group. Do not measure and reward each individual supervisor. This is a group measurement and works best if done by physical location.

Sometimes it's appropriate to break down turnover among the hierarchical levels of the organization. Make sure the breakdown is reasonable. If you measure every supervisor on turnover, the number of employees is too small for the percentages to make any sense. A group of supervisors with a total of one hundred employees is about the smallest I've found to be effective.

Sales   Some people might argue that sales is a questionable leading indicator of performance for all employees. People in the back office or factory can't affect sales. They're not out on the road. They may never see customers. But the old line "Nothing happens until you get an order" is probably fair. As organizations expand the role of employees from being bound by their job descriptions to one of corporate citizenship, an argument can be made for sales as a measure to apply to every employee. I remember the reaction of a ten-year veteran of a customer service operation when a big sale was announced over the public address system. He shook his head and said, "Hell, more money for the sales guy and just more work for me."

Sales are often influenced by the way the telephone is answered or by how quickly the company responds to requests. How the last order was filled often determines the next sale. And employees are also doing more team selling. The sale is not necessarily made by just the salesperson but by a whole team of people working together.

While sales is currently a very uncommon measure for nonsales employee performance, so was customer satisfaction a few years ago. And sales probably has a better LoS than profit or return on net assets.

Level of organization to be covered: Sales numbers relate to business units and, sometimes, geography. Whatever makes sense to the business is what should be measured and rewarded.

Market Share   Market share is also a rare measure for all-employee group incentive plans. Measured as a percentage of the available market captured by the organization, it has a very long LoS. The biggest problem is the reliability of the available market numbers. They are good indicators of trends, but often they are not solid enough to use for reward purposes.

Level of organization to be covered: Market share should have the same coverage as sales.

Operational Measures

Operational measures are not as commonly used by top management as financial ones. Top management is often somewhat skeptical of the value that operational measures deliver to the bottom line, and they therefore demand that these measures be scrutinized more closely.

Productivity   Productivity has many definitions—from the broad, macroeconomics view to the individual's personal productivity. The only agreement among economists, industrial engineers, and line managers is that productivity is always a ratio. It is either output divided by input or input divided by output, depending on which is easier to communicate to employees. The measure can be as broad or as narrow as you wish.

The challenge in setting the productivity measure is to define output. It looks simple. Output can be anything the organization produces. The original Scanlon gain-sharing formula (Chapter Three), a reasonably complex formula (net sales divided by a cost figure), is applied to manufacturing and uses net sales as output. Some manufacturers use an equivalent units methodology that applies an indexing approach to all products produced for a common output measure. In a service organization, output is generally much more difficult to identify. It might be number of customers served, number of weighted customers served based on their value to the organization, number of claims processed, number of transactions, or number of transactions weighted by the nature of the transaction.

Output becomes more difficult to determine as the organization is broken down into smaller units. Frequently, the output measure can't be easily carried down to lower levels. Number of widgets or customers served may not translate into real output for the units deeper within the organization.

Input is easier to determine. Input is always characterized by some combination of costs or a physical unit easily translated into costs, such as number of labor hours or pounds of raw material. Input could be financial, and stated as total cost of labor or total cost of labor minus benefits. I have found that using controllable costs as the denominator works well, because these costs are perceived to be things that people can influence. Controllable costs tend to be labor, materials, and supplies. In fact, controllable costs are easier to describe by the things they do not include: rent, corporate allocations, heat, light, and other fixed expenses.

Productivity measures, therefore, are customized by the very nature of the organization. If you don't already have a productivity measure, your design team should be able to pound one out in a reasonable time. Remember to take quality into consideration in any productivity measure. Output should be reduced by things like rejected widgets or returned merchandise or number of claims reworked.

Just one note of caution about productivity as a measure: Labor (organized or not) sometimes sees it as another way to push people to do the job faster or harder, resulting in layoffs. Only a fool would participate in a plan that, if successful, would cost him his job. In fact, productivity has been improved dramatically in the United States through technological improvements, which in combination with economic downturns and restructuring have caused massive layoffs. Group incentive plans have not contributed to layoffs. Their primary focus is to use resources and systems more effectively.

The best measurements of productivity are those that can be connected to the P&L statement and understood and influenced by everybody in the organization. Once you determine your productivity measure, try to look at your ten-year productivity history and ten-year profit history and see if there is any correlation. If you can take into account controlling factors such as market conditions or other influences, there may be some statistical correlation between the two histories that would give you a greater argument for how productivity affects the P&L.

Level of organization to be covered: You can generally use productivity for relatively small organizational units—if you can figure out the output number. Productivity changes at lower organizational levels. The nature of output and input changes as the function changes. Again, be careful. Shortening LoS by moving the measure and reward to cover smaller organization units not only increases cycling but can cause suboptimization between the organizational units.

Internal Quality   Since there are so many legitimate and self-appointed gurus on the subject of quality, how to value and measure it is one of the more hotly debated topics in U.S. business. What has essentially been ignored is the role of rewards in quality improvement. I suggest Stephen B. Knouse's *The Reward and Recognition Process in Total Quality Management* (1995) for a more complete discussion of W. Edwards Deming's and others' views on rewarding quality. My experience is that practical necessity for reinforcing quality improvement can live quite nicely alongside the views of the purest of quality experts. (See Figure 8.3.)

The quest for quality is a process, not a destination, but putting some focus on results provides balance to the process. A results focus also provides some good signposts during the quality journey and some protection from the potentially fickle management team that is focusing on the quarter's financial statement.

A results focus provides good signposts during the quality journey.

W. Edwards Deming's continuous quality improvement strategy attempts to engage employees by emphasizing education. Deming wanted to integrate a passion for quality into the bloodstream of each employee, to educate employees on how to use the tools of quality, and to reinforce them by giving them more pride and satisfaction in their work.

All the gurus of quality agree on the necessity of a formalized process that enables educated employees to make a contribution. Part of such a process is using employee teams to monitor process variability and generate quality improvement ideas. But extrinsic rewards or recognition for these contributions have been largely overlooked. Lip service has been paid—"quality team of the month/quarter/year," "Here's your coffee cup for completing training," and so on—but reinforcement plans have been poorly designed and implemented. Some gurus have even argued that rewarding results is anti–Deming. While some pats on the back or symbolic recognition have been OK, formalized reward plans such as group incentive and project team incentive plans have been counter to the quality movement.

The subject of rewards is for the most part simply ignored in writings about quality. In Deming's *Seven Deadly Diseases*, (Walton, 1986, p. 89), he argues that merit ratings and the evaluation of individual performance should be replaced by equal pay. That position has been taken out of context and blown up into "all reward plans are bad."

I've attended a number of seminars led by Deming and have read most of his work (along with that of the other important contributors to the field), generally with an eye out for comments on reward plans. Because his teachings have had such a powerful impact on American business, I believe it is worthwhile to summarize his views on the subject and comment on them.

Like all great men, Deming was capable of changing his mind and had no problem admitting it. That was true when it came to his views on reward plans. In 1988, two years after he published *Out of the Crisis*, Deming said in a conference that he believed everyone in an organization "from the president to the janitor" should be rewarded equally, for "they were all doing the best job they knew how." He opposed bonuses and all incentives. In 1990, at a General Motors seminar he led, Deming revised his earlier positions. He thought that incentives were appropriate as performance rewards if they were commensurate with, and contingent upon, impeccable employee performance improvement (100 per-

FIGURE 8.3. TQM and Incentives: W. Edwards Deming.

cent attribution). He believed that incentives were permissible in three situations:

1. When equal awards were given to all members of a group operating within the control limits of a stable system
2. When individual awards were given for those performing consistently outside the high side control limit of a stable system
3. When awards were given for using the operating system rather than for the results achieved by the system

Remember that Deming was first and foremost an authority on a scientific approach to performance improvement that included a preoccupation with measurement. He was, in my conversations with him, supportive of team idea plans and ad hoc team plans (described in Chapter Nine). He also supported my approach to recognition plans (described in Chapter Seven).

Deming was, however, opposed to group incentive plans. It is my opinion that his negative position on numerical goals, something so necessary in group incentive plans, was rooted in poorly developed plans. He believed that most measurement systems punish rather than reinforce (which I agree with, but I will show how they can be reinforcing). He believed that most measures are poorly chosen and outside the control of the very people being asked to effect the measures (which I agree with, but I have shown in this chapter how to choose measures, in addition to financial ones, that accurately reflect your objectives, and how a good line of sight addresses the issue of control). Finally, Deming felt that the engineered standards on which so many plans are based had, in his experience, no basis in reality (which I also agree with, and that's why I argue for baselines for group incentive plans and that they be based on history).

I do not mean to suggest that with these changes Deming and others would have wholeheartedly embraced incentive plans. I don't know. The art of developing these reward plans is just emerging, and the science of cost justification is in its infancy. But most of the nationally known experts on quality have their roots in manufacturing, with its command-and-control, short-term, financial mentality. Their mission is to change that focus, and quality is their rallying cry. Most of their objections address removing reward plans, particularly compensation, as obstacles to continuous quality improvement. From my perspective, well-designed group incentives, project team incentives, and recognition plans are change agents in support of just that.

Look to whomever has the leadership, coordination, or official responsibility for quality in your organization, and get their help in developing measures. The simplest and most obvious measures—reducing scrap, improving utilization, reducing rework or redos—have been used for years in manufacturing and today are being adapted to service industries. For more information, look to your local business bookstore for this week's latest publication on the subject.

Level of organization to be covered: I have found quality results difficult to measure on a company-wide basis. Quality can be incorporated into a productivity measure by measuring output in good units only. To provide greater emphasis on the importance of quality in a productivity formula, some companies deduct one bad unit as two, reducing output disproportionately. Another way to have the same effect is to double count the dollars spent on rework or redos in the input. Either way, quality becomes even more important in the productivity ratio. This approach makes the productivity ratio more difficult to explain and communicate, however.

Quality often relates to an organizational system rather than to an organizational unit, but I've found that relationship difficult to incorporate into a plan design. Most other measures do relate to organizational units. Unless quality is your only measure in the plan, I would try to measure performance results on the same organizational level as productivity.

Cost reduction isn't generally successful as part of a group incentive plan.

Cost Reduction Cost reduction isn't generally successful as part of a group incentive plan. Telling employees that you want to cut budgeted costs from $1,000,000 to $900,000 and then giving them a portion of the savings is like legislated welfare. It never seems to work quite right. Budgets, advertising, new product development, making sure you have enough people to answer the phones, and new systems projects are all designed to accomplish specific objectives for the organization.

Cutting budgets often reduces the level of service or the number of services. If that is management's intent, fine. But if the hope is that people will find ways to save money while maintaining the same level of service as an integral part of their day-to-day jobs, I wouldn't use a group incentive plan. I would use a type of project team incentive plan, the team idea plan, which is described in Chapter Nine.

Level of organization to be covered: Cost reduction in a group incentive plan is against budget. Wherever you have a budget, you can measure performance improvement.

Attendance   Attendance tends to be most important in lower-paid jobs. When a retail business needs people on the sales floor during lunch hours or holiday rushes, attendance is crucial. The same is true for a service organization that needs people available to answer phones. Although some people have a philosophical problem with giving extra rewards for people to come to work, there are businesses that have a legitimate need for people to be at a particular place at a defined time in order to handle a specific responsibility. Although most of these nonexempt, full-time people don't get paid (expect for sick leave, vacations, and holidays) if they don't show up, some organizations do get value for the extra amount paid for attendance incentives.

Attendance measurement can be handled in two ways. Absenteeism is counted as the number of people absent (tardy or absent for quarter, half, or whole days) over and above excused absences as a percentage of total available days. The reverse process is presenteeism. It's more positive. Presenteeism counts the percentage of people who are on the job 100 percent of the time (you can use any percentage that works for your organization).

Level of organization to be covered: Attendance can be measured from the organizational unit down to the individual.

Safety   Safety is used as a primary measure for group incentive plans in 25 percent of the CARS database. While safety incentive plans abound, improving safety is best effected by an awareness, training, and recognition plan to reinforce the process rather than by a measure in a group incentive plan. Awareness and education are more effective at supporting safety efforts than are the rewards from group incentive plans. People don't stop themselves from being hurt so that they can earn a reward. This is not to negate the importance of safety, however. When it is included in a group incentive plan, the objective is to remind people how important safety is in the organization. Safety is generally measured by a reduction in reportable injuries or by activations and audit ratings. Inclusion in a group incentive plan can create positive peer pressure for people to watch out for their fellow employees, to drive carefully, and to take safety training to heart. If the amount of payout is large enough, however, it can reinforce the wrong behavior, such as not reporting an injury or seeking medical help.

If safety is an issue for you, you probably have a safety officer who would love to include his objectives in your plan. Just make sure you don't reinforce the wrong behavior. You want people to report injuries immediately and get attention.

Level of organization to be covered: To make people aware of this issue, I suggest measuring safety separately at each physical location.

Output or Volume

This measure is not the same as productivity, which is a ratio of output to input. Output or volume is simply total units produced; input is not considered. Output is generally paired with quality measures as part of performance improvement efforts. Quality is always a concern when rewards are based on output. It is common to deduct any defective product or cost of redos from the output measures, sometimes at a penalty of two times the value.

An output or volume measure was used in almost half of the plans in the CARS study, and it clearly has value. The most common use of an output or volume measure in a group incentive plan is in a situation where production is bound by the capacity of the machines and quality is built into the system. A paper mill is a good application for an output measure.

Level of organization to be covered: It depends on the business, but output or volume should not be measured any higher than physical location. Many companies try to wrap output from feeder plants with that of the finishing plant. Even with a high degree of codependency, I find that the LoS is too long to make the total measure effective. Many managers argue that combining these outputs reinforces the importance of the feeder and the finisher working together. That would be fine for a management-only group incentive plan, but it is of little value if the plan includes all employees.

If cooperation is that critical to the organization, I would recommend that some percentage (perhaps 75 percent) of the reward for output be based on each plant's output and the rest on the combined performance. To support this plan, cross-location teams should be developed to work out problems and encourage the idea of the "greater team."

Cycle Time

The most encompassing measure of cycle time is from the minute an order is received until it is paid for. Reducing that time can be worth money to the organization. Cycle time can also be measured from the time the order is received until it is shipped or the service is completed.

Reducing cycle time has been a primary focus of reengineering efforts, because the notion that time is money is truer today than ever before. Cycle time is a message everybody, from the receptionist to the manager, can touch.

Getting new products to market is often the first thing companies think about when the topic of cycle time comes up. Depending on the organizational unit covered, new product development is not influenced by the majority of employees—an important requirement of a group incentive plan. If the measure includes development, prototyping, production engineering, materials sourcing, production, and shipping, and if it engages the majority of the employees, then it is certainly applicable. If not, consider using a project team incentive plan.

Level of organization to be covered: It depends on the cycle you are measuring. If it is important enough to include in a plan, include everyone in the physical location.

Projects The appropriateness of projects, including new product development, in a group incentive plan is a function of the number of people who are involved. Most companies limit participation. If there is limited participation in the organizational unit, look for input on improving performance in Chapter Nine, which discusses project team incentive plans.

If in your company, the majority of the employees are constantly involved in projects, a broad attainment of project milestones is a good measure of performance. MIS organizational units are a good example. Most have a myriad of projects that engage or at least touch almost everyone in the organization. It is important to make all employees, whether assigned to a project or not, aware of how vital the projects are to the overall business.

Level of organization to be covered: The best way I've found to measure success on an organizational unit level is to total up all of the completed milestones (approved by management as complete) and to divide the total by the total number that could have been completed. For example, an organization might have twenty ten-person teams—a significant portion of the employee population—working on different projects. Each project has milestones with time frames. A certain number are to be completed within the first measurement period. A predetermined formula for accomplishment and reward is put in place. If 75 percent of the milestones are met (that's a baseline), everybody in the organization will be rewarded. The higher the percentage, the larger the award. (If you decide that because of changing conditions, the project milestone *should not* have been accomplished in the time period assigned to it—because the milestone is dependent upon what was accomplished by a previous one, upon the work of another team, upon new technology, and so on—you can elect to take it out of the numerator *if* you also deduct it from the denominator. You can't punish people for something that should be changed for the good of the project.)

In larger organizations with matrix management, or those that have a lot of projects going on at one time, everyone needs to be engaged in meeting the project objectives, directly or indirectly. If the person sitting next to you is on a project team, you need to be sensitive to how important it is to cover for her and still get the organization's work done. You don't have to be assigned to a team to be a player. A group incentive plan gives everyone the same focus and makes it worth it to them to work as a contributor to the larger team effort.

Lag (Financial) Measures

Financial measures are bottom-line measures and use one or all of the following methods:

1. Profitability, earnings, or revenues
2. Return calculations (return on equity, return on assets, and so on), economic value added, total shareholder return, cash value added, or cash flow
3. Publicly traded stock price

Profits are by far the easiest financial measure for organizations to address, no matter how long the LoS tends to be in larger organizations. It would make sense that the profit LoS would be relatively short in small organizations; there are fewer people, and generally they are familiar with the nature of their markets. However, if the small organization is privately held, the owners may not want to share profit information, so once again, profit has a long LoS.

The other measures of financial performance have a longer LoS than profit. If the objective is to increase employees' awareness of these measures, do not expect much change in the rank and file.

Level of organization to be measured: Most financial measures are organization-wide, generally crossing physical locations. If you can develop or use an imputed operating profit for a location, it will improve your LoS. Remember, you must be willing to share all the information with the rank and file if you want the measure to be effective.

Can financial measures work? Look to open-book management. In Jack Stack's groundbreaking book, *The Great Game of Business* (1994) and John Case's recent *Open-Book Management* (1995), you can find success stories that demonstrate that financial measures work. If you engage, educate, trust, and reward your employees in the business of improving performance, you can use financial measurements as effectively as any other measure—and you can change the rules of the game as often as necessary for the health of the business. Most but not all of the businesses described in these books are relatively small and located at a single site. When management is willing to share all the data (financial and otherwise) with all employees, to teach them how to use the information, and to reward them fairly for improvement, the results are nothing short of spectacular.

Can financial measures work? Look to open-book management companies.

I think if you are willing to practice the precepts of open-book management, financial measures as a basis for payouts can be a dynamic call to action. As I said before, financial literacy combined with employee involvement and accountability makes lag measures into operational ones. It allows you to reduce the LoS and make people feel they can make a difference. If you haven't done that, you may be distributing funds to simply reinforce employees' awareness of the financial measures.

An Example of a Group Incentive Plan

Table 8.3 illustrates how this discussion of measurement can be applied to the objectives, broad measures, and weightings provided earlier in an earlier example. I realize that for those of you in the service industries, most examples of group incentive plans are for manufacturing. Each of the measures in Table 8.3 can be applied to a service business, depending on what you can measure. Table 8.4 is an example from a financial institution.

Participation

If you have a plan that improves business performance, *should* you include everybody in it? On the surface, the answer looks simple: involve everybody. It isn't always that easy.

Participation

Most organizations already have individual incentive plans for

Table 8.3. *Midwestern Company Example: Basic Parameters.*

OBJECTIVE	BROAD MEASURE	WEIGHTING	LEVEL OF ORGANI-ZATION COVERED	SPECIFIC MEASURE
Financial performance	Profit or return calculation	• 25%	• Company-wide	Net income before taxes
Productivity	Output divided by input	• 25% for plants • 0% for headquarters	• Each plant • No measure of headquarters	Number of pounds shipped per controllable cost dollar
Cycle time	Order to payment in days	• 25% for plants • 50% for headquarters	• Each plant • Headquarters measured on overall performance of all plants	Order to payment days
Quality	Cost of poor quality	• 25%	• Each plant • Headquarters on performance of all plants	% of labor hours spent on rework and redos

Table 8.4. *Financial Services Company Example: Basic Parameters.*

OBJECTIVE	WEIGHT	LEVEL OF ORGANI-ZATION COVERED	MEASURE
Employee satisfaction	30%	Each physical location	Two attributes with greatest importance-satisfaction gap
Customer satisfaction	30%	Company-wide	Two attributes with greatest importance-satisfaction gap
Asset quality	20%	Company-wide	Dollars defaulted ÷ loans
Productivity	20%	Each physical location	Controllable costs ÷ assets

executives that take an inordinate amount of human resource and consultant time. Less time and money are spent on plans for second-level management, and even less on first-line supervisors and professionals. There is little left for the rank and file. Group incentive plans break that mold. Plans reported on in the CARS research essentially included everyone. When there was an exclusion, it was the top manager of the organizational unit.

The best plans include everybody, with one exception. People on probation should not be eligible for awards. On an individual performance rating scale of one to five, if one is given to a person who should look for another line of work and five goes to outstanding performers, ones and perhaps twos should not be eligible for rewards. This rule tends to tighten up some individual performance reviews and give them a bit more teeth.

Middle Management and First-Line Supervisors

Middle management and first-line supervisors often have the most difficulty in accepting group incentive plans because these plans often demand a cultural shift on their parts in order to be effective.

Many middle management and first-line supervisory groups are accustomed to a traditional hierarchical structure in which top management makes the decisions and passes them down the chain of command. Thus, the management group is often uncomfortable with a system that encourages the rank and file to think for themselves. In the old system, management thinks and rank and file does, thereby creating a limited information flow, as well as regulated power, at each step in the organizational food chain. When you begin to reward people based on a preannounced formula that everybody understands, mid-level managers and first-line supervisors often feel like they're losing control. (Figure 8.4 illustrates how these people feel.)

SALLY FORTH

Figure 8.4. *Changing the traditional structure can be difficult for middle management and first-line supervisors.*
SOURCE: Reprinted with special permission of King Features Syndicate.

In this case, you might be wise to set up a management-only plan at first (it could go all the way down to first-line supervisors and may even include professionals). The people in this group are the primary resisters to change, and if they do not embrace the plan, it has less of an opportunity to succeed with all employees. This step may be appropriate to allow these people time to become comfortable with the incentive system and its measures. It can also buy time to refine some shaky measures with a smaller population (management only) and the limited total payout cost before moving to the total employee population and greater payout cost.

The design process for a management-only group incentive plan is exactly the same as the process described in this chapter. A management-only plan, however, is simply an interim step before the plan flows to all employees. Beware of the attitude that says, "*They*—the rank and file—can't influence that." If everyone isn't included in the plan, "they" surely can't influence results because they won't have the chance.

Including Salespeople in Group Incentive Plans

Salespeople were among the first, after executives, to receive rewards for improved performance. For that reason, they aren't usually included in group incentive plans. My belief is that this ought to change in organizations where sales are tightly linked to the manufacture and/or service process.

Traditionally, salespeople's activities and behavior have been directed by management and the commission plan. Their connection to the organization and the production process hasn't been very tight. But as companies move to real-time deliveries and consultative selling, the sales force becomes more of an integral part of the total employee team. The salespeople become concerned with more than just sales. Now they are part of a whole team of people who see installation, service, price, and delivery as elements that are as important as the sale itself. In these companies, salespeople whose efforts are part of the integrated process probably should be included in group incentive plans. Monsanto Chemical includes all salespeople in their group incentive plan for plant employees because of the tight interdependence of sales and production.

Here again, it's a LoS decision. The further removed the salespeople are from the plant or headquarters operation itself, the less they need to be connected to a plan.

Group Incentive Plans with Unions?

Many people assume that it's difficult to use a group incentive plan in a unionized organization. That's not necessarily true. Group incentive plans that were reported in the CARS study covered about 1.3 million employees, of which about 20 percent were union members. If your organization is unionized, don't write off these plans. In fact, unions generally accept these plans without a vote. Only 35 percent of the organizations studied in the CARS project said their union voted as part of the approval process. Over the past twenty years, unions have been awakening to the importance of working with management for everyone's mutual benefit. The idea of a group incentive plan is generally appealing to unions because everyone earns equally (at least the same percentage of base pay).

Group incentive plans often are not negotiated in a contract with the union. They may negotiate entitlements, but not business strategies. The company wants the right to change objectives and measures, depending on the financial rationale of the plan, the changing market conditions, and the plan's business objectives. To work, the plan has to be in everyone's best interests. Cooperative planning and assessment, including union representation on the design committee, are becoming the norm rather than the exception.

A Vote for Broad Participation

Broad participation provides an excellent opportunity for mentoring and cross-functional communications. When bank tellers are in the same plan as back-office people, everyone has the opportunity to step out of their prescribed roles and begin working cross-functionally. If industrial engineers are on the same plan as the production people, they will work toward the same objectives and be prone to defend their turf.

When people work in silos, prone to suboptimization, they do what is best for their own jobs, whether that supports organizational performance or not. Group incentive plans that cover everybody can break down many of those barriers. By breaking the barriers, the organization can often respond more effectively to what needs to be done for the organization to be successful.

Another strong argument is that broad plans help organizations become more flexible. If yours is a traditionally submeasured and suboptimized organization, management's job becomes schizo-phrenic—maintain the silos and yet make the silos work together. Flattening organizations, redesign, and self-directed work teams are methodologies for reducing silo-thinking. Group incentive plans can certainly accelerate the process.

Baselines and Goals

Setting Baselines

Baselines
and Goals

A baseline is the point at which you begin to measure performance improvement.

The simplest definition of baseline is that it is the performance you would expect if you didn't have a plan. Performance above this baseline is meaningful to the organization, financially and/or oper-ationally. A baseline can be set on any measure. Even a project has a baseline: completed, or not. The baseline is the point at which you begin to measure and reward performance improvement.

The best first step in setting baselines is to look at the company's history with each measure. It could be the last twelve months, or several years. If you have a highly cyclical or seasonal business, you could use the previous equivalent period. If you don't have a history, you can use your best judgment of what is reasonable. But I would not recommend running a group incentive plan if there were no history on any of the measures selected.

Another way to set baselines is through competitive bench-marking or industry standards. These methods are relatively new, and with the creation of the American Productivity and Quality Center's Benchmarking Institute, I expect to see more of it in the future. It was surprising to find in the CARS research that engi-neered standards ("It should take six labor hours to make this wid-get") played a relatively small role in plans that had productivity measures. At best, these standards are benchmarks against which history is measured ("Our historical performance is 70 percent of standard").

Baseline doesn't have to match history exactly. If, for example, your measurement is productivity, sales may be divided by labor hours. You know you're going to have a 3 percent price increase, which will increase sales by 3 percent. You should include the 3 percent in the baseline. That's known as *packing the base*. Be warned that management can get greedy (or nervous about their financial risk) and overpack. Overpacking creates a baseline that may be perceived by the rank and file as unattainable. It defeats the whole purpose of the plan.

When setting financial baselines, it's often important to consider any significant changes that are planned. If your measurement is return on net assets and you're going to significantly increase assets in the short term by refurbishing your facility, take that into consideration.

Operational measures can be affected by gyrations in the market, product availability, and all kinds of other internal and external influences as well. It's helpful to look at the last four to eight quarters and see what variations the company has experienced. This will give you some guidance on adjusting baselines for inflation and new technology and for changes in organization, work flow, size, or the workforce. These are all things to take into consideration when you set the operational baselines.

There is a natural inclination to make baselines equal to the business plan. The accuracy of the business plan is often looked upon as wishful thinking rather than as realistic. If the measure in the business plan was developed in the way I've described for setting baselines, then use it as a baseline. More often than not, the business plan is closer to a goal than baseline and is not the appropriate performance level to begin measuring improvement. In the CARS research, 34 percent of the plans set baselines for financial measures at plan, while 51 percent set baselines according to history (the rest were based on competitive benchmarking, and so on). Operational measures relied even more heavily on history, with generally less than 15 percent using planned performance equal to baseline.

Sometimes a company doesn't have a measurement history, or that history is not appropriate. Project businesses with highly fluctuating revenues or costs from one year to another may require a best guess for a baseline.

A final word on setting baselines: people spend a good deal of time and energy arguing about baselines. During reassessment, they usually agree that too much time was spent trying to cover every possibility. Unfortunately, setting baselines is much more of an art than an exact science.

> *Unfortunately, setting baselines is much more of an art than an exact science.*

Setting Goals

A baseline is where you start measuring performance improvement. A goal, or target, is where you think the organization can get if the plan works. "Goal setting" is a powerful process when all of the people covered by the plan participate in the setting of the goal.

***Goal setting is a best
guess of what would
be accomplished if
the plan worked.***

The fine art of team goal setting does not apply to establishing a goal for a group incentive plan. The goals are set by the design team. It is not a sophisticated process. In this case, setting goals is figuring out what feels reasonable. It's saying, "If this plan works, what could we probably expect?" Every measure has its baseline and goal. One way to look at it is: baseline is what we would probably get without a plan; goal is a fifty-fifty chance.

Some people look at the company's history of peak performance to set goals. They take the average of the best of several months' or years' performances and make that the goal. Moving the average performance to the previous peaks is reasonable and attainable, and demonstrates real improvement.

The hardest part of setting goals is to establish some equity in the *degree of difficulty* between measured organizational units. The reward for reaching goal should be the same for all organizational units. This equity should apply to every organizational unit, with its set of measures, baselines, and goals, which may be compared for fairness (equity).

Here's a simple example: organizational Unit A is measured on profit, productivity, and customer satisfaction. Organizational Unit B is measured on economic value added (EVA), quality, and cycle time. The task is to set the goals on all three of both units' measures at a point where it will be seen by all employees as equally difficult to attain.

A second example: Organizational Unit C is measured on objectives from sales to controllable cost ratio. The history of organizational Unit C is one of running a tight ship and being a top performer in this measure. Organizational Unit D is measured in the same way but has one of the poorer performance histories. It may be as difficult for Unit C to hit a 5 percent improvement goal as it is for Unit D to hit a 10 percent improvement.

The focus is on degree of difficulty, not on how much more is saved by D's increasing by 10 percent than by C's increasing by 5 percent—nor on one measure having a significantly lower baseline than the other. The perception is that if the plan works as it should, the reward opportunity to reach the goals is about the same.

Once you go through the goal-setting process (sitting around the table and figuring out what feels right), you end up with exact numbers for baseline and goal that reflect each of the measures you want to reinforce by organizational unit. You then round them off to make the process simpler. This is going to be a tough concept for the engineers on the design team, but getting too precise in the calculation adds to the complexity of the communication and feedback process. I actually saw a manufacturing company that was dominated by engineers calculate their baselines and goals to a 1,000th of a percentage point. Most data systems are not that sophisticated.

It is easiest for the designers to work with a percentage improvement over baseline, such as 10 percent. In communicating the plan, however, I find it more powerful to express goal in terms of the measurement itself, that is, as baseline = 1 widget per hour; goal = 1.1 widget per hour.

It probably sounds simplistic, but the questions are always the same: What do you want to measure? What can you measure? Where do you want to measure it? How long do you want to measure it? How do you know you've been successful?

A manufacturing company, dominated by engineers, calculated their baselines and goals to a 1,000th of a percentage point.

At-Risk, Payouts, and Period

At-Risk

My favorite tough-minded managers often demand that future merit increases, CoLA, and or base pay be reduced to create even more of an incentive for the employees to perform. There is a wrongheadedness about approaching an at-risk design element from this point of view. It suggests that a group incentive plan is more a punisher than a positive reinforcement.

About 20 percent of the plans in the CARS database were considered themselves to have an at-risk element. This at-risk characterization, however, was limited to reduction of future merit increases. This only reinforced the degree to which merit increases had become an entitlement. There are a variety of ways to reduce merit pay pools and relate that reduction to the group incentive plan. The two most common ways have been to index the merit budget on overall business performance, with the group incentive plan providing the upside opportunity, and simply to divert all or a portion of the merit budget into the funding stream of the incentive plan.

These approaches have the effect of reducing entitlements. They also move the focus onto improving performance and the additional rewards that would bring. Considering that payouts from group incentive plans are not added to base pay, a 1 percent reduction in merit increase each year will be worth a compounded

At-Risk, Payouts, and Period

About 20 percent of the plans in the CARS database have an at-risk design element.

12 percent to the organization in ten years. The amount will be even more if you elect not to base benefits on the incentive amount.

There are no real data on what risk/reward ratios are being used. It seems rational that if employees give up 1 percent of merit pay or CoLA, they should be able to earn two to five times that amount at goal. It depends on how much they give up. My rule of thumb is that if 1 to 2 percent of base pay is taken out of the merit pool, 5 to 8 percent is a reasonable incentive for performance at goal. If they give up all of the merit increase pool, about 4 percent these days, an 8 to 10 percent payout at goal makes sense.

The CARS research reported that "perhaps the most interesting finding, given some of the publicity surrounding at-risk plans, is that plans [with this element] did not report more unfavorable results in any area [of effectiveness]. An at-risk plan sends a clear message to employees: some portion of future 'people costs' must vary with organizational performance. Employees will be partners with the company, sharing both the rewards and risks" (McAdams and Hawk, 1994, pp. 28–29).

As I have discussed before in this chapter, reducing base pay is very rare. It usually happens when the business is about to go under or labor rates are considerably above the competitive market. This move puts a great deal of pressure on the group incentive plan to be accurate in its measurements. (Reducing merit pools also applies pressure, but not to the same extent.) The risk/reward ratio in this scenario would be closer to one to ten, or a 1 percent reduction in base pay with a 10 percent opportunity at goal.

The Art of the Payout

Payout is initially determined based on how much is needed to motivate employees to reach goal on all the measures, assuming proper communication, education, involvement, and feedback. Take a look, for example, at Table 8.5 and think about what percentage of base pay would be necessary to do the job.

There is some relationship between LoS and the amount of payout. The longer the LoS, the more you have to reward people if you want them to figure out how to improve upon the measure. There is some relationship between the amount of communication, education, involvement, and feedback and the amount of payout at goal. The fewer the communications, education, and so on, the more you have to reward people.

There is also a relationship between the *intent* of the plan and the amount of payout. If the plan is just for awareness, you do not have to pay out as much as you would if you wanted significant improvement in a measure that can be directly affected by the people. If there is a mix of intentions—such as awareness for profit and direct influence on productivity—you may wish to rethink the weighting. You could reduce the weighting on profit and increase it on the others. Determining payout involves many variables.

Setting the Payout at Goal   Much like the subjective process used to set goals by measure, setting the payout for meeting all the goals is more often than not based on a gut feeling.

There is some folklore, some helpful, some misleading. There is some research, primarily CARS, and it saves the design team time. What is not folklore, however, relates back to the discussion about the degree of difficulty in reaching goal among organizational units with different measures and baselines. The total earning opportunity, at goal, should be about the same for all employees in the plan. Organizational Unit C may have to improve 5 percent over its baseline in order for each of its employees to earn 8 percent of base pay. Employees in organizational Unit D may have to improve 10 percent to earn 8 percent of their base pay. Different measures or the same. Different goals or the same. Equity should be attempted in both the degree of difficulty in reaching goal and the amount of the award at goal.

Here are some folklore and reality about setting payouts:

Folklore: You have to have pay from 20 to 30 percent of base pay to get someone's attention and be meaningful. *Reality:* Rarely.

There are two situations in which paying 20 to 30 percent may be a good idea. First, if the base pay is quite low, then significant percentages are necessary to develop a reasonable reward-performance linkage and fair and competitive pay. This usually occurs in individual incentive plans, generally in piece rate plans, and it is considered in base compensation. Group incentive plans that have little communication, education, involvement, and feedback and that just ask people to work harder or smarter in their jobs usually require high payouts at goal.

The second situation is a function of the employee's level in the organization. Organizations have developed an overwhelming need

TABLE 8.5. *Variations in Percentage of Base Pay at Goal in CARS Research.*

LEVEL OF EMPLOYEE	TARGET % OF BASE PAY AT GOAL
Top management	25%
Middle management	20%
First-line supervisors	13%
Exempt professionals	10%
Nonexempt	5%

Source: McAdams and Hawk, 1994, p. 160.

to make the well-to-do even more so. The CARS research found that about 150 plans of the 737 surveyed varied the percentage of base pay at goal by type of employee, with the median ranging from 25 percent for top management down to 5 percent for nonexempt employees (see Table 8.5). These median data were consistent for the 40 percent of the plans that targeted a payout at goal. These plans did not perform any better, however, than those that had the same percentage of base payout at goal for all employees or those with the same dollar value.

Does this mean that 5 percent should be your target? Certainly not. You establish what is appropriate for your culture; the LoS; the degree of communication, education, involvement, and feedback; the types of employees to be covered by the plan; the nature of the measures; and the levels at which you set the baselines and goals. The CARS plans reported targets from 3 to 30 percent.

The CARS research also showed that plans that target higher payouts often perform better on their measures and make higher payouts. They also report larger gains and better net return on payouts—at least for plan participants at exempt/management levels. These plans also report consistently better nonfinancial results. It makes sense that by offering bigger earning opportunities, organizations can expect better results.

Folklore: The way to determine a payout is to figure out how much you are going to gain (save) at goal and pay back 50 percent to the employees. Fifty-fifty splits are a design dictum. *Real-*

ity: Put the horse before the cart. The objective is to develop a reasonable payout that will influence people, not just reward them after the fact, and check it against your ability to pay.

More than fifty years ago, the original Scanlon gainsharing plan had one measure—productivity—and was designed to pay out 75 percent of the savings from the improvement to the employees and 25 percent to the company. Variations of the plan have subsequently moved that split to the easily communicated fifty-fifty split. For public relations, it looks and sounds fair. From a design point of view, it is irrelevant. Most plans have more than one measure, some whose gain can be valued in dollars and some whose gain can't, but both are still terribly important to the company.

If you follow my approach to design, you will end up with some split of gains between employee and company, but the design is not driven by a predetermined split. Group incentive plans are proactive. They are designed to get people to make changes that will improve the measures. That means determining what is necessary for a meaningful payout at goal, then calculating the value of the gain at goal, then comparing the two for a split return on payout. If the return is unacceptable, go back and adjust any of the variables that meet the needs of all those affected by this plan.

The Form of Payouts   Generally, payouts provide an equal percentage of pay or an equal dollar amount to everybody in the plan. About 30 percent of the plans studied by CARS paid an equal percentage, and about 30 percent had an equal dollar payout. (The rest had a graduated scale that paid a higher percent of base pay for employees in positions higher in the organization.)

The decision is based on the message the organization wants to send to employees. An equal percentage of pay might reflect the perceived level of each employee's contribution. Equal dollar payouts probably support better teamwork and a sense of equality. For purposes of designing the payout strategy, use an equal percentage of base pay target at goal. It is the easiest way to ballpark your financial exposure at goal. You can adjust to the other options rather easily later.

Does It Make Sense?   I always suggest a sanity check. Take the targeted percentage of base pay of each type of employee at goal and see if the dollar amount feels right when compared to what you are asking from the employee population. If the majority of your employees are making $20,000 per year, a 2 percent payout at goal is $400 per year before deductions. If you pay out monthly, that would be $33 per month, again before deductions. If there are three measurements, each weighted equally, that's $11 per month before deductions. Is it worth it? Probably not. Do you need 10 percent at goal? That's $166 per month, $55 per measure. Only you know your organization well enough to decide, but make sure you look at the plan from the view of its participants.

How About Payouts by Measure?   Table 8.6 shows baselines and goals for the Midwestern Company Example's set of objectives and measures. Remember that this example demonstrates the process and is not intended to be a recommendation for your plan.

In the example, the weighting that was determined by top management or the design team is equally applied to the total award at goal to distribute it among the measures, as shown in Table 8.7. It should be pretty obvious why you don't want more than five measures: it dilutes the payout at goal too much. The same point applies to weighting any one measure less than 10 percent, unless the measure is there just to remind employees of the objective, such

TABLE 8.6. *Midwestern Company Example: Incorporating Baselines and Goals by Measure.*

OBJECTIVE	MEASURE	WEIGHTING	BASELINE	GOAL (% IMPROVEMENT)
Financial performance	Net income before taxes	25%	$10,000 million	$10,500 million (+5%)
Productivity	Number of pounds shipped per controllable cost dollar	25%	1.90 lb./$	2.0 lb./$ (+5.3%)
Cycle time	Order to payment days	25%	100 days	90 days (+10%)
Quality	Percent of labor hours spent on rework and redos	25%	15%	10% (+33%)

TABLE 8.7. *Midwestern Company Example: Incorporating Weighting to Payout at Goal by Measure.*

OBJECTIVE	MEASURE	WEIGHTING	PAYOUT AT GOAL
Financial performance	Net income before taxes	25%	25% of 5% = 1.25% of base pay
Productivity	Number of pounds shipped per controllable cost dollar	25%	25% of 5% = 1.25% of base pay
Cycle time	Order to payment days	25%	25% of 5% = 1.25% of base pay
Quality	Percent of labor hours spent on rework and redos	25%	25% of 5% = 1.25% of base pay

as safety—although there are better ways of doing that. (See the section on modifiers later in the chapter.)

When Do You Begin to Pay Out? It's important to determine when to begin payouts. If you reach baseline, is that the only point at which you start rewarding people? It depends. Most traditional group incentive plans pay nothing upon reaching baseline. Employees have to improve over the baseline before earning anything. However, if you have been giving out payments on a previous plan that has become an entitlement and you're now converting to a more performance-based plan, then that amount of money might be the amount you would expect to pay out at baseline.

I once converted a management-only plan that over the years had become a variable entitlement. Top management chose about 30 percent of the managers for a bonus that varied based on top management's opinion of their performance. When the company went to a group incentive plan, 100 percent of the managers participated, so I used what they had previously paid out in variable entitlements (several millions of dollars) as their reward at meeting baseline. The reality is they would have spent that money anyway, and it was basically considered a fixed cost. Using it as the reward for hitting a slightly packed baseline, but spread out over all the managers, sent a powerful message to everyone that the business was now performance-driven and would be in the future.

When Do You Stop Paying Out?   *Stretch* is the payout cap—the point at which you're no longer willing to pay for additional improvement. Management is often concerned about having a windfall due to outside influences, unconnected with what the employees have done. As protection for the organization, they set a payout cap. Depending on the stretch performance level, this could send a negative and misleading message. Baseline is the opportunity to communicate what you expect to do without a plan. Goals communicate what you think can be reasonably accomplished. Stretch tells people that there is a limit to what they can earn. It also gives people the subtle message that this is the most management thinks they can accomplish. Finally, it says we are not interested in improving above this point.

Windfalls can occur. If you're worried about windfalls, it's better to exclude the effect from the plan's performance measurement when the data come in than to have a stretch point that is too low. (If you take this approach, be sure to communicate what you are doing when the windfall occurs. It will reinforce your fair and objective approach to both the employee and the organization.) Are stretch points or caps always inappropriate? Not if they are high enough.

I find that most payout caps are imposed by managers who are bound by budget-think—"We manage to the budget." Obviously, budgeting is a critical and appropriate process in the business life of companies, but it can be counterproductive to group incentive plans. Companies are only used to variable budgeting in sales plans, where they understand that if sales sky rocket, so will the commission cost. That is usually fine, because companies make more gross margin on incremental sales, assuming they don't have to increase capital expense. "Sell big, earn big" is the old sales commission mantra.

With some limitations, the same approach applies to nonsales employee group incentive plans. If you are making a good return on your group incentive plan investment, don't put a payout cap on the measure. If you only want or are willing to pay a certain amount for improvement on all or just one measure, use a cap. They limit what people can do, but they also limit the financial exposure of the organization. About half of the plans studied by CARS had caps on payouts. The median cap was 10 percent of base pay (McAdams and Hawk, 1994, p. 165).

Here's an explanation from an announcement of a group incentive plan explaining the cap on earnings: "You may ask why we have an upper limit on the amount you can earn. That's because the top level of performance is exceptional and is unlikely to be bettered in the plan year. We realize that business success depends on balancing several factors. So, it's possible that too high a score on one measure indicates insufficient attention to the others."

How Often Do You Pay Out?   According to the CARS research, plans based on lead and lag measures tend to pay out annually. Operational measures allow more frequent measurement, and payouts are made monthly or quarterly (McAdams and Hawk, 1994, pp. 170–171). More frequent payouts clearly reduce LoS. It is possible, but rare, for plans using a combination of measures to pay out at different frequencies—for operational performance plans to pay out monthly and lead or lag performance plans to pay out annually. Another option is to use the financial performance as a multiplier. Improved financial performance is rewarded with a year-end bonus. The bonus is determined by multiplying what has been earned in operational performance during the year by a factor indexed to financial measures. (This topic is discussed in greater detail in the sections on line of sight and rules structure.)

What Do Plans Pay Out?   The median CARS data on payouts (within the plan period, not deferred into a retirement plan fund) show a consistent range from $800 to $2,000 per employee per year, depending on the type of plan, industry, and so on. For the employee covered by these plans, the median payout ranges from 3.0 to 5.4 percent of base pay. (See Table 8.8.)

TABLE 8.8. *Median CARS Data on Payouts.*

	ALL PLANS	MANUFACTURING	SERVICE	PLANS WITH FINANCIAL MEASURES ONLY	PLANS WITH OPERATIONAL MEASURES ONLY	PLANS WITH BOTH FINANCIAL AND OPERATIONAL MEASURES
75th percentile	$2,960	$2,868	$3,122	$3,594	$2,028	$4,467
50th percentile (median)	$1,175	$1,123	$1,125	$1,393	$833	$2,028
25th percentile	$587	$596	$486	$695	$274	$795

Source: McAdams and Hawk, 1994, p. 204; updated 1995.

Setting the Plan Period

The plan period is always preannounced; it defines the plan from starting date to reassessment date. It is important to make clear to employees in the preannouncement that at the end of the period, one of three things will happen:

1. The plan will be kept exactly as it is, with minor changes in the baseline or the point at which measurements and payout are made. These are minor adjustments to account for the previous year's experience. The adjustment is to numbers, but not to the measurement itself. Some plans announce in advance that they will change the baseline on a rolling average, using a three-year period. Each year, the last three years are used to revise the baseline.

2. The measurement and/or rules will be changed. This is a significant revision. Usually, organizations add measurements. They seldom get rid of them. This may happen because they have discovered some area of performance that is important to the business that they were not measuring and rewarding previously. People also become comfortable with the plan, so adding a new measurement is less problematic.

3. The company will kill the plan. Out of the 737 plans in CARS, there were about 80 terminations. Little difference could be found between the plans that terminated and those that didn't. Most of the time, they were not getting the performance they wanted (McAdams and Hawk, 1994, pp. 275–285). That's good. The plan is a dynamic process. You don't want to keep one that doesn't work.

> *A group incentive plan is a dynamic process. You don't want to keep one that doesn't work.*

On the right side of the reinforcement model, particularly in group incentive plans, you need plan periods, because you never want to suggest that the reward is a guarantee or entitlement of any kind. It must be re-earned every single time.

The most common plan period is twelve months, and it tends to dovetail with the fiscal year. There are some exceptions. Plans range from six to eighteen months between reassessment periods. Some run indefinitely with yearly reviews but with little expectation of significant changes. These latter plans run the risk of becoming an entitlement. That's okay, if you use that portion of the total reward opportunity to keep you competitive in the labor market.

Value of Gains

Performance goals are key elements in the design process because they determine a consistent point at which gain to the organization can be measured. Gain can be direct or indirect. It can be visible on the bottom line, or it can have an imputed value to the corporation. Valuing gains is the most difficult part of this process, and the most critical.

> Value of Gains

The Watergate rule of "follow the money" plays to the sensibilities of most top managers. Organizations often get buy-in from top management on plans because they make financial sense, because it seems like the right thing to do, and because it feels right for all the stakeholders. Commitments for more training plans are a classic example of funds committed in good faith and withdrawn at the first sign of an organization's financial hiccups. A solid, financially justified group incentive plan will not be as subject to managerial shifts in focus as one not so justified.

If you want to get management's attention, grab them by the P&L, and their hearts and minds will follow.

My golden rule: if you want to get management's attention, grab them by the P&L, and their hearts and minds will follow.

Calculating Gain by Types of Measures

This discussion about calculating gain is intended only to give readers a simple way to look at the subject; it is not a "how to" primer on calculating gain. Calculating gain can be a complex exercise best left to the financial member of your design team. However, it is important that other design team members have a basic understanding of gain when determining measures.

Suggestion plans were the first to use a "sharing of the gain" concept. If an employee or team suggestion saved the company a million dollars, part of that money was shared with the employees. That was a simple calculation, once you decided that the suggestion could or did save the million dollars. Getting agreement on the value of a cost reduction is the most straightforward of the various gain calculations. Suggestion plans have a particular advantage over all others in that management is pretty sure they wouldn't have saved the money without the suggestion. The gain is directly attributable to the idea and its implementation. (This is an example of a project team incentive plan that will be discussed further in Chapter Nine.)

Measurement and how to use measurements as part of a performance improvement process have been documented to death. But the amount written about putting a dollar value to the gain in that performance is pretty limited. That's because it is difficult and unique to each application and also because the organization probably didn't involve its financial staff in the process early enough. I suggest you initiate a "take the CFO to lunch program" when you start this journey.

Leading Measures

About every business I know would love to be able to put a dollar value on this first one:

Customer Satisfaction   It looks like we're a long way off from being able to measure improvement in customer satisfaction. Some data are available indicating that it costs seven times as much to get a new customer as to keep an existing one. That number would obviously vary with the type of business, but when you consider the cost of advertising, promotion, research, and so forth, it rings true. Organizations have always put more emphasis on getting new customers than on keeping those they already have. This approach is akin to getting more sales rather than cutting costs. In both cases, the latter is probably easier to do, and it will have a greater effect on the bottom line.

Management does understand, however, that customer satisfaction is important. At best, it is a macromeasurement of an indirect link to financial measures, reflecting the larger organizational performance. The Profit Impact of Market Strategy (PIMS) database includes more than 2,700 business units. The data show that business units with high quality (as perceived by their customers) get price premiums and increase their market shares with the same or lower costs as those with low quality. The measurement of high versus low quality is far more complex than the simple methods I've described. Gale (1994) demonstrates how PIMS can be used to draw linkages between market perceived quality and relative price, direct cost, return on investment, market share, cash flow to sales, and market value.

Do these data give you a dollar value on the gain in customer satisfaction? Hardly, but it is the most solid information I've found to reinforce the wisdom of organizations' focus on and reinforcement of customer satisfaction.

Employee Satisfaction   It's not practical to calculate gain on pure employee satisfaction; however, turnover can have a dollar value attached to it. Turnover can be a big expense. In very high turnover businesses, like fast food restaurants, turnover rates regularly exceed 150 percent. By the time you interview, hire, train, and then lose employees, it will probably cost between $300 to $500 for every one lost. This is a relatively straightforward gain calculation.

In organizations where turnover ranges from 15 to 30 percent—a much lower turnover rate, but still not acceptable—the cost can be much higher. A reasonable calculation is based on the fully loaded cost of a person for a year. Again, this is a subject for finance and human resources, but always keep in mind that by reducing turnover you may realize a significant gain for the company.

Sales   If sales is a measure in your group incentive plan, you have to value the gain based on the contribution to the bottom line, such as net income before taxes.

Market Share   Gain would revert back to any increase in sales that improved market share, and the incremental profits those sales bring.

Operational Measures

Productivity   Productivity is the most common measure for calculating gain, and it is by far the greatest contributor to the dollar value of a group incentive plan. Readers who are industrial engineers might be interested in the detailed financial calculations of the financial incremental value of productivity found in John Belcher's book *Gain Sharing* (1987) and in Tim Ross and Brian Graham-Moore's *Gainsharing: Plans for Improving Performance* (1990).

Because this is a book for nontechnicians, I begin with a simple example of the process of putting a dollar value on productivity gains—just to provide a basic understanding. Your design team member from finance will use her own process and do the work.

If you produce a thousand widgets with a thousand total labor hours, you have one widget per labor hour, or a productivity ratio of one. Over the measured payout period, the productivity ratio has improved to 1.1 widgets per labor hour. That may have happened because you made 1,100 widgets with 1,000 labor hours or 1,000 widgets with 909 labor hours, or some other combination, but it's a 10 percent improvement either way.

What is the 10 percent improvement worth to the company? At the very least, the cost of 91 labor hours. More likely, the value is based on the incremental gross profit on each item produced and sold. The cost of raw material per widget stays the same. The cost of the labor component goes down. If you produce more widgets, overhead is spread over more production, so overhead goes down. In the real world, both output and input vary from minute to minute, and the best we can do is create a reasonable ratio to reflect overall performance.

The median gains were about $2,200 per employee per year. $1,100,000 for 500 employees.

The CARS data for gain from operational measures (not financial) that can be valued in dollars is primarily driven by productivity. To normalize the data, the reported gains by plan were divided by the number of employees, and the result was annualized. The median gains were about $2,200 per employee per year. The top 25 percent of the performers got two to three times that amount. The bottom 25 percent got half that gain. So the median gain for a five-hundred-employee population would be $1,100,000 ($2,200 x 500 employees) for the year. Tracking that money to the P&L is one of the challenges of the accounting profession. It is not a matter of legitimizing the savings, but rather of having the ability to track the savings with existing accounting systems. It's the plan's job to deliver the grizzly bear and finance's job to skin it.

Valuing gains is a matter of legitimizing savings with finance. It's the plan's job to deliver the grizzly bear and the finance's job to skin it.

Internal Quality   Quality improvement must be measured as a result in order to be rewarded in a group incentive plan. The following are the simplest and most common examples I've seen.

Reduction in scrap is a straightforward quality measure. If you have 1,000,000 pounds of scrap and you reduce it by 500,000 pounds, you have saved the value of 500,000 pounds of scrap. The gain is clear.

Rework is another simple quality measure that allows for calculation of gain. However, the amount of rework done on products under warranty moves the measure from an operational indicator to a lagging indicator. You don't know that a hair dryer has failed warranty until you repair it. The measure comes too late to affect operations. The same applies to complaints on hard goods. A product or service with a faster customer feedback mechanism might be a candidate for a quality measure on which a value could be placed.

In white-collar office environments, records are seldom kept on the amount of rework done, so a quality measure for gain calculation is rare. Most organizations just don't keep records on retyping or redoing work. If you do, it is an opportunity for valuing gains in quality. In the banking industry, the loan decision process can be a measure of quality. The ratio of the value of bad loans to the total number of loans outstanding is a common measure of asset quality.

The "hidden cost of quality" in lost customers, credibility, and redundancy of systems has been a primary theme from the beginning of the quality movement in the United States. Many more dollars of savings could be made through quality improvement than in the examples I've given and than can be generated from these simplistic approaches. Look to your quality coordinator for support on gain calculations. (If you do not feel comfortable using these "hidden" costs in the gain calculation, at least put them in a footnote in your plan's financial rationale statement.)

Cost Reduction   Fewer than a quarter of the organizations in the CARS study use cost reduction against a goal or budget as a basis for payouts. Cost reduction is reported in dollars, but it is an operational, not a financial, measure. Because the improvement is reported in dollars, the gains are clear. The assumption, however, is that you would have spent the budget if the plan had not been in place.

I've seen companies use cost reduction in a group incentive plan to ease the pain of making the budget cuts work. It is a bit of a strange approach—almost like buying compliance. As I suggested earlier, cost reduction is best addressed by a project team incentive plan (Chapter Nine).

Attendance   Measurement of attendance is reasonably straightforward. Organizations usually can account for every hour worked by an hourly worker, and every hour lost costs the company in production or service or quality. Attendance may also save the cost of a more expensive substitute player who may not do the job as well.

Exempt employees are usually paid a salary, and their absenteeism is generally not as well reported as that of nonexempt employees. There is also a developing mind-set that a salaried hour isn't worth focusing on, at least to the degree that an hourly person is. If you are going to attempt to measure the value of gain due to a reduction of absenteeism or an improvement in presenteeism, make sure you include all types of employees.

Safety   The primary funding from improvements in safety is due to a reduction in workman's compensation costs that parallel health care cost increases year to year. Developing a value in safety performance improvement is surprisingly straightforward. It generally comes from a human resources or safety staff function.

Output or Volume   Output or volume has the same gain issues as sales. The contribution is at least equal to the incremental gross profit on the increased production. In some operations the influence on customer satisfaction is equally important.

Cycle Time   Gains on cycle time can be calculated based on cash flow. The faster you can get an order, fill it, bill it, and receive payment, the sooner you will have that money in hand. Depending on the volume, gain could be calibrated in terms of getting the money earlier rather than later. In reality, it takes a huge cash flow to make this calculation large enough to make a difference.

The real value of cycle time is that it reflects the organization's ability to respond, to be flexible, and to achieve high levels of customer satisfaction—assuming that quick response time is important to the customer.

Project Milestones   Project milestones are much the same problem in gain calculation as cycle time. Remember that group incentive plans focus on a cumulative performance of steps in projects and that such plans include all employees in the organizational unit. Gain calculation is difficult in that project completion tends to be critical to the operation of the business or worth a good deal of money when completed regardless of milestone completion. Assigning a dollar value as a gain is not common.

Lag Measures

Logically, the easiest gain calculation should be on lag measures, because they stem from accounting ledgers and P&L sheets. Historically, organizations have relied on financial statements to determine how well they're doing. It is easy to calculate the dollar value of the gain in financial measures. Going from $10 million to $11 million in profits is clearly a $1 million gain. And yet, very few of the plans in the CARS research that had financial measures were willing to put a dollar value on the gain.

I believe that this reluctance is due to attribution: what caused the financial performance to change? (The very nature of operational measures assumes attribution, for the most part, to the people and the plan.) The CARS respondents were unwilling, rather than unable, to put a dollar value on the gain, because of their inability to identify a connection between the changed performance and the group incentive plan. Too many things that can affect financial statements are simply outside anyone's control.

In addition, financial measures have a long LoS, and the perception is that most of the rank and file cannot affect them. Sometimes, financial plans are not intended to affect how people do things. They are simply an awareness exercise, although few top managers would admit that. Most plans based on lag measures are simply ways to distribute funds created by improved financial performance. They have become entitlements, and there is little understanding or appreciation within the company of their importance.

I find it very strange that a company would put a project team through the ringer to cost justify a new piece of machinery or system, and yet spend millions each year on a profit sharing bonus without evaluating its effectiveness. Some companies use profit sharing or some other version of financial group incentive plan to fund retirement plans. Some pay under the competitive market, with the objective that profit sharing will make up the difference—plus a little more. If that is their objective and their rationale for spending the money, then it makes sense. I am surprised, however, that many managers believe that the profit sharing package really makes a difference in the performance of the two thousand employees covered by it. For example, Chrysler employees were elated to get an average of $7,000-plus as a profit sharing bonus for 1994, but I doubt that anyone would strongly argue that it was earned as a direct result of employee performance.

There has been some research done in this area. Douglas Kruse of Rutgers University published a review of the research on profit sharing plans, deferred and current, in *Profit Sharing: Does It Make a Difference?* (1993). He found that profit sharing plans were associated with (not caused by) higher company performance and productivity increases of 3.5 to 5 percent. Such plans work better in smaller companies, and if they pay out currently, not deferred. Yet, most profit sharing plans are in larger companies, and they are deferred. The connection between profit sharing and improved performance of larger companies is a tenuous one at best.

I suspect that management's fondness for financial measures is rooted in a number of things:

- Top management is familiar with profit and return calculations and accepts them with little question of their value.

- Financial measures are supported by the existing accounting systems.

- Payouts are made from a pool created by (typically) profits and the assumption is that "as long as there is a pool, the payouts are justified."

- Financial measures add to the total earning opportunity in the hope that they are attractive to outsiders and substantial enough to retain the current people.

- The organization's financial stakeholders are protected. "No profit, no payout" is the only simplistic soundbite of plans based on these measures.

My question is, "Are you convinced that the money paid out is related to the contribution of the employees?" If that is not the issue, fine. If it is, it is time to reexamine your plan.

What's the Best Measure?

The best measure is a combination of measures that accurately reflect the operational and financial success of the organization. One or more of the measures should be able to be assigned a dollar value of the gain to the improvement. Table 8.9 shows Midwestern Company's basic parameters with an added estimated value of the gain from baseline to goal for each measure. Note that cycle time gain could only be expressed in terms of the measure itself.

There are as many creative measures as there are creative people and organizational functions. Measures can be as broad as an overview of what has been accomplished after the books are closed, or as focused as a totally redeveloped measure of a specific need of the business for a specific period of time.

Here's just one note of caution: be wary of rewarding on activity measures (number of meetings held, and so on). They can mask accomplishment. Obviously, some activity measures are appropriate. Some customer service operations swear that the number of calls answered in thirty seconds is a direct indicator of customer

TABLE 8.9. *Midwestern Company Example: Incorporating Value of Gain at Goal for Each Measure.*

OBJECTIVE	MEASURE	WEIGHTING	BASELINE	GOAL (% IMPROVEMENT)	PAYOUT AT GOAL	GAIN AT GOAL
Financial performance	Net income before taxes	25%	$10,000 million	$10,500 million (+5%)	1.25% of base pay	$500,000
Productivity	Number of pounds shipped per controllable cost dollar	25%	1.90 lb./$	2.0 lb./$ (+5.3%)	1.25% of base pay	$130,000
Cycle time	Order to payment days	25%	100 days	90 days (+10%)	1.25% of base pay	10 days less cycle time
Quality	Percent of labor hours spent on rework and redos	25%	15%	10% (+33%)	1.25% of base pay	$625,000

service and a good measure of performance. Perhaps, but it may also be the only thing they can measure. Answering the telephone is an activity and does not necessarily improve results. (I think that reinforcing activities are best addressed by recognition plans, discussed in Chapter Seven.)

Return on Payout

Return on payout is the relationship between how much money you're going to make as a result of the reward plan and how much you will have to spend. There is a simple way to look at it:

Return on Payout

$$\frac{\$1,000,000\ (gain) - \$400,000\ (payout)}{\$400,000\ (payout)} \times 100 = \frac{\$600,000}{\$400,000} \times 100$$

$$= 150 \text{ percent } net \text{ return on payout}$$

In other words, take the dollar amount calculated for gain. Subtract the amount you will have to pay out at goal, divide by the same payout amount, and multiply by one hundred to get a percentage. This is a simple *net return on investment* figure. The *gross* return on payout is $1,000,000 (gain), or a $2.50 gain on each $1 of payout, with a total payout of $400,000. In addition, there may be an improvement on performance measures that cannot be given a dollar value.

So, you spent $1.00 and made $2.50, a 150 percent net return on your investment. I realize this is not very sophisticated, but it is as good as anything that is available. Compared to many of the capital requests made in major organizations, it is just as logical. I realize that capital has depreciation and accounting principles written all over it, but there are just as many dogs and ponies—not to mention smoke and mirrors—in those requests as in one for a group incentive plan.

Table 8.10 illustrates the Midwestern Company example.

If we assume that each measure reaches goal, the payout will be 5 percent of base pay, or $625,000 for five hundred employees. The gain would be overstated if all the gains from each measure were totaled, because we would be double dipping (counting the same dollars twice). Since in the example, controllable costs do not include labor, the gains from productivity and quality could be combined for a total of $755,000. The return calculations are:

$$\frac{\$755,000\,(gain) - \$625,000\,(payout)}{\$625,000\,(payout)} \times 100 = \frac{\$130,000}{\$625,000} \times 100$$

$$= 21 \text{ percent } net \text{ return on payout}$$

The *gross* return on payout is $755,000 (gain) on a total payout of $625,000, or a $1.21 gain to $1.00 of payout. In addition, there is a 5 percent improvement in profit and a ten-day reduction in cycle time.

TABLE 8.10. *Midwestern Company Example: Gain at Goal by Measure.*

OBJECTIVE	MEASURE	GAIN AT GOAL
Profit	Net income before taxes	$500,000
Productivity	Units shipped per controllable cost dollar	$130,000
Cycle time	Days from order to payment	10 days less cycle time
Quality	Labor hours for rework/redo as a percentage of total hours	$625,000

After you have calculated your gross or net return on payout, you can decide if it will be acceptable to management. If it is not, you can decide to change the payout rates, the measures, or the goals to improve the return. The process is iterative; you adjust it as you proceed, always remembering that the plan must be fair both to the organization and to its employees.

If your payout exceeds your gain, then you've spent money to accomplish the objectives. It is an investment. In this case, the design team must decide: "Is the expense worth the improvement?" In the example, let's assume the design team decided only to use the gain from productivity—$130,000. The plan still met goal in all measurements. Would the net expense—$625,000 in payout less $130,000 gain for a $495,000 net expense—be worth a 5 percent profit improvement, reduction of cycle time by ten days, reduction of rework by 5 percent, and the soft stuff—alignment of employees with objectives, and improvement in communications, education, feedback, and involvement? Each organization must decide for itself.

What Does the Research Show?

In the CARS data, 232 plans reported their gains and their payouts. To determine the median net return on payout, it is necessary to calculate the net return on each plan and take the median of the calculation value. In the CARS data, the median is 122 percent net return on payout. That's $2.22 for every dollar spent on payout (McAdams and Hawk, 1994, pp. 194–200, Rev. 1995 data).

In the CARS data, the median is 122 percent net return on payout.

How Much of the Gain Is Real?

To be fair, there are a few things to remember when considering the data and the calculations. Not all of the gains are represented. This is an extremely conservative approach. Remember, we're usually only putting a dollar value on one or two measures of gain. We can't count the performance-gain linkage because we can't calculate a gain on customer satisfaction, projects completed on time and on budget, cycle time, and so on, for which we may reward.

Another consideration is attribution. Just how much of the gain came from the plan? Of course, no one knows for sure. When people in the CARS research were asked to estimate, the guesses were consistent. Plans with operational measures or in combination with financial measures attributed about 70 to 80 percent of the gains to the plan itself. Those few plans using only financial measures that reported gains estimated that less than 20 to 30 percent was due to the plan. Compared to the other elements of the reinforcement model, however, only project team incentive plans (discussed in Chapter Nine) can take credit for essentially all the results.

The other issue is that the payout number doesn't represent all of the costs. Training, consulting, communications, measurement, and other plan support aren't included. It's surprising that most of the organizations in the CARS study didn't keep any records on this cost. When they did, it did not significantly affect the net return on payout. The median cost was reported to be about $40 per person, with a minimum of $5 and a high of $200.

It's comforting to know that most of the costs are in the payouts and not in the administration. But a low per-person cost also indicates that organizations are not spending much on what makes group incentive plans really work—good implementation. Most group incentive plans are treated as if they were compensation plans, with little follow-through on communications, education, feedback, and involvement.

Clearly, the net-return-on-payout formula is not meant to be a hard and fast financial statement that you can take to the P&L. The connection between group incentive plans and profitability is difficult to prove. I certainly wish this were a more exact science, but it isn't. Organizations guess at what it will take to motivate people to reach a nonscientific goal, and they estimate the dollar value of the performance gain on just a few of the measures on which the rewards are based. The research from CARS and many other researchers at least gives some idea of what to expect and some comfort that there is a real opportunity to show a return on investment in people.

Structure

Structure

Creating the reward structure involves a simple matrix connecting the performance with the reward. I do not recommend a continuous payout schedule driven by a formula. Table 8.11 provides an example of a continuous payout schedule using the Midwestern Company quality measure.

TABLE 8.11. *A Continuous Payout Schedule.*

OBJECTIVE	MEASURE	BASELINE	GOAL	PAYOUT AT GOAL
Quality	Labor hours for rework/redo as a percentage of total hours	15%	10% (33%)	1.25% of base pay

If the organization reaches a goal of 10 percent, there is only one payout at the end of the year, and all employees get the same percentage of base pay as a payout. The award for quality only would be (remember the hours are the total for the organization of five hundred employees; this not an individual incentive plan):

$$\text{Total hours worked} = 10,000,000$$
$$\text{Hours spent on rework/redo} = 1,156,000 \text{ or } 11.56\%$$
$$\text{Employee payout} = (15\% - 11.56\%) \times 0.25\% \text{ of pay} \times \$25,000 \text{ base pay}$$
$$= 0.86\% \times \$25,000 = \$215$$

A continuous formula gives away money. Nobody decides they are going to perform 11.56 percent instead of 11.57 percent of total hours on rework. Yet, with a continuous payout formula, organizations pay for that 0.01 of a percentage point. Remember, this is a precise measurement of a somewhat imprecise performance measure.

Continuous formulas eliminate "breakage" for the organization. Breakage occurs when you have incremental steps of performance and payout. If the performance is within the incremental step, the difference between the actual performance and the payout level below it is free. That's breakage. The organization makes incremental payouts and doesn't pay anything until the next level of performance and payout is reached.

I have no data on this, but my experience is that performance ends up going about 25 percent into the next earning increment. Of course, performance might go 90 percent into the next increment, which means the company would get 90 percent of that increment for free. Breakage can amount to quite a bit of improved performance at no cost, depending on number of measures and frequency of payout. The more measures and payout periods there are, the more breakage there is.

Here's the quality element in a matrixed, performance-payout step design:

$$\text{Quality measure} = \frac{Labor\ hours\ on\ rework/redo}{Total\ labor\ hours}$$

Table 8.12 contains a reward schedule encompassing five levels of performance improvement to goal for the Midwestern Company example. There is a natural cap on this schedule when no labor hours are spent on rework, resulting in a payout of 3.75 percent of pay. If the performance improvement is unlimited, you must decide if you want to cap the performance you're willing to pay for.

Be careful not to make your increments of payout performance too big—only baseline and goal, for example—because people will see that as unfair. It also creates a goal that's perceived to be too high for them to reach. It's important that you reward fairly, so try to find increments that people can relate to; three to five between baseline and goal is a good rule of thumb. One increment is too few. Fifty increments is coming close to a continuous formula and is tough to communicate.

Just look at baseline and goal measures and see how they break down readily into chunks of improvement. Most design teams try to show the improvement in percentages because it is easier to calculate. (Quality ratio = 15 percent; 1 percent improvement earns $x; 2 percent improvement earns $y; and so on.) But it is not as effective to communicate percentage improvement as it is to communicate in terms of the measurement itself. Reducing days of cycle time to chunks of one day for each level of payout is clearer than a 1 percent improvement.

TABLE 8.12. *Midwestern Company Example: Single Measure Reward Schedule.*

BASELINE	LEVEL 1	LEVEL 2	LEVEL 3	LEVEL 4	LEVEL 5 (GOAL)
15%	14%	13%	12%	11%	10%
1,500,000 hrs on rework 10,000,000 total hrs	1,400,000 hrs on rework 10,000,000 total hrs	1,300,000 hrs on rework 10,000,000 total hrs	1,200,000 hrs on rework 10,000,000 total hrs	1,100,000 hrs on rework 10,000,000 total hrs	1,000,000 hrs on rework 10,000,000 total hrs
Payout = None	Payout = 0.25% of pay	Payout = 0.5% of pay	Payout = 0.75% of pay	Payout = 1% of pay	Payout = 1.25% of pay

Payouts as Points or Percentage of Target

If you have more than one measure and several levels of payout, consider using points. Points are an extremely flexible tool, because you can make a point worth whatever you want—$1.00, 1 percent of base pay, .001 percent of base pay—and they also can be redeemable for time off or stock or catalogue merchandise. Points are flexible in another way, too: a point can have a different value depending on the employee's level or organizational unit. If you want to use a nonegalitarian plan in which the CEO makes 25 percent of base pay and the lowest level person makes 5 percent at goal (not that I'm suggesting that), then a point is worth a whole lot more for the CEO than for the janitor.

Converting the quality measure example to points (see Table 8.13) is a matter of deciding what looks easiest to communicate. In the figure, a point is worth 0.025 percent of pay.

TABLE 8.13. *Midwestern Company Example: Quality Reward Schedule in Points.*

BASELINE	LEVEL 1	LEVEL 2	LEVEL 3	LEVEL 4	LEVEL 5 (GOAL)
Payout = None	Payout = 10 points	Payout = 20 points	Payout = 30 points	Payout = 40 points	Payout = 50 points

A second approach to easing the communication challenge is to translate the reward structure into a percentage of the employee's targeted payout—his or her payout at goal. On the quality measure, the payout target at the performance goal is the same as the weighting given quality—25 percent. The payout structure would look like Table 8.14.

TABLE 8.14. *Midwestern Company Example: Quality Reward Schedule in Percentage of Target Payout.*

BASELINE	LEVEL 1	LEVEL 2	LEVEL 3	LEVEL 4	LEVEL 5 (GOAL)
Payout = None	Payout = 5% of target	Payout = 10% of target	Payout = 15% of target	Payout = 20% of target	Payout = 25% of target

Balancing Increments

If your first measure has five increments to goal and the next one has two, and the next has four, it gets confusing. I always suggest trying to leverage down to a constant number of increments from baseline to goal, ideally three to five. The points will change within the increments depending on the measure's weighting, but the number of increments will remain constant. Table 8.15 converts the quality example to the same number of performance levels and payouts in points. Table 8.16 does the same thing using a percentage of target payout of 5 percent at goal.

You may need to adjust your goal a bit or tweak baseline or increments to make the numbers as round as possible so they'll be easier to communicate. That's okay. Anything lost in the rounding process will likely be made up through clearer communications and breakage.

If you need a stretch or cap, you can have it on one measure and not on the next. You can have different caps for each measure. I suggest you just note the cap in the increment box in the appropriate row.

TABLE 8.15. Midwestern Company Example: Total Reward Schedule in Points.

OBJECTIVE	BASELINE	LEVEL 1	LEVEL 2	LEVEL 3	LEVEL 4	LEVEL 5 (GOAL)	INCREMENTS
Financial performance	$10 million	$10.1 million	$10.2 million	$10.3 million	$10.4 million	$10.5 million	Each $100,000 increase earns
Points	*0 points*	*10 points*	*20 points*	*30 points*	*40 points*	*50 points*	*10 points*
Productivity	1.90 lb./$	1.92 lb./$	1.94 lb./$	1.96 lb./$	1.98 lb./$	2.0 lb./$	Each 0.02 lb./$ reduction earns
Points	*0 points*	*10 points*	*20 points*	*30 points*	*40 points*	*50 points*	*10 points*
Cycle time	100 days	98 days	96 days	94 days	92 days	90 days	Each 2-day reduction earns
Points	*0 points*	*10 points*	*20 points*	*30 points*	*40 points*	*50 points*	*10 points*
Quality	15%	14%	13%	12%	11%	10%	Each percentage point reduction earns
Points	*0 points*	*10 points*	*20 points*	*30 points*	*40 points*	*50 points*	*10 points*

TABLE 8.16. *Midwestern Company Example: Total Reward Schedule in Percentage of Target Payout.*

OBJECTIVE	BASELINE	LEVEL 1	LEVEL 2	LEVEL 3	LEVEL 4	LEVEL 5 (GOAL)	INCREMENTS
Financial performance Points	$10 million 0% of target	$10.1 million 5% of target	$10.2 million 10% of target	$10.3 million 15% of target	$10.4 million 20% of target	$10.5 million 25% of target	Each $100,000 increase earns 5% of target
Productivity Points	1.90 lb./$ 0% of target	1.92 lb./$ 5% of target	1.94 lb./$ 10% of target	1.96 lb./$ 15% of target	1.98 lb./$ 20% of target	2.0 lb./$ 25% of target	Each 0.02 lb./$ reduction earns 5% of target
Cycle time Points	100 days 0% of target	98 days 5% of target	96 days 10% of target	94 days 15% of target	92 days 20% of target	90 days 25% of target	Each 2-day reduction earns 5% of target
Quality Points	15% 0% of target	14% 5% of target	13% 10% of target	12% 15% of target	11% 20% of target	10% 25% of target	Each percentage point reduction earns 5% of target

The reward schedule is laid out for the length of your payout period. If you're going to pay out once a year, the reward schedule is for that year. If you're going to pay out monthly, you will need to create a monthly reward schedule.

Remember, a critical design criterion is finding a balance between a reasonable reward schedule and an objective that, with a little education, everyone can understand and act upon. Keep asking yourself, "What is the most important message? Where do we want the focus?"

Line of Sight and Cycling

Line of Sight (LoS) and cycling are the good guy and bad guy of group incentive plans. They both exist and must be considered. I will cover them briefly now because they are so critical to consider during design. But at the end of the chapter I discuss in more depth how to handle them.

Reassess: LoS, Cycling and Protection

Line of Sight

The term "line of sight" (LoS) comes from the military; it refers to distance from a target. The farther away you are, the more you have to adjust for the trajectory of the bullet and the harder it is to hit the target. *LoS is the employee's perceived ability to affect a measure on which rewards are based.* The farther away the measurement is thought to be from the employee, the longer the LoS and the harder it is for the employee to influence the result.

A very long LoS design—such as a single profit sharing plan for a ten-thousand employee, multilocation organization—ends up being just a method for distribution of funds, with little effect on people, other than increased awareness. Long LoS plans invariably become entitlements. A very short LoS design—such as an attendance plan for a work group of ten people—can be directly influenced by people's behavior.

> **LoS concerns usually mean you cannot be simple _and_ fair. I prefer being fair. "Simple" is a communication and education problem.**

There is no optimum LoS, just trade-off in the design. LoS concerns usually mean you cannot be simple *and* fair. Long LoS plan designs are often simple (one profit measure), but not fair (the rank and file cannot relate or affect the measure). I prefer fair over simple. We will continually come back to this idea as we explore how LoS can affect a group incentive plan.

Four characteristics of the design affect LoS:

1. *Number of physical locations of the organizations covered.* People relate first to their work group, then to their department, then to their division, then to the physical location of their office, and then to the corporation. LoS gets disproportionately long when you combine the measurements of one or more physical locations. I suggest you avoid combining different physical locations for measurement and reward, if at all possible.

2. *Size of the organization covered.* If a lot of people are covered by one or more organization-wide measures, then you have a very long LoS. How many are "a lot"? No one really knows. Conventional wisdom argues for less than five hundred to six hundred people in a single plan. That seems to be the greatest number of people you can comfortably cover with one or a set of measures. I suggest if you have a large number of people at one location, use a mix of measures and move some of them lower into the organization, customizing for smaller organizational units.

3. *Type of measure.* LoS is affected by the employee's understanding of a measure, his perceived ability to influence it, and the amount of information the organization shares about it. Employees relate to operational measures—productivity, quality, cost control, and so on—much more than to financial measures. The exception is in open-book management companies. They reduce the LoS to financial measures through financial literacy education. I suggest having at least one operational measure in the plan, OBM company or not.

4. *Frequency of payout.* Plans that measure performance and pay out at least a portion of the earnings more often than each year clearly have a shorter LoS. I suggest that if everything else has a reasonably long LoS, try to have more frequent payouts.

Apart from changing the plan design, you can shorten LoS by increasing communications, performance feedback, and employee involvement efforts.

Cycling

If most of the measures have a short LoS, it can cause serious administrative and financial risks in larger companies. These risks are called cycling. Cycling is the net effect of performance that varies from group to group, period to period, measure to measure, or a combination of any of these elements. Cycling is only significant when performance drops below baseline or a group, measure, or payout period. Here's an extreme example: two organizational units of equal size and different physical locations are rewarded on the same reward schedule but earn based on their own performance on the same single measure in the same time period. Unit A improves its performance by 20 percent. Everyone earns. Everyone is happy. Unit B—for whatever reason—underperforms baselines by 20 percent. No one in Unit B earns. Unit A's performance is offset by Unit B's performance. The company, however, must pay for whatever Unit A earned. There is a cost with no net gain. Now, in support of the separate location plan design, you could argue the following:

Cycling has a negative effect on the return on payout when performance drops below baseline in a group, measure or payout period.

- People do not do worse because of an incentive plan.

- Unit B may have done even worse without the plan.

- The good tracking, feedback, employee involvement, and management support of the plan will spot Unit B's problem and take action. After all, the incentive plan is not a compensation plan but a strategy to improve business performance.

And all of it is true. But with a net improvement of zero and an expense equal to the earnings of Unit A's payouts, someone is not happy (the CFO). You can watch his black socks turn white. Obviously this is an extreme example, but the message is clear. Minimizing cycling possibilities is a primary design challenge—to keep the LoS short enough to make the plan actionable by the people.

No Cycling, No Risk

You can design a plan with no cycling possibilities, if the plan covers the entire organization, has only one measure, and measures and pays out once a year.

In this scenario, the LoS becomes rather long in all but smaller organizations. The plan runs the risk of simply being a way to distribute money and not a way to motivate people. That's why most profit sharing plans are not considered motivational to people and are viewed as an entitlement.

Remember, cycling can occur to some extent among group measures and payout periods. If performance does not drop below baseline in any one group, measure, or payout period, it has no effect on the plan's financial rationale.

I've tried to resist the "no pain, no gain" line—which is somewhat true in exercise and in group incentive plans. Organizations must find that delicate balance between acceptable LoS and cycling.

Balancing LoS and Cycling

Number of Physical Locations   The examples used so far in this chapter have not defined the number of physical locations of an organization that might be involved in a plan. It is possible for a plan to apply to several locations, with the measures covering all of them. Such a design has a long LoS and would not be as effective as one calibrated for each location—but that, of course, increases the possibility of cycling. If management is willing to take the risk, it is better to design by location. Usually, management thinks of each location separately anyway. They certainly evaluate the local management by location, so why not reward them and their employees based on location performance?

If that is unacceptable, try splitting the difference: make the financial measures include all locations, and develop operational measures by location. In the example, profit would be for the entire company, and productivity, cycle time, and quality would be for each location. The baselines and goals would reflect the reality at each location.

If your design team is at headquarters, be sure to adapt the basic design approach to the location with a design team from the location. The most feared words in business are "Hi. I'm from Corporate, and I'm here to help you." You may find that it will be necessary to slightly modify the measurement itself in order to accurately reflect the contribution each location can make. Failing that, try to make the majority of the measures cover all locations, with just a few (at least one) calibrated to the individual locations.

The most feared words in business are "Hi. I'm from Corporate, and I'm here to help you."

If you must measure and reward the organization as a whole, propose doing that for the first year and then roll the measurement down into each physical location the next year. The first year, 100 percent of the payout would be organization-wide, and each location's measurement, reflecting its contribution to the overall measure, would be communicated to everyone but not rewarded. The following year, 75 percent of the payout could be based on company productivity performance and 25 percent on the productivity performance of each location. That could continue until everyone is comfortable with the balance between organizational units.

This approach allows time for all employees, particularly middle management, to become used to the measurement, to learn about it, and to become comfortable with being rewarded for improvement. Of course, the LoS is long in multilocation companies, and there will be little connection between the performance of the measure and what people do.

If top management demands that all locations be wrapped together forever, crank up your communications, promotion, education, and involvement efforts. That is the only way to make the LoS somewhat shorter for the employees.

Size of the Organization   As I discussed earlier in this chapter, if your company has more than six hundred employees and certainly more than a thousand, you should consider breaking the organization down into logical units and calibrating the plan measures accordingly. If the organizational units are really in different businesses, I would argue for customizing to each business. All the arguments and fallback positions suggested in the earlier section about the number of physical locations apply here as well.

Type and Number of Measurements   You've chosen your measures, and that determines the LoS. Just be aware of how much education you will have to do if the types of measures are unfamiliar to the rank and file.

Number of measures also affects cycling. Here are some ways to minimize cycling in a plan with multiple measures.

1.   *Require balance.* If cycling between measures is risky—you've financially justified your plan by showing a dollar value of a gain in just one or two of the several measures—you don't have to pay out on individual measures. A "balanced scorecard" or "family of measures" approach creates an index of performance derived from the performance and weighting of each individual measure. The payout is based on a minimum index number that reduces cycling's effect on payout. If the index for all of the measures does not equal or exceed the minimum, you don't pay out at all.

Each of the options reduces the effect of cycling between measures. The point system, which was illustrated in Table 8.15 for the Midwestern Company example, handles this option quite well. (A total of forty points must be earned before any payout is made, or baseline must be achieved in each measure before any payout is earned, or the profit measure must reach baseline before any payout is earned.) Using the percentage of target approach (Table 8.16) would be slightly more difficult.

2.   *Install a gate* (a qualifier or a trip wire). In such a plan, you don't pay off anything unless a key measure not included in the plan reaches a certain level. This measure is usually some financial measure such as net income before taxes or a certain level of sales. I argue that gates should be set at disaster levels. The firm has to be in the dumper before the gate is involved and all payouts are off.

Gates can create employee cynicism and distrust. Depending on the level of employee cynicism, your plan has to be sensitive to anything that can be interpreted as manipulative. Rank-and-file employees have often not been educated about the finances of the business. If they have done a great job on the plan's measurements and earned a payout, closing a gate that has been triggered by a financial measurement considered out of their control is cause for concern.

One chemical company had an excellently designed plan that addressed a plant's productivity, operating income, quality, and EPA conformance to standards. Their gate was corporate profitability and return on net assets (RONA). If profit or RONA was less than the previous year, there was no payout. The plan was introduced in January and all measures were improving, along with the payout opportunity at the end of the year. Then, profit dropped for the corporation due to a management decision to acquire a new business. As good a decision as this was for the corporation, it had nothing to do with any of the plan measurements, and although the plant improved on three of the four measures, all payouts were canceled. The action was viewed as unfair, and it set the operation's performance improvement efforts back significantly.

3. *Use a modifier.* A modifier is a soft gate. Modifiers are another way to deal with those long but important LoS measures. In the example used in this chapter, profit was included as one of the measures. An alternative approach is to use profit to increase or decrease the total payout earned on productivity, cycle time, and quality. If someone earns $1,000 annually based on the three elements and profitability is up by 20 percent, the company could apply a multiplier of 1.2 for $1,200 profit. The opposite could be true if profitability goes down.

Common modifiers are based on profitability, a return calculation, market share, and customer satisfaction. Generally, it should be possible to measure the modifier as frequently as the direct measures of the plan. If you have monthly payouts, a yearly modifier doesn't make much sense. Modifiers are ways to communicate the importance of a long LoS measure.

4. *Use point indexing to add protection.* Another way of protecting the profit line is to make the point value in your rules structure vary with profit performance. While this adds a good deal of complexity, increases the LoS, and may appear to the employees to be too conservative (and therefore too hard to earn), it does integrate into the plan structure quite nicely. A simplistic example would be if profit were at last year's level plus x percent, each point would be valued as announced in the plan. If profit dropped below a certain level, points would lose value. If profit exceeded the last-year-plus-x-percent level, the point value would increase. This schedule of point indexing would be published in the plan announcement and rules. (Obviously you can only use points with this option.)

Frequency of Payout and LoS

The more often you pay out, the shorter the LoS. To dampen cycling, consider using reserves.

Reserves are an approach to handling cycling between payout periods that was designed by Joe Scanlon in the late 1930s as part of the original Scanlon Plan. Reserves hold back part of the payout to go into a year-end account. The reserved amounts are paid out at the end of the year based on how the plan or some other measure did overall. It's even called the "thirteenth payment" in a year of monthly payouts. Some companies pay interest on the reserved amount. If the overall performance fails to reach the goal, however, the reserve reverts to the company.

If you have reserves, make sure you explain them under the reward schedule—something like, "For every two points earned, one point is deposited to the reserve bank. These points will be rewarded based on overall performance of the plan according to a separate reward schedule." This tells employees that one-third (in this case) is being put into reserve. Remember to reduce the value of a point by the equivalent amount.

Although reserves make the plan more complex to explain and understand, I much prefer them over gates.

Striking a balance between LoS and cycling risk is a judgment call. As with almost all LoS considerations, reserves are part of a mosaic that has to be arranged and rearranged to get the best and most pleasing composition.

Some General Observations on LoS and Cycling

When in doubt, the most powerful way of reducing LoS is by increasing the frequency of payouts. If your objective is awareness, take your risk in frequency of payout. It has great communications capability, and cycling can be dampened by reserves.

If you can't pay out frequently, the next best thing is to pay out by measure (which means you don't require a total point amount for all measures). Paying out by measure helps make the plan more real to employees and demonstrates that performance improvement comes in many forms.

I try to structure plans first by physical location. I'd sacrifice almost everything else to insure that people are operating under a single location plan. The primary LoS and cycling levers, therefore, for maintaining the balance between keeping the plan motivational and protecting the organization are, in order of effectiveness:

1. Measuring by facility
2. Frequency of payout
3. Paying out by measure and not having any restrictions on the measure (such as total points)
4. Applying modifiers to the overall performance of the plan, based on the overall performance of the organization

The Role of Subjectivity in Distributing Rewards

For a good portion of this book, I have railed against the evils of subjectivity. I still believe that objectivity is the heart of group incentive plans, but it is also important to "practice the art of the possible."

Management discretion can be used in the distribution of a portion of the rewards generated by a plan. I recommend applying this process to management only. So, if you want discretion, you will have two plans—one for management with discretion and one for nonmanagement without discretion.

For the management plan, scale back the value of the points by the percentage of the total reward you wish to make discretionary. (The number of points at each level of performance doesn't change, just the value of the points.) The discretionary pool is created by the plan performance. No points, no pool. The points are distributed by top management to individuals based on their judgment. One thing is helpful: use the gravity rule. The discretionary funds can flow down, but not up.

Here's an example. For management, each earned point is worth 3/4 of a percent of base pay, rather than the 1 percent that would be used without a discretionary element. The incentive payment from the group's performance is handled normally. The pool, funded by the remaining 1/4 percent of everyone in management's base pay, is distributed based on the discretion of top management. If there are more funds allotted to a second-level manager for distribution to her direct reports than she feels are warranted, they cannot go to her or her boss. They flow down or not at all.

Conclusion

Group incentive plans are one of the most powerful of the reward plan options for improving organizational performance through people. They are customized to meet the needs of each organization. The customization process uncovers opportunities for improvement, and more often than not, it is the most cost-effective strategy. The very nature of the plan directly addresses issues that organizations have been wrestling with for years: consistency of message and organizational focus, consensus on those few critical measures that in part define an organization's success, and opening the door for teamwork with teeth, providing an umbrella under which organizations can, and must, do things they should have been doing all along.

Group incentive plans are not a panacea. They are the actualization of a strategy to engage everyone in the business of the business. Combined with recognition plans and, where appropriate, project team incentives, group incentive plans complement the individual compensation plans in the most positive ways. They directly improve organizational performance.

The design process is a rich one. It is also a tiring one. The trap is obvious. So much energy is expended in designing a good plan that there is little left for implementation. You would be better advised to put your money and energy elsewhere if you are not willing to commit to an implementation strategy as complete and compelling as your design effort.

Project Team Incentive Plans

Project team incentive plans reward contributions made by employee involvement teams on a preannounced reward schedule. They reinforce employees for putting their ideas and expertise into action to improve performance. They have a great deal in common with group incentive plans in that they require focus, objectives, measurement, feedback, and rewards. They can stand alone or operate in support of group incentive plans. Project team incentive plans can be designed to reinforce the following common processes of involving employees: individual suggestion and team idea processes, ad hoc project teams, and quality action teams. Project team incentive plans can be applied to almost any team that is formed for a specific purpose or objective whose contribution can be measured and valued. Every attempt should be made to value the contribution to the organization in dollars. In some cases, management will agree to implement a project team incentive for a contribution that cannot be valued financially but can justify a payout because the contribution is good for the organization.

> **Project Team Incentives**
> *Engage and involve employees; measure and reward project results*

What You Will Find in This Chapter

A large part of this chapter is devoted to the most powerful employee involvement effort to be reinforced by a project team incentive plan—the team idea process. I also discuss:

- Project team incentive plans that support group incentive plans

- When a project team incentive plan is most appropriate

- Types of processes and related design considerations

- Individual suggestion and team idea processes

- Ad hoc project teams

- Quality action or continuous improvement teams

I will discuss the team idea process more thoroughly than the others. It focuses on cost reduction, quality, and customer satisfaction improvement.

The Nature and Scope of Project Team Incentive Plans

Our desire to label things for the quick fix is clearly alive and well in the business community. Organizations have been *Zapped*, *One-Minute Managed*, and *Performance Managed* through hundreds of books, articles, and seminars for twenty years. Most of these approaches focus on the individual employee and what managers can do to encourage, reinforce, and—here's the *E* word—empower them.

The E Word

"Participatory management" didn't take hold because management didn't want to participate.

Empowerment stems from the practice of allowing an employee, with the proper training, to service a customer without running to his or her supervisor for permission. For employees who have little outside customer contact, empowerment means giving them the right to make a difference by making decisions on their own or with a group. The problem, however, is that there are so many organizationally imposed obstacles to making empowerment real—not to mention that many employees feel they barely have enough time just to do their assigned jobs. As attractive as the idea may be, the pitch for a general environment of empowerment raises many managers' eyebrows, probably because they believe that the workforce has not been educated or trusted enough to allow it to work. Years ago, the business community was all abuzz about "participatory management." It didn't take hold because management didn't want to participate.

Empowerment without direction, focus, education, and structure can be fractured, inefficient, and frustrating to both employees and the organization. I could give Ryan, my fourteen-year-old son, an Uzi and he would be empowered. He'd also do a lot of damage. A team of employees told they are empowered to "make things better" without the proper support and environment can be damaging. Another E word, *engagement,* describes the environment of formalized structures that is necessary if employees are to apply their newfound power positively. (Effective environments engage empowered, educated employees efficiently—sorry.)

Employee Involvement

Most companies have employee involvement processes in place. These plans range from the social planning committees (a picnic, working for the United Way, and so forth) to formalized continuous process improvement teams (under the quality, continuous, or customer-satisfaction improvement banner) to self-directed work teams, as an organizational design strategy.

Open-book management is dependent upon employee involvement for its success. More than any other approach I've seen, OBM focuses on employees taking responsibility and being accountable for results. Involvement is part of each person's job or role.

The OBM reward system, however, tends to be a group incentive plan rather than a project team incentive plan. The more financially literate employees are, the more effective their involvement will be directly reinforced by the group incentive plan. Eventually, as OBM matures with more and broader applications, organizations may find they need project team incentive plans for focus on specific organizational needs. But for now, the individual's reward for working within his or her organizational unit, characterized by OBM as a "team," depends on the performance of the whole team. The reward for working on a project that crosses over units or teams is a function of the performance of the whole group.

Certainly, not all employee involvement efforts are, or need to be, tangibly rewarded. The continuous process improvement team that includes a few employees in the work group and that solves daily problems is a function of the employee's job or role. The picnic planning committee is made up of volunteers who want to do something different and enjoyable as a part of their work life. The individuals and teams involved in these efforts may or may not be recognized for their activities and performance. If they are, it is generally after the fact, as an expression of the organization's appreciation (see Chapter Seven).

The self-directed work team is an organizational unit that may or may not be measured and rewarded based on its performance. If it is, the process is part of a group incentive plan. Table 9.1 illustrates the many differences between group incentive plans and project team incentive plans.

Project team incentive plans can be individually based, despite the obvious contradiction, such as in the case of an individual suggestion process whose primary objective is cost reduction. (Most individual suggestion processes allow groups of employees to submit suggestions, but groups or teams are not the foundation of the process.) Other than that, project team incentive plans are team-based.

TABLE 9.1. *Differences Between Group Incentive Plans and Project Team Incentive Plans.*

	GROUP INCENTIVE PLANS	PROJECT TEAM INCENTIVE PLANS
Measures	Organizational unit measures of success (top-down)	Targeted improvement opportunities (bottom-up); most successful with cost reduction, revenue enhancement, customer satisfaction, continuous quality improvements, and (obviously) specific projects.
Participation	Usually everyone in an organizational unit	Just those assigned or those who volunteered for the team. Not an organizational unit.
Baselines and goals	Required	Function of the project team's focus: cost reduction and revenue enhancement—how much money is saved or made? System improvement—project completions, contributions within time and cost guidelines.
At-risk	Possible	Rarely, if ever
Payout size	Function of value of improvement	Same
Structure	Formula-driven	Will always be formula-driven but could vary by objective. Cost reduction and revenue enhancement have same formula for each project team; other objectives may have different formula for each project team.
Plan period	Usually a year	Plan is not time bound, although some projects may be.
LoS, cycling, and protection	Considered in design	Not a concern
Results attributed to plan	Something less than 100%	Generally 100%

The New Team Environment

Managers are being bombarded with articles, books, and consulting advice on how to develop teams and/or a spirit of teamwork in their organizations. Some companies have reorganized employees around a product or service rather than in departments, with all functions represented (for example, an accountant now works in the line organization rather than in the finance department). Self-directed work teams do much that previously was the responsibility of the supervisor or direct manager. They tend to be cross-trained, which allows them to meet the needs of the organizational unit (now dubbed a "team") more efficiently and effectively. Even in traditionally structured organizations, management sometimes tries to energize a "team spirit."

Most discussion about this new environment revolves around how to manage individual compensation of team members. The use of 360-degree reviews to determine an employee's merit increase is one way to reinforce the team approach. Having a team actually sit down together and decide who gets what is risky but has been a successful way of making teamwork a reality. In Chapter Six, I described the variety of plans that can be used to reinforce and develop individuals. In particular, the use of "facilitation" competencies development, paid for or not, can assist individuals in working more effectively in a team or team environment. For purposes of reward plan design, I define "team" in two ways: as either an organizational unit, which would be covered by a group incentive plan, or a project team formed for a specific purpose, which would be covered by either a recognition or a project team incentive plan.

Supporting Group Incentive Plans

Project team incentive plans help reduce the line of sight (LoS) in group incentive plans by providing the path that connects employee involvement contributions to group plan measures.

When you introduce a group incentive plan, the first reaction of the rank-and-file employee is a tactical one: "What do I have to do to earn?" For plans that have a long LoS, the answer is, "Pay attention to the organization's objectives as you do your day-to-day job, and behave accordingly." Even though the LoS is long, employees will be more likely to embrace change, be more informed, and be more willing to do their share as contributing stakeholders than

> **When you introduce a group incentive plan, the first reaction of the rank-and-file employee is: "What do I have to do to earn?"**

they would be without a plan. A good implementation of a group incentive plan moves the measures, but not necessarily the rewards, down into the work group to demonstrate what the group members can do to make a difference.

The purpose of a project team incentive plan is to invite people into the process of improvement. It is a tactical, immediate way of getting people involved. Joe Scanlon understood this principle when he designed his group incentive plan in the late 1930s, the Scanlon Plan. The reward in this plan was based on a long LoS measure (net sales/cost ratio for a whole plant). An integral part of the Scanlon plan was the employee suggestion process. The suggestions themselves were not rewarded, but the improved performance of the plan measure resulting (hopefully) from the suggestions was. In this case, the suggestion process was an employee involvement effort, not a project team incentive plan. Since Joe Scanlon's days, the strong sense of community and "do the right things and you'll get yours" have been replaced by the need for more immediate gratification.

Do you have to reward everything? Of course not. The decision to reward is a function of how much extra you are asking people to do. It is also a matter of activities versus results. You *recognize activities* and *behaviors*. You *reward results*. You also reward employees for taking the risk of generating an idea that may change things, particularly if it is contrary to the organization's or the supervisor's view of how things should be done.

> *You recognize activities and behaviors. You reward results.*

Companies are often concerned about "double dipping" (counting the same savings dollars twice) when installing a group incentive plan and a project team incentive plan together. The concern arises when the group incentive plan is designed to measure and reward improved financial performance, and the project team incentive plan is designed to reward cost reduction or system changes. The fear is that the measure used for the latter plan will "double count" the financial gain. It probably will to a degree, but I find it is difficult to follow the accounting trails from the measure to the effect on the bottom line in most plans. The necessary new cost or activity-based accounting techniques are not a reality in most organizations. Rewarding the same results twice can be completely avoided, however, by deciding what you are going to include in your *return on payout* calculation. You can include (or exclude) any gain you wish in the design and in the reassessment phase. (See Chapter Eight.)

Project team incentive plans are one way to involve people in a meaningful way to make the longer LoS group plans work. Group incentive plans reward results. Project team incentive plans reinforce the *process* of improvement as well as making unique contributions. They can stand alone or work together, but with careful attention to financial justification, both plans working together offer the best hope for real performance improvement.

Group incentive and project team incentive plans working together offer the best hope for real performance improvement.

When a Project Team Incentive Plan Is Most Appropriate

There are four business objectives that can be most directly influenced by project team incentive plans, whether a group incentive plan is in place or not: cost reduction and revenue enhancement, customer satisfaction, and continuous quality process improvement.

Cost Reduction and Revenue Enhancement
Cost reduction and revenue enhancement aren't very successful as measures in a group incentive plan for nonsales employees. (The exception, discussed in Chapter Eight, is in OBM or very small organizations.) Management-legislated budget reductions certainly cinch up the company's belt, but they also tend to reduce services, programs, and morale. Increasing revenue has been the primary charge of the sales team, although nonsales employees can affect it.

When cost reduction and revenue enhancement are measures in a project team incentive plan, opportunities to cut costs and enhance revenue are identified by employees, idea by idea (or project by project), rather than being handed down by management. Cost reduction and revenue enhancement have been more effectively accomplished as a bottom-up (project team) rather than top-down (group incentive) process. The old belief that employees have the best ideas because they are closest to the work has certainly been borne out.

Customer Satisfaction
In Chapter Eight, I described how to measure customer satisfaction to shorten the LoS, by asking customers (or statistically deriving) what drivers of service they consider important and how satisfied they are with those drivers. By focusing on the elements that are considered most important with the lowest satisfaction ratings, rather than on the numbers provided by a traditional index of customer satisfaction, employees gain a sense that they can directly influence the outcomes.

Customer satisfaction is fundamentally a policy, systems, and employee satisfaction issue. Organizations have traditionally focused on the attractiveness of the facility, the "empathy" and friendliness of the customer contact person, and the speed of response. All are important. But what really makes the difference to customers is employees who do what they say they are going to do, and if they don't, the next best thing is to demonstrate a "remarkable recovery." Systems are the biggest drivers in helping employees live up to what the company has promised. When employees work together, they can make the systems more customer sensitive.

Continuous Quality Process Improvement   Then, of course, there's everything else that needs to be improved. Today, most of these efforts are under the quality banner. Special task forces need to be set up to solve the account systems problem. Ad hoc teams need to be formed to speed up getting supplies from one place to another. Cross-functional teams need to try to solve the communications problem between marketing and sales. Quality action teams need to work on improving the cycle time for blueprint updating. And then there are all those little (and sometimes not so little) changes, adjustments, and improvements that make things work more smoothly. These continuous process improvement opportunities are everywhere. It seems as if the rank and file see them and can fix them better than anyone else.

Processes Supported by Project Team Incentive Plans

The four most common employee involvement efforts supported by project team incentive plans are:

1. *Individual suggestion process,* which exists in most larger organizations and is commonly understood.
2. *Team idea process,* which will be extensively described in this chapter because of its recent success and ability to support so many performance improvement opportunities.
3. *Ad hoc project teams,* which are more commonly reinforced with recognition but can be reinforced with project team incentive plans. Frankly, there's not much to say. They either finish the

project on time and in budget or they do not. What is somewhat original is to reward an ad hoc project team on the effects of their work.

4. *Quality action teams,* or *continuous improvement teams,* generate results that the organization may or may not be able to measure and value objectively. If the results can be measured and valued, the team is addressed in this chapter. If they cannot, look to Chapter Seven, on recognition plans.

The real issue with the last three efforts, all team-based, is whether they are to be rewarded on a preannounced, formula-driven reward structure or simply recognized for their contribution or activity. The "reward or recognize" issue is whether or not the contribution can be measured and valued and whether it is worth the time and effort to do so.

Individual Suggestion Processes

Individual suggestions have been encouraged by organizations for some time. In 1741, Sweden established a Royal Commission to evaluate the suggestions of citizens, but Japan had already beaten them to the punch. In 1721, Yoshimune Tokugawa, the eighth Shogun, installed a suggestion box outside the palace with the inscription, "Make your ideas known; rewards are given for ideas that are accepted."

There are those who say that the individual suggestion process hasn't improved much since then. A Far Side cartoon shows several devils standing around in hell laughing hysterically at the contents of a suggestion box. The caption reads, "Where they *really* go." Another cartoon shows a cleaning lady collecting trash, including the contents of the suggestion box. Employee cynicism runs high in individual suggestion processes.

Focus on Cost Reduction   In the United States, the traditional individual suggestion process has focused on cost reduction, but it has expanded to include almost anything that will make things better. One of the problems with traditional plans is that they require little of the suggester and a great deal of management. The suggester has an idea, thinks about it a little, writes it up, and puts it into the system—electronically, through the mail, or into the box. The clearing office or the suggester's supervisor reviews the idea and either takes on or assigns the responsibility of "checking it out," which involves:

- Determining whether the suggestion makes any sense

- Determining the cost savings (we know we'll save the money) or avoidance (this is money we can avoid spending)

- Making sure that it follows the rules for suggestions (can't touch base pay, organizational mission, and so on)

- Getting agreement from everyone affected by the suggestion

- Calculating the award

- Giving the suggester the award, or telling her she'll have to wait until the suggestion is implemented and has proven its worth

Turnaround time in the traditional process can run into months, even years, with little feedback about the suggestion's status. Devaluation of the suggestion's estimated savings tends to be high, probably because the suggester estimated high and the finance department had other ideas. An average of about 6.5 percent the employees in U.S. organizations participate by making a suggestion at least once a year. The average approved idea is worth $7,900. Overall, the average suggestion earns about 10 to 15 percent of its approved value for the suggester (Employee Involvement Association, 1994).

The root problem in the traditional individual suggestion process is lack of teamwork, responsibility, and accountability. Teamwork is important if the idea needs some work or is big enough to involve several operations in the company. One person generally can't take, won't take, or isn't allowed to take the time to do the necessary research alone. So the responsibility shifts to management.

When an employee off-loads the responsibility and accountability for a suggestion onto management, she doesn't have to learn about the process, consider the ramifications, understand what's behind the costs or potential savings, or be concerned about implementation. She just waits for the check. And waits. Even when the check comes, the amount isn't anything near what she thought it would be.

Not all individual suggestion processes that focus on cost reduction are this dire. Some work just fine—they are consistent with the amount of effort and money that management wants to put into them. Most processes, however, are like some employees. They retired several years ago; they just keep coming to work.

The Kaizen Approach
The fodder for suggestions can come from far more than cost reduction. The most popular Japanese suggestion plans follow the Kaizen notion that continuous improvement is an integral part of everyone's job. The objective of the Kaizen approach is participation and generating lots of ideas. Suggestions become the vehicle for constant interaction among all the members of an organization.

Use some caution when looking at the numbers of suggestions publicly reported for these types of processes. There is the story about a suggestion to outline tools on a pegboard to make them easier to return. There were forty tools, so the organization counted it as forty suggestions. Few people can argue, however, with those firms that target one hundred suggestions per employee per year, as Toyota does, and that firmly believe their outstanding quality is due, in part, to their suggestion process, as part of their continuous improvement process.

According to Toyota, in Japan it is common practice for an employee to give his entire award for an idea (when there is an award) to his co-workers to grease the skids for the next idea. I'm hard pressed to think of many U.S. companies that have such a collectivist culture. Japan is a society in which workers are culturally groomed to place self-interest below organizational interest on the totem pole of values. Kaizen-based suggestion systems mirror these cultural norms (Yasuda, 1991, pp. 36–37).

Many of the practices have been installed in Japanese-owned and operated companies in the United States. Here's an example of one effort of rewarding for suggestions in a U.S. organization with a Kaizen environment. The suggester does his best in justifying his suggestion, but just having and submitting it is what's important—certainly more than its quality and cost savings. The suggestion works its way up the normal hierarchy of the organization for approval. The greater the cost reduction or process improvement opportunity, the higher it has to go for approval.

If the suggestion has a savings value, a small percentage (around 5 percent) goes to the suggester, half upon approval and half upon implementation. If the suggestion has no savings value and is approved, it earns a token amount ($10 to $15). Celebration events

Most individual suggestion processes are like some employees. They retired several years ago; they just keep coming to work.

are held to recognize departments for the volume of suggestions submitted, the number of those approved, and their dollar value. Participation rates are high; 70 to 90 percent of the employees submit at least one suggestion per year, but five to ten are more common. The total economic value of the suggestions isn't tracked because the point is participation, not savings.

Of course there are a number of U.S. owned and operated firms that have successfully practiced the continuous improvement process for decades, a part of which is soliciting and expecting employee suggestions on all aspects of the business. At Milliken & Company's textile manufacturing operations, giving suggestions for improving performance, particularly customer satisfaction, is an integral part of an employee's responsibility. In Chapter Six, I briefly referred to the Lincoln Electric plan in which the number of ideas offered by an employee is one of the four elements of his performance review (along with production, quality, and teamwork). These forms of employee involvement are endemic to these operations but still the exception in the United States.

Clearly, the key element of making a Kaizen-based suggestion process work is the company's culture. If your organization's culture is not such that suggestions for improvement flow from employees as naturally as taking a lunch break, you may want to consider the team idea process.

Team Idea Process

It may be the people closest to the job who know best what needs to be improved, but individuals often need support, guidance, and resources for perspective—to see themselves as contribution stakeholders rather than as cogs in the wheel. The team idea process is a powerful tool for the rank and file to become stakeholders.

In the mid 1980s, employee involvement took a leap forward with the introduction of a new process based on generating ideas for cost reduction and revenue enhancement (and subsequently all kinds of improvement) from teams of employees. Certainly, groups of people have been allowed to contribute ideas in traditional individual suggestion processes, and the practice of team suggestions is an element of the quality movement—but the focus and results have not been significant. A team idea process combines the discipline of positive reinforcement (positive, immediate, and, in this case, certain), the emerging power and flexibility of the personal computer, and the synergy of teamwork. It can do double duty—as support for group incentive plans, and/or by improving performance in their own right.

This kind of process moved Mildred from clerk to contributing stakeholder. Presented with a bank-wide profit sharing plan, Mildred felt powerless to affect the results. A team idea process—introduced to support the profit sharing plan—enabled her to save her company $60,000.

Mildred is a fifty-seven-year-old grandmother who has worked as a bank billing clerk for eighteen years in a large city. She wrote checks for accounts payable, first by hand and later on a computer.

Two years ago, the bank moved from its downtown location to a suburb. The move was expensive because the bank had a lot of fine antiques that needed special handling. As Mildred paid the bills for the move, she noticed a monthly $5,000 bill for leased warehouse space. She could think of no reason for still needing the space.

Mildred went to her supervisor who said—in his best hierarchical fashion—"I'm the manager, you're a billing clerk, go back to work."

A few months later, the bank announced a profit sharing group incentive plan and a team idea process with its own project team incentive plan. Mildred and six other women who often had lunch together decided to form a team. After brainstorming for a while, Mildred thought about the mysterious warehouse bill. They questioned the leasing company about the space but didn't get a satisfactory answer. The team pooled enough money for Mildred to take a cab (it was her first taxi ride ever) from their suburb location to the warehouse. When she got there the door was locked and she couldn't see in since she is only five feet and one inch tall. I know this sounds like a Ron Howard movie, but she really pulled a wooden box under a window, climbed up on it and looked through the window, and saw . . . an empty warehouse.

Mildred took the cab back to work and told the team what she had seen—and not seen. It turned out that the company's antiques had been stored in the expensive humidity-controlled fine arts warehouse for a brief period during the move. A bank employee had arranged for the lease space, and since he didn't know how long the move would take, he got an open-ended contract. He had since changed jobs, and he had assumed that his successor would handle the cancellation of the warehouse agreement. Well, he had no successor. His job was farmed out to a number of people, and the cancellation of the agreement fell through the cracks.

The bank canceled the contract at the team's suggestion and saved $60,000 the first year. No one at the bank wanted to think about how many years they would have been paying the warehouse bill if Mildred hadn't been given the opportunity to act. The company paid for Mildred's cab ride, and awarded about 20 percent of the savings to the team, which amounted to about $1400 in catalogue merchandise, tax-paid, for each team member. After all, this had not been a one-woman effort. A good deal of work had been done by the other team members. The team's next idea was driven by another team member, and Mildred contributed to the implementation of that idea as well and was rewarded as a team member.

There are thousands of team idea stories like Mildred's, of people who have been encouraged to step out of their traditional job roles into greater roles as corporate citizens and have been rewarded for doing so. Like Mildred and her team, they see how they can have an impact on their organization's success.

The key difference between team idea process and the traditional individual suggestion one is that the responsibility rests on the idea-generating team. It generates the idea, researches it, costs it out, discusses its acceptability with those affected, writes it up, and submits it to a evaluation committee for approval. The more guidance the team gets from managers, the better the idea will be. The more a company supports the process through training, on company time, celebration, and reinforcement, the more effective the process will be.

Quick Hit or Long Haul Short-term team idea versions usually allow ninety days for idea generation and about a year for implementation of each idea. Another installment of the short-term process is operated two or three years later. Long-term versions may start with a short-term effort but quickly evolve into an ongoing one in which the generation of ideas never stops.

Short-term idea processes generate "highs": high excitement, high intensity, high workload for management, high participation, and high savings. It takes about two to four months to prepare for introduction. They operate outside the normal managerial hierarchy. Ideas "leap frog" from their source to a level of management to approve and support them, often bypassing layers of management in between.

Everyone responsible for the operation of the team idea process receives training before it goes into effect. (The training is limited to the mechanics of the process itself, rather than the creative process of thinking up ideas or business/financial educational preparation.) Implementation of the process then begins with a two-week period in which employees form their own functional or cross-functional idea teams. During the ninety-day period of idea generation, teams generate, research, cost out, check out, write up, and submit ideas to management-staffed evaluation committees, which turn them around in nine to ten days. Any cost-reduction ideas are evaluated for their potential net savings for the first year after implementation, although the average idea's value generally lasts for about three years. The awards, which are based on a preannounced schedule, are made equally to all team members.

While short-term idea processes generally save and make more money in a shorter time with more employee involvement than any other intervention, they can be a shock to the organization's system. Of course, if a jump start is needed, few things work better or faster. In a number of cases, short-term efforts are the beginning of a long process of employee involvement. Over time the process may be integrated with the organization's continuous improvement process and become the "normal" way of doing business. Thus, employee involvement produces a significant change from what was previously "normal," making the business better and allowing the company to show a return on its investment in the process.

Table 9.2 conveys the impressive results of 185 short-term plans covering 700,000 employees and 79 long-term plans covering 115,000 employees. All of the plans used noncash awards from a catalogue of merchandise. The data show that as the long-term idea process, whether or not it develops from a short-term process, becomes more integrated with the hierarchical organization and/or the existing continuous improvement process, participation goes down and savings per idea go up.

One of the reasons for the reduction in return on investment in long-term plans compared to short-term plans is the expanded focus of long-term plans to include non-cost-reduction ideas. These ideas are rewarded, thus increasing costs; their value does not show up as savings.

Management Commitment Is a Must   Like any other business strategy, a team idea process requires management commitment and involve-

TABLE 9.2. *Results of Short-term and Long-term Idea Processes.*

	SHORT-TERM PLANS	LONG-TERM PLANS
Participation rate	70 to 90%	30 to 40%
Number of ideas submitted	290,000 or about 3 to 4 per team	33,500 or about 2 to 3 per team
Number of ideas approved	77,000 (36% approval rate)	13,500 (40% approval rate)
Savings per idea approved	$23,588 (first year only)	$34,320 (first year only)
Average return on investment (awards, communications, administration software, etc.)	Net: 200% Gross: $3 saved, $1 spent	Net 100% Gross: $2 saved, $1 spent

SOURCE: Maritz Idea System Data Base, Maritz Inc., 1995.

> *There's almost as much value in management learning about the creativity and power of employees as in the money saved by their ideas.*

ment. Managers are sometimes less excited than employees about team ideas. They view the necessary time spent in evaluation committee meetings or acting as resources as just another thing to do on their already long list. Some managers have to be convinced that employees are, in fact, savvy enough to come up with valuable ideas, research their ramifications, and present them convincingly. Luckily, this usually isn't too difficult as the process progresses and proves to be saving money and improving a lot of systems. There's almost as much value in management learning about the creativity and power of employees as there is in the money saved in implementing their ideas.

In addition, any employee involvement effort must have the assurance of management that no employees will be laid off as a result of the process. It would be foolish to install an intervention that had the vaguest implication that, if it is successful, those very people who were responsible for making it successful might lose their jobs.

Setting up a Successful Process   Much of the process I describe here applies to both short- and long-term versions. The approach you take is a function of your needs. If you want to save a good deal of money quickly, jump-start your employees and management into taking an active look at the business, and see quick improvement, a short-term process may be the answer. However, because of their design and timing, short-term plans can be disruptive. The changes in process they require may seem insensitive or punishing to the management team (although there are rewards for management performance as well). The ultimate team idea process is a long-term, continuous employee involvement effort, and it should be thought of that way as you consider instituting it. Figure 9.1 on page 239 illustrates the players in the process, the roles they play, and the relationships among them.

Everybody Plays a Role The first step in establishing the process is approval of the process by top management, followed by the appointment of a *process manager.* This person will drive implementation and operation. If an outside agency is used to assist the organization, the process manager will be the primary liaison with that agency. Process management will be a full-time job.

The process manager and top management create a *steering committee* and together they are responsible for, as their name implies, steering the entire process. The committee includes an *information coordinator,* who becomes the hub of the process. This person receives and enters all of the idea data into a computer (software systems are available for customization), routes idea files, prepares summary reports, generates award checks, and more. The information coordinator reports to the program manager. Other members are selected from top management.

The organization's designated *resource managers* are a vital part of the whole process. Their importance can't be overstated. People throughout the organization are suddenly going to be given the right to get whatever information they need to develop their ideas. It's important that resource people be able—and willing—to provide any data requested by the teams. It's also important that the data be up-to-date and available in a form that's easily accessible. That may require some work before the process rolls out. Having the right resource managers, and enough of them, is often underestimated. Don't let that happen.

Evaluation committees are selected by top management coordinated by the process manager. These committees should always be cross-functional, representing all functions (or as many as possible). They are responsible for accepting or rejecting ideas. How they do both is critical to success. This is a real opportunity for managers to teach and to use the skills of coaching and mentoring.

Ideas that are valued at more than a certain amount (generally $500,000) are reviewed and approved by an *executive evaluation committee* of the organization's top management. (It could also be the same as the *steering committee.*) Most organizations generate at least one million-dollar idea.

Top management, along with the process manager, also appoints *team sponsors,* generally lower-level managers or staff assistants, to handle the myriad details that go into supporting the team idea process in action. Each sponsor works with ten to twelve idea teams, both driving and supporting them to generate, research, and document ideas.

Implementers are assigned on an ad hoc basis to implement the ideas. Implementation could be handled by a team or by an individual. Usually, it involves at least the manager of the area most affected by the idea, or an expert in the subject of the idea. The process could also be implemented by the idea-generating team itself.

Participation in an idea process team is completely voluntary. Employees usually form their own teams of seven. They may consist of co-workers from a work group, a lunch group like Mildred's, a bowling team, or just people who know and like each other. The most effective teams are self-formed and cross-functional. If some employees wish, the project manager can assign people to a team. Once the teams are formed, they each choose a *team leader.* The primary training I referred to earlier is for the team leader. It focuses on the mechanics of the process itself. Most of the team's training is "just-in-time"—that is, they get it when they need it, when they are working on a specific idea. Getting advice, support, and coaching from managers, as well as from the resource managers, is the best training.

Idea Flow   Now that all the roles have been defined, you can get a good picture of how the process actually works by following the idea as it flows through the system (Figure 9.1). Solid lines are idea flow. Dotted lines are feedback. The idea team generates, researches, and puts a value on its idea. It writes up the idea and its justification on the idea submittal form.

The idea submittal form includes registration data, an explanation of the idea, the cost justification, operations affected (and sometimes the operation manager's signature), and the budget line-item codes indicating to which budget to charge any expenses, cost

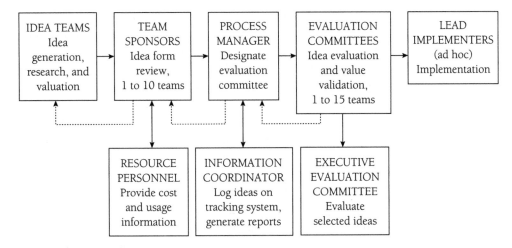

Figure 9.1. *The Idea Flow.*

reductions, or revenue enhancements due to the process. The form itself is not complex. The reason for putting a team through such fact-finding and education to complete the form is to ensure that they have thought the idea through, developed a business case, talked to those affected, understood the financial side, and taken responsibility and ownership of the idea. That's quite a step for the rank and file, from knowing only enough about the business and its finances to do their job to being required to know enough additional information to change an aspect of how an organization works.

The idea is reviewed by the team sponsor and discussed with the team if necessary. Generally a team sponsor would work with the team to contact the right resource personnel for costing and usage information. It would also be important to facilitate a discussion between the team and the person directly impacted if the idea were implemented. Once the team sponsor agrees, the idea is properly documented (no judgment of its worthiness) and all the agreements are made, it is sent to a process manager for assignment to an evaluation committee. The idea is also logged into the tracking system by the information coordinator.

The evaluation committee rules on the idea and on its value. If the idea is particularly big, either in value or impact on the business, it is sent to the executive evaluation committee for action. If ideas are approved, all parties are notified and it is assigned an implementer.

Everyone Gets a Reward   Everyone except the executive evaluation committee is rewarded in this process. Team sponsors are rewarded as a function of the performance of their teams. The evaluation committees' rewards are based on turnaround time, number of ideas handled, and so forth. Implementers' awards are based on the value of the ideas implemented. The process manager, her steering committee, and the resource managers earn a flat amount. The process provides a reward schedule for all participants. Table 9.3 shows a typical reward schedule for teams. It shows the increasing award value per team member relative to the amount of savings approved by the evaluation committees. The awards can be in cash or noncash (generally merchandise from a catalogue).

Teams that reach a certain level of savings for all their ideas often qualify for a grand award. A hospital in Tennessee sent their qualifying teams, with spouses and significant others, to Paris for a week. A manufacturer in Florida awarded a four-day cruise to all high-performing team members and their guests. An airline takes their qualifying teams to a merchandise warehouse in a metropolitan city for the weekend for a "Run Through the Warehouse." Complete with brass bands, running outfits, new tennis shoes, and their spouses, team members have a minute to select anything they want. The run is usually videotaped for use in motivating others. The "Run Through the Warehouse" awards plus an all-expenses-paid week-end away make for a very exciting event.

An Opportunity for Mentoring   An evaluation committee knows how to say "yes" to an idea. Saying "no" is another matter. I argue for a rule: a "no" must be delivered in person, not in writing. One objective of the team idea process is to improve the communication flow between management and the rank and file. When an idea is not accepted, there is an opportunity for a manager on the evaluation committee to play the role of mentor, to work with the team sponsor and the team to turn a negative experience into a positive one. Most rejected ideas have not been completely researched or thought out. If they had been more carefully considered, they would have been approved or not submitted in the first place. A mentor can really help a struggling team.

One team, for example, suggested eliminating the company's main computer backup data feed cable. They determined how much was being spent to maintain and test it and how much it would cost to take it out. The potential savings were significant,

TABLE *9.3.* *Typical Reward Schedule for Team Idea Process.*

NET SAVINGS APPROVED	AWARD VALUE PER PERSON ON TEAM
$0 to $500	$0
$501 to $1,000	$25
$1,001 to $2,500	$50
$2,501 to $5,000	$75
$5,001 to $7,500	$100
↓ **INCREASING INCREMENTS**	↓ **INCREASING AWARD VALUE**
$500,000 and above	$5,000

particularly after the first year, after incurring the initial costs of removing the cable.

The team's evaluation committee turned down the idea as too risky, but one committee member saw this idea as an opportunity to get to know and coach the team. He met and talked to them, told them that it was a great idea but that they hadn't thought it out clearly enough. He suggested things they might do to make their process more realistic. He told them if they wanted to pursue the idea, he would support them.

The team did some more research and found that in more than a decade nothing had ever happened to the main cable. The only time they were without the feed was when the power was down, but then the backup cable didn't do them any good either because both relied on the same power source.

They resubmitted the idea, and once again they were turned down. The committee told them that while it was true that the main cable had never failed, it might. The manager met with them again and told them to keep thinking. They had a brainstorming session and decided to research all the reasons the cable might fail. They found out that about the only time cables fail is when someone accidentally digs them up. Interestingly, as a result of this research they also found that the backup cable was in the same conduit as the main feed cable. If the main cable were broken, the backup would be, too.

That did it. The company pulled the backup cable and saved well over $100,000 a year net, after costs. Each of the seven team members earned $3,000 in noncash awards from a catalogue. That's a cost of $21,000 for a $5 savings for every $1 in payout; a 500 percent gross return on payout.

There are two points to this story: (1) team idea process provided an opportunity for managers to mentor employees, and (2) it engaged people in a meaningful and profitable way. The personal relationships developed within and outside the team while working on an idea are invaluable to the future. The most important relationship that develops is that among team members and managers who probably would not otherwise have had the opportunity to meet during their normal work day.

Documentation   Documentation is necessary at every step in the process, even before teams write down their first ideas. Research, feedback from people potentially affected by an idea, sign-off by managers affected by the idea, approvals, and implementation all require careful documentation. It's no small job and a good paperwork system is essential. Most companies use commercially available customized software for team idea processes, which require less paperwork but no less expertise.

The idea tracking system keeps a record of when each idea was submitted, where it is in the system, how it is valued, which financial accounts are affected, the progress of its implementation, and the associated award costs. The system also generates the necessary tracking and feedback reports to the teams (for example, the status of their ideas, or when awards will be issued), to evaluation committees (such as how many ideas they have received, how long they've taken to process them, and what's coming) and to management (for example, how many ideas have been submitted and their value, the number approved and their total value, the number implemented and their total value, team and evaluation committee activity, and total financial statements for the process).

Do These Plans Work Over Time?   You would think the well would run dry after a few years of operating a team idea process, whether independently, with a group incentive plan, or integrated with the continuous improvement effort. But there are a few cases with enough years of experience that can be used to argue that there is always another dollar to save and another process to improve.

An American Airlines program, "IdeAAs In Action," has been running since 1986. It began with a ninety-day, short-term process, but the system has steadily improved its savings record over the long haul. As Figure 9.2 illustrates, after an enthusiastic start and an initial burst of savings, the results decreased in the second year as the company converted to a long-term design. As the organization has learned to use its employees as corporate citizens, it has continued to be a laboratory for long-term success.

Rewarding Other Ideas   Ideas for improving processes—particularly ideas that make systems more customer sensitive—are difficult to cost justify. Just like many of the measurements in group incentive plans, there are ideas that are good in themselves but that will not reduce costs or enhance revenue; they should be valued as such.

The simplest way of reinforcing approved ideas is with a flat award, as in the Kaizen continuous improvement approach discussed earlier. Regular awards can also be given to operations or teams that generate more approved ideas than targeted. The objective is to generate lots of ideas and keep the involvement going.

Another way to reinforce process ideas is to create a simple matrix (see Table 9.4) that determines the value of the idea on a subjective evaluation on a scale from one to ten, and the scope of the idea's effect, from affecting just one person's job to the whole organization. An initial subjective evaluation of where the idea lies—"goodness" and scope—is done by the generating team. The

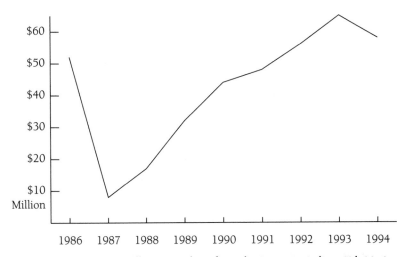

Figure 9.2. Savings (in Millions) Resulting from the American Airlines "IdeAAs In Action" Process.

SOURCE: American Airlines.

TABLE 9.4. *Process Ideas Reward Matrix.*

	HOW GOOD AN IDEA IS IT?									
	1	**2**	**3**	**4**	**5**	**6**	**7**	**8**	**9**	**10**
Individual	Coffee and donuts	Lunch in cafe	Reserved parking place for week	Reserved parking place for month	$10 award value	$12 award value	$14 award value	$16 award value	$18 award value	$20 award value
Work group	Lunch in cafe	Reserved parking place for week	Reserved parking place for month	$10 award value	$15 award value	$20 award value	$25 award value	$30 award value	$35 award value	$40 award value
Department	Reserved parking place for week	Reserved parking place for month	$10 award value	$20 award value	$30 award value	$40 award value	$50 award value	$60 award value	$70 award value	$80 award value
Division	Reserved parking place for month	$10 award value	$30 award value	$50 award value	$70 award value	$90 award value	$110 award value	$130 award value	$150 award value	$170 award value
Company	$30 award value	$60 award value	$90 award value	$120 award value	$150 award value	$180 award value	$210 award value	$240 award value	$270 award value	$300 award value

Scope (indicated vertically on left margin)

award value is for each team member. If the team size varies significantly, the value number can be adjusted to a total team award. When the idea is accepted by the evaluating committee, they also rate it on both scales. Depending on the level of understanding and trust in the organization, the final award could be either what the team or the evaluators say it is worth, or they could split the difference.

Another reinforcement option is to issue a "lottery" card whenever an idea is approved. Each card contains a range of award values. Each team member scratches off a square to reveal the amount earned. There could be one card per team, with the total award being equal to the square scratched off, or each team member could have their own card.

Not All Teams Are Created Equal   I've made the point that, for group incentive plan purposes, a group is a unit within the organization that shares commonality of focus, responsibilities, and tasks. Teams are treated as any other organizational unit is treated, and they are rewarded on the basis of improvement in measures. The definition of team in a project team incentive plan is slightly different. Members of these teams often work together outside their job descriptions, and their sole purpose is to come up with ideas. These teams are rewarded based on the value of those ideas.

It is possible and often practical for a group and team to be the same—for instance, a research and development team or a long-term new-product development team—to wear two hats. They can be a team eligible for reward based on their performance as an organizational unit under a group incentive plan. They can also be an idea team in an employee involvement process.

Ad Hoc Project Teams, Quality Action Teams, and Continuous Improvement Teams

Ad hoc teams are created for particular purposes and are often made up of management and professionals. This makes them something of a special case relative to the other employee involvement efforts discussed in this chapter. Top management often questions whether they should be rewarded in project team incentive plans. It depends. The honor (or sense of responsibility) of being asked to participate in such teams is often a reward in itself. What team members can learn is extremely valuable, including what they will learn from the upper-level managers with whom they will be associating. It may be more appropriate to simply recognize their efforts (see Chapter Seven) as a way of saying thanks. In many organizations, however, you can't swing a dead cat without hitting a project team formed by management to focus on a business issue. People don't look on it as an honor to serve, but as just another part of the job, role, or responsibility. Schedules are juggled, pressure is applied, and good project management is essential to accomplish much of anything. If the project is important enough and it may be less of an honor and more of a burden, consider a project team incentive.

Quality action or continuous improvement teams are always working on special assignments from management (they may be the same as the ad hoc project team described above) or in their work group improving quality, systems, or anything else that reflects the needs of the customer. They are the most common of employee involvement efforts in U.S. business. They are often not measured on their results, however, nor are their contributions given a financial value. If they are measured and valued, a straight-forward design process can be used to create them. (These teams have a short LoS, and they provide a real opportunity for cycling and cost exposure if a significant portion of the company's population is on project team incentive plans. See Chapter Eight.)

The project team incentive plan design process would consider the following elements:

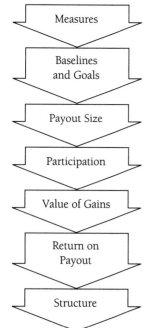

• *Measures:* What are the objectives of the team, and how do they know when they are successful? The measure can be outcomes, time lines met, and/or evaluation of the quality of the work. The measure can also be the effect of the work. An example may be improving a customer satisfaction system, for example, the dispatching process for on-time deliveries. The team could be rewarded for the completion of the project and/or for the effect of the project on on-time delivery. The first measurement option would be straightforward—finish on time and in budget. The second could have a number of levels of success, requiring baselines and goals.

• *Baselines and goals:* For simple project completion, I find a baseline to be less appropriate than a simple goal. It is less common for the measurement to be a graduated level of accomplishment than a yes or no: "It was accomplished" or "It was not accomplished." One exception is when the work is done sooner than planned, which could be the basis for greater awards. If the measure is the effect of the project, then the same, if abbreviated, design process used for group incentive plans is applied here. The baseline might be 75 percent on-time delivery with a goal of 85 percent and levels of improvement in between. In this example, the steps of improvement would continue to 100 percent. Each step would carry a payout. You could even pay out at baseline performance as a reward for completing the project.

• *Size of payouts:* The payout for these plans is determined in the same way as for group incentive plans, described in Chapter Eight. Determine first what is necessary to motivate the members of the team to accomplish their objective, and estimate the total cost. Financial justification will come later.

• *Participation:* People may move in and out of a project team, but there is usually a core group. Whether or not these temporary members are eligible for awards could be determined by their degree of participation (for instance, individual hours spent on a project could be viewed as a percentage of the total of all hours spent, which could determine how much the individual receives). Some people argue for more subjective criteria—such as level of involvement and quality of contribution—to determine the amount to be received by each full-time or part-time team member. But I've found that process to be more divisive than it is worth. Regardless of the "fairness" of the process, feelings get hurt and bridges get burned if you don't make the rules of the game (the reward structure) clear in the beginning.

• *Value of gains:* The dollar value of the team's contribution is much more difficult to determine than cost reduction or revenue enhancement. If the plan designers and management can agree to the financial value, you're ahead of the game. If not, you can simply state what was accomplished. Any reward is an investment in improvement.

• *Return on payout:* If you can put a dollar value on the contribution, a simple return on payout calculation (gain less payout divided by payout times one hundred) will give you the net return, not including time and resources. If you can estimate the cost of time and resources, or anything else related to the project, add it to the payout for a more accurate calculation of net return on payout. If you cannot value the gain in dollar terms, you cannot calculate the return on payout.

• *Structure:* The reward structure can be boiled down to "accomplish this and earn that" for simple project completion. For those measured on their effect, it looks a great deal like the one for group incentive plans, with a reward amount for each level of performance.

• *About milestones:* I have been studying ways of rewarding project teams for years. Some of the most complex measurement and reward schemes have developed around teams formed to complete projects within time frames, according to customer specifications, and within budget. Measuring on milestone attainment is an attractive option, but the milestone better be solid. Project team incentive plan design often ignores the inevitable questions about how accurately the milestones were set in the first place. And then there are milestones that should be moved because of technical problems or developments outside the control of the project team. Milestones offer so many possibilities for counterproductive micromanagement and micromeasurement, that unless you can solve the inherent problems, I don't think rewarding by milestone is the way to go.

I suggest that you focus on the objective—the what—and leave the process—the how—to the team. Base rewards on project accomplishment and value—either in dollars or in management's valuation of the contribution. Most milestone plan designs tend to die of their own measurement and administrative weight. Organizations are very used to thinking in terms of time frames, but events might be just as important. One drug company reinforces its research and development teams whenever they complete a step in the development process—from getting approval to proceed with the project to final FDA approval. The reward is set for accomplishing the step, which is an event. It is not about meeting a time line, but the sooner they complete the step, the sooner they get the award.

For a more detailed description of project team incentive plans at work, I suggest *Learning Partnerships* by Bob Mai (1995). It provides an overview of how reward and communication plans are being used effectively to implement organizational learning. The learning, specifically, is that of management about the power and creativity of employees when they are given the opportunity and the reinforcement.

Conclusion

Rewarding project teams that have been created by management is something everyone wants to do but can't quite figure out how to—and if they do, they can't quite get it to work smoothly. Exceptions, modification of the rules structure, and concern that the wrong behaviors are being rewarded (ones that may work against the integrity of the project) keep cropping up. The bottom line, again, is pragmatism. Set up the team, measure and value its contribution either on a time, project-completion, or effect basis, and reward them according to a reward schedule. Leave it up to the team to determine how they are going to accomplish their objectives. Milestone measurement invites micromanagement, and that is counter to the purpose of employee involvement.

I spent most of this chapter describing the team idea process because of its unique benefits: it pays for itself, it is voluntary, and everyone can participate. It is the essence of employee involvement with measurable outcomes, and it can prove to management what engaged employees can accomplish. Alone, it can save and make a lot of money. Under the umbrella of a group incentive plan, it answers the rank-and-file employee's question, "What can I do to improve performance?" in a way that can satisfy and delight everyone.

CHAPTER 10

Types of Awards

Society's basic medium of exchange is cash. We earn it, spend it, invest it, and even use it to keep score. Organizations deal almost exclusively in cash. Our systems are developed to write checks, figure taxes and deductions, account for and distribute cash. Most payments are made in cash. Benefits are delivered as insurance, vacations, days off, and so on. Cash is the currency of all entitlement-based compensation systems. Stock, or at least the option to buy it, can also be an element of compensation plans. It is not surprising, then, that plan designers rarely consider any type of award but cash.

Cash is the most common extrinsic award. It is the only choice when the reward adds to base pay. Reward plans that do not add to base pay but are offered as unique awards come in a variety of types. Research shows that what people want most in their jobs is recognition for having made a contribution to the betterment of the organization. They want to be valued. It makes sense, then, that the more you can tie rewards to the message "you are valued," the better off you are. The best way to say "you are valued," with extrinsic awards is to use a variety of them: cash, trips, valued merchandise, time off, stock, training—and the list goes on. A variety of awards works best because people have different psychic needs. By using different kinds of awards, organizations can meet those differing needs and therefore tap more people's creativity and enthusiasm.

What You Will Find in This Chapter

Cash (or financial) awards include cash added to base pay, cash not added to base pay, deferred cash, prepaid or partially paid services (such as insurance, pension, and employee assistance programs), and stock (grants or options). Most companies are already familiar with these types of awards, so I'll spend this chapter on non-cash awards and then compare them to cash awards. The chapter covers:

- The types of noncash awards

- Reasons to consider awards other than cash

- Use of noncash awards in each type of recognition and group-based incentive plan

- A comparison of cash and noncash awards

Why Consider Anything Other Than Cash?

I rarely hear, "No more money for me. It just wouldn't be fair."

When employees are surveyed about what type of tangible awards they would like, the consistent answer is cash. This is not unexpected. My guess is they are not thinking so much about money as about the things money can buy. If your manager asked you what you wanted as an award and you answered anything other than cash, you'd get some pretty strange looks. What are you saying, that you are now being paid exactly what you're worth? I rarely hear, "No more money for me. It just wouldn't be fair." Well, of course we want more money. Yet, what employees say is really important to them at work is "full appreciation for work done, being involved, and sympathetic help on personal problems" (Kovach, 1980, pp. 54–59). Consequently, as it becomes more important in plans to reinforce performance improvement and to motivate—proceeding from the entitlements of compensation to recognition to group-based incentive plans—the *recognition* or *trophy* value of awards must increase.

The research in this area is best expressed in *People, Performance, and Pay* (O'Dell and McAdams, 1987), which showed that trophy value is the primary reason that noncash awards of significant value (generally over $400) are used. Every time an employee looks at the lounge chair or uses a set of golf clubs earned for improving performance, he or she is reminded that it was earned for a particular accomplishment. This continual reinforcement has a quality that a cash bonus does not have.

I was making a speech in Boston a few years ago, and I asked someone in the audience to let me know if they had ever received a noncash award of significant value. A number of hands went up, and I chose one man who said, "In 1969—about 20 years ago—I earned an award I still have. A clock radio."

"What was its cost?" I asked.

"About $30." A little surprised that he could remember a $30 item earned twenty years earlier, I asked, "How did you earn it?"

"I was on a team of engineers at RCA and we came up with an idea to change a screw size in a machine. We saved the company enough money to earn each of us a choice of merchandise from a catalogue they gave us. I picked a radio. I still have it, although it doesn't work now."

"Do you get a cash bonus in your job now?"

"Well, I left RCA a long time ago, but I've gotten a bonus for several years now."

"How many years ago? Can you remember how much it was?"

"Five, no, four, I guess."

"What did you do with it?"

"Can't remember. Probably paid some bills, went for a special dinner with the family—something like that."

I'm not suggesting that a $30 radio is as important as the man's bonus, but look at what RCA got for $30. He remembered the award, the company, and what he did to earn it—more than twenty years ago. That's trophy value. It would have taken a good deal more than $30 to make a cash award memorable. Plus, you can talk about a noncash award to others, even brag a little. It is socially acceptable to show off your new camcorder to your neighbor and say, "I earned this for working with a team on improving our process." It is tacky to go from door to door showing your W-2 form.

> *It is OK to brag a bit about earning a noncash award. It's tacky to pull out your W-2 form.*

Noncash awards cannot be confused with base pay or compensation. There can be little or no entitlement. You don't expect to live off noncash awards. They are extra. This makes it easier for the organization to reassess the plan from period to period to meet the demands of the business. There is less likelihood of people being upset than if they thought their cash income (and hence their standard of living) might be reduced.

The research reported in *People, Performance and Pay* covered 330,000 sales employees from 607 organizations. It provides some evidence that plans that use noncash awards can produce the same results as those that use cash awards, but at a lower cost (O'Dell and McAdams, 1987, pp. 73–83). I have some concerns about applying research findings on sales employees to nonsales employees, so take that into your consideration of these data. My experience is that the results don't differ much if employees (sales or nonsales) perceive they are being paid fairly. There is an argument in favor of looking at the sales performance-reward experience and applying the appropriate knowledge to the nonsales employee population: sales has been doing it for fifty years.

The research found that cash incentives beyond the base-salary-plus-commission plan improved sales performance 13 percent. Noncash awards for the perceived equivalent value improved performance about the same amount, 13.3 percent. The cost of the cash awards was approximately 12¢ on every additional dollar in sales. The noncash awards cost about 4.1¢ per incremental dollar—which is a significantly better return on payout. I'm not suggesting that noncash awards are three times more cost effective for all performance improvement efforts, but they have demonstrated an ability to improve performance at a lower, or equal, cost.

In addition to their trophy value, noncash awards get more attention than cash in any recognition and group-based incentive plan. Catalogues of merchandise and brochures on travel opportunities can be sent to the home, merchandise can be displayed in the cafeteria, and time off and educational opportunities can be aggressively promoted to encourage employee involvement in the plan. Going over the catalogue with one's team or family and choosing the awards as a goal-setting process is a lot more involving than offering a flat cash award.

So, Which Is Better?

It depends on the nature of the plan and its objectives. Table 10.1 summarizes the advantages and disadvantages of each approach.

If your objective is to create excitement, involvement, and action by employees, noncash awards may be more appropriate.

Cash awards are more traditional and therefore more readily accepted. There is certainly less hassle. But if your objective is to create excitement, involvement, and action by employees, noncash awards may be more appropriate.

Merchandise and travel tend to get people's attention, while cash awards can be lost in an employee's cash flow, regardless of the plan type. The use of an award medium that provides additional recognition of the objective makes a lot of sense. This is particularly true

TABLE 10.1. *Advantages and Disadvantages of Cash and Noncash Awards.*

CASH	NONCASH
Easily understood	More difficult to explain
Administration systems in place	Unique administration system
Flexible; employee may use in any way	Flexible; employees have wide range of possible awards
Expects tax deductions	Tax paid by employer; included in the financial rationale
Limited recognition and trophy value; quickly spent	High recognition and trophy value
Can become confused with compensation; same award media	Cannot be confused with compensation; different award media create greater attention
Can become an entitlement or considered a part of compensation, depending on plan and amount	Tends not to become an entitlement
Will not be accumulated	Will be accumulated
Adds little excitement	Adds a good deal of excitement
Communicated at work	Communicated at work and home

when you're trying to teach people how to understand and affect productivity, quality, cost reduction, safety, attendance, project milestones, and other business objectives.

The decision about whether to use cash or noncash awards is a function of what you want to accomplish. Adding trophy value to any award enhances it, whether the employee wants to "go public" or not. Once you have determined that a type of award is attractive, then the decision about what type of award to use with which plan is a function of what will produce the best return on your investment. Table 10.1 lists the awards most commonly used in each type of plan.

The decision about whether to use cash or noncash awards will affect the degree to which an employee attributes her award to the organization's plan. With cash, there is clear attribution when the award is received, but it goes away when the money is spent on things other than a large, tangible item. There is greater attribution to the plan when the employee uses points to get something from a

Compensation	Capability	Recognition	Group Incentive	Project Team Incentive
Cash, stock, benefits, services	Cash, symbolic, personal development	Symbolic, tangible and nontangible, "Thank you"	Cash, noncash of significant value	Noncash of significant value

FIGURE 10.1. *Most Commonly Used Awards by Plan Type.*

store, for a trip, or from a catalogue. The item earned (or the memory of travel) stays in the employee's mind for years and is connected to the organization. The smaller the value of the award, however, the less significant it will be over time. With catalogue merchandise and award points, the award is attributed to the organization and reinforces the employee's contribution for as long as the item lasts.

The Point System

95 percent of points earned by an individual are accumulated for an award of greater value.

Most noncash awards are delivered as points (award credits), valued at whatever the design team decides. The flexibility of points allows them to be paid out in any amount, from a value of a half-cent to one dollar. While employees are free to use award points at any time, 95 percent are accumulated for an award of greater value, and in this lies their significance. The greater the value of the award, the greater will be its long-term trophy value. By contrast, small amounts of cash will be spent as discretionary income, quickly forgotten.

The opportunity for accumulation is particularly important when the amount of earned payout is relatively small, due to a small improvement or frequent payout periods. The smallest payout in a team idea plan is about $25. The median payout for group incentive plans with operational measures, in which monthly and quarterly payouts are common, is $833 per employee per year or 3 percent of base pay (McAdams and Hawk, 1994, p. 206). If you break $833 down into monthly payments and take out taxes, the net award is about $55 per month, which can get lost in the employee's normal cash flow.

If there is a reserve feature in the design, at least 25 percent of the cash reward goes into a year-end bank, reducing the monthly payout to $40. Forty dollars worth of points, however, tends to be accumulated. People save their points until they have enough to buy that large-screen television, dining room suite, or tennis racquet. They end up with something they appreciate and will remember for a long time.

Types of Noncash Awards and How To Use Them

The most popular noncash awards of significant value for improving performance or recognizing improvements are merchandise, travel, educational opportunities, earned time off with pay, earned-value credit cards, symbolic (often known as recognition) awards, and social awards.

Merchandise Awards

Merchandise as an award is different from what you normally buy in a store. In order to have trophy value it must be special—generally something the employee would not normally buy for himself. The key to merchandise awards is variety. For that reason, they are made available to employees through award catalogues that have been expressly designed to present awards, not just merchandise. The awards are "purchased" by the redemption of award points (or credits). They are considered of "significant" financial value, generally totaling more than 2 percent of annual salary. The rewards may also be distributed in the form of merchandise certificates that can be used at the local branch of a national retail chain, but merchandise presented in this manner loses some of its award appeal, compared to the catalogue approach.

Award Catalogues from Performance-Improvement Agencies   Award catalogues are various sizes. Some offer nearly two thousand high-quality items, selected to be appealing to a broad range of tastes. While they offer a broad selection of functional items, the intent is to focus on their special value to the individual or family. Recently, these large catalogues have evolved to reflect new employee lifestyles. Health insurance and other forms of insurance, education and training, memberships, and access to specialty catalogues

are now included. The next smallest award catalogue generally has about eight hundred items and is limited to quality merchandise. Minicatalogues are really booklets containing ten to fifteen items each, in value groupings from $25 to $500.

Accompanying these catalogues are price lists shown in points or award credits. When a plan is introduced, levels of performance are directly related to the award value in points. Checks for points are issued by the organization or the agency supplying the merchandise.

Award catalogues are supplied by full-service performance-improvement agencies that also administer plans. These agencies issue and mail the point checks based on performance information supplied by the company or the plan participants. The agency takes care of lost checks and refunds (when participants send in more points than necessary for their order). All record keeping, tax and management reports, order entry, shipping, customer service, auditing, and billings are also handled by the agency. Some agencies also offer a bank account system, which deposits the points into an account in the participant's name, issues balance statements, and allows ordering by telephone or mail.

Award earners have higher expectations when using points than they do when buying something using cash.

To award earners, the service provided by these agencies is a critical element. People have higher expectations of product quality, delivery, and customer service when using points than they do when buying something using cash. They have earned the award, they want it as soon as possible, and they don't want any problems. If there are any problems, they demand quick, fair, and empathetic service. A good agency will stock items that make up from 60 to 75 percent of their orders. Some items such as clothing, furniture, and large appliances have to be shipped from the factory. The size and buying power of the agency has a strong influence on the service that an award earner will receive on their drop shipments. If the desired item is not in the award catalogue, some agencies also offer special ordering services.

Agencies usually bill the firm for the value of the award points *redeemed,* plus transportation and sales tax. This gives the organization cash flow benefits that are unique to merchandise incentives. Because the vast majority of merchandise-award winners save their checks until they have enough to get a larger award, a lag time occurs between the actual performance improvement. And the cost of awards is actually incurred by the organization. The billing for awards is at redemption, often eight to twelve months after point issuance (except for bank account plans, which generally are billed when points are issued). The company has the benefit of improved performance without incurring the cost of an award until the time of point redemption and billing. The positive cash flow can be significant.

Other Merchandise Options Some organizations offer employees a general-purpose catalogue from a traditional department store from which to make their award selections. This kind of catalogue is designed to meet everyday functional needs, and not every item in the catalogue would be considered an award. There is quite a difference in the merchandise selections among these catalogues and those designed specifically to offer awards.

Companies can also buy merchandise awards directly from a manufacturer. Many major manufacturers of popular consumer goods (such as General Electric, Motorola, Sony, Thomasville, and so forth) have incentive divisions that focus on selling a limited selection of their products directly to companies for their incentive plans. The buyer—in this case the company—has to decide what will be most appealing to the targeted population. A common approach is to create a booklet of a few items (TVs, VCRs, cameras, golf clubs, and so on) that should be of interest to anyone in the audience. That's not always the case, however. If you already have three TVs, it's hard to get excited about earning another one. Trying to guess what is valuable to people is a frustrating and often hopeless task. Offering a broad range of awards is the safest approach.

Full-service performance improvement agencies (Maritz Inc., Carlson, S&H-Citadel, and Business Incentives are the largest) generally are not involved in incentive plans when companies purchase their own merchandise awards. In this situation, companies often make use of brokers who represent a number of manufacturers for direct sales to organizations. Brokers seldom offer any additional services (such as design, communications, promotions, administration, assessment, customer service, tax data, award point issuance, and so on). If a company decides to buy merchandise from a manufacturer, then the company handles all of the administrative work itself. This may not be very burdensome if the number of items is limited and all merchandise is drop shipped (that is, shipped directly from the manufacturer or distributor to the employee). If, instead, the company buys a number of items and stocks them for redistribution, it must take all of the accompanying costs into account when designing the reward plan.

Unless you have a drop-shipped-only purchase arrangement, there is little cash flow advantage with this approach, because award payment is made when the shipment is made to the company's stock. Demands for good customer service are equally stringent with a preselected merchandise approach, and the company's staff is responsible for providing that service. Because of the complexities involved, few firms take this approach, at least not the second time around.

Employees who earn merchandise awards feel cheated if they have to pay taxes on them.

Paying Taxes on Merchandise Awards   Merchandise awards are subject to federal income tax withholding, state and local taxes, and both the employee and employer portions of FICA (Social Security). Employees who earn merchandise awards feel cheated if they have to pay taxes on them. Here is a rule to count on more than your thumb: include in your financial rationale for any plan the cost of all taxes on noncash awards. Do not have your employees pay any taxes on them.

The process for handling taxes is common and simple. Firms "gross up" the fair market value of the awards when reporting them on each employee's W-2 form, and then they pay all the taxes. There is little or no tax consequence for the employee, assuming that he or she isn't moved into a higher tax bracket.

There are two acceptable ways to gross up awards for tax purposes: (1) look at the award value itself and apply a flat 28 percent federal withholding tax rate; or (2) assume that the award will be incorporated into the lower-wage employee's income and allow for an alternative 15 percent rate. Table 10.2 presents a typical scenario for each alternative, assuming that state and local income taxes also exist.

Tax considerations for merchandise obtained from department store catalogues and directly from manufacturers are the same as for the award catalogue approach.

Travel

The all-expenses-paid vacation has been touted on TV for thirty years as the ultimate award. The expense of such an award is far more than the median award in any of the reward and recognition plans I've discussed. But the travel industry has changed and is offering the opportunity to supply certificates for all or part of hol-

TABLE 10.2. *Grossing Up Noncash Awards.*

	28% FLAT FEDERAL WITHHOLDING TAX RATE	ALTERNATIVE 15% FEDERAL WITHHOLDING TAX RATE
Fair market value of all noncash awards	$100.00	$100.00
Federal withholding tax	46.40	20.45
State income tax (at 3%)	4.97	4.09
City income tax (at 1%)	1.65	1.36
Employee's portion of FICA (at 7.65%)	12.68	10.43
Gross amount of award (reported as W-2 compensation)	$165.70	$136.33
Employer's portion of FICA (at 7.65%)	12.68	10.43
Total cost to employer of awards	$178.38	$146.76

iday travel. For this reason, travel awards are becoming more popular because they feature many of the benefits of an award catalogue plan.

Travel certificates can be issued in various denominations of "travel value," usually $50 to $100, according to a preannounced schedule that relates to levels of performance. A book of travel destinations is given to employees at the beginning of the program. Certificates can be accumulated by the employees and redeemed for the travel awards. These certificates may be used to pay for all of the cost of the award or any part of it.

One of the appeals to this approach is its ability to offer participants a wide range of destinations (one hundred or more) in a promotional kit. All administrative needs, including certificate redemption and travel arrangements, are handled by the individual award earner directly with the airlines, hotels, and other travel suppliers. The certificates are used as payment directly to the supplier for the cost of the travel award.

Full-service agencies offer a catalogue of award travel destinations designed to promote resorts and other locations. Their primary award-travel business is designed to serve participants from any part of the nation or world, and they are staffed to deliver this service. Customer service in this case is the responsibility of the hotels, airlines, and other travel suppliers, with the support of the agency. Regardless of how you handle travel awards, the participant will hold the sponsoring company responsible for the quality of service.

Taxes on travel awards are also handled by grossing up. The cost of the travel certificates is billed to the company when they are issued, so there is no cash flow advantage to the company. If the certificates are issued in exchange for points, however, the cash flow advantage is the same as with the award catalogue plan.

Educational Opportunities

A frequently overlooked award is to give employees the opportunity to expand their knowledge—both in general and of the business. Attending professional seminars sounds great, but it is clearly limited to a few people. The cost per person is high, unless it is a local conference or seminar.

Attendance at company meetings that are generally reserved for sales or general management is a far more affordable educational opportunity, and it enables the award earners to get to know people they may not see every day.

Firms regularly use special team-building training as an award. The event is held in a special place, like the Rocky Mountains; it lasts a week and is highly prized as a benefit to the company as well as an award to the employees. To be considered an award, however, participation must be purely voluntary. Even implied pressure to participate eliminates any award aspect of such an activity.

Earned Time Off with Pay

As the stress of modern life increases, special time off is considered a powerful award. It is given in addition to time off with pay for sickness, vacation, or disability.

Most companies that give time off make it *paid* time off. Otherwise, it may not be considered an award. Time off without pay, however, can be a positive way of capturing productivity improvements. Many employees would be quite happy to get a day off without pay if it would not jeopardize their job status.

Selectively used, earned time off can be used in two ways. First, employees can be allowed to take a day (or days) off when a specific goal or objective has been reached. Some companies allow people to accumulate days for additional vacations or vacation extensions. There could, however, be a philosophical conflict with this type of earned time off. What message does such a plan send? Do we really want to reinforce the idea of not coming to work? Some believe that such a plan should only be applied in organizational units in which attendance is not a problem or the loss of critical customer contact is not a risk.

Second, company celebrations may be held that take people as a group off company premises. Most of these activities, such as company picnics, are considered entitlements, but they can also be effective awards. When goals are met, everyone celebrates. If your company already has traditional events that are not considered awards, don't try to convert them into awards. Some creative thinking, however, can bring a company real benefits through group activities.

Companies using this type of award find administration to be more complex with nonexempt and shift workers than with those in the exempt and professional ranks. Unlike the other types of awards described, the cost of this award is something to consider. Companies should be aware that the limitations of accounting systems can mask the real cost of this award. Many firms consider professional, exempt, and management earned time off to be of no cost to the company, depending on how much time off is given. Nonexempt and shift worker's earned time off is generally considered to carry a real cost.

Earned time off is probably most effective when used on a limited basis and driven by the nature of the operation, timing, workload, and how critical the individual is to the organization. Also, earned time off generally provides no tax consideration to the employee.

Earned-Value Credit Cards

Earned-value credit cards are the newest idea in noncash awards, and they are particularly well suited to today's more diverse workforce—from full-time employees to contingent and/or part-time workers.

Earned-value credit cards look like regular credit cards, but they can accumulate credits toward the purchase of merchandise or travel from catalogues or participating stores. Earned points are credited to employees' accounts. At any point, they can take their card to an ever-increasing range of local suppliers, and 800 numbers can be used to order from specialty catalogues (such as Eddie Bauer, Spiegel, and many others). In addition, minicatalogue merchandise or travel selections can be provided by the company.

The cards give employees great freedom in selecting their own awards when the organization has decided it wants to maintain the advantages of noncash awards and yet give employees even greater flexibility in selection. Each month, employees receive their earning statements. The statement builds rather than bills—in fact, it's not a bill, it's a credit, and that's powerful. As people begin to see that credit, they start to do more goal setting. Frequent flyer programs are a classic example of storing up credit. These programs encourage people to plan their travel carefully in order to earn the maximum amount of miles. When employees have earned-value credit cards, they become more engaged in the importance of meeting their organization's business objectives because they can see their own accounts building as a result.

A fast food employee accumulating credits for a mountain bike is more likely to stay the extra six months to earn it.

Contingent and part-time workers don't usually make enough money for companies to be able to give them big cash awards. Turnover is often an issue, too. In the fast food industry, for example, earned-value credit cards are a viable way to reduce turnover. In addition to offering credits for improved performance, organizations can offer additional credits to employees who stay with the chain for three months, six months, a year, or longer. Cumulative credit is potentially more powerful than telling people they will get a bonus of an equal amount, because the earned credit has more intrinsic recognition value. If an employee is saving for a mountain bike from a catalogue or local store, she is more likely to stay the extra six months to earn the credits needed.

Earned-value credit cards are yet another way of engaging people in the process of performance improvement. They offer considerable leverage to companies with limited amounts of money available for group incentive plans. Earned-value credit cards are only available from full-service performance improvement agencies who handle all the administrative details.

Symbolic Awards

A trophy is a symbolic award. It has more meaning than financial value to an employee. Examples are plaques, rings, desk sets, pins, publicity, free lunches, jackets, hats, reserved parking places, memberships in advisory councils, and so forth. Not all symbolic awards are inexpensive, however. Company rings or pins can cost hundreds of dollars.

Symbolic awards are used for two purposes: to raise awareness and to grant recognition. Awareness is acknowledging the importance of an objective or goal. Organizations have program themes printed on selected items to distribute to all members of the organization, regardless of their performance. These items are good communication tools and tangible, ever-present reminders of the strategic objectives.

Symbolic items are more commonly used for recognition. Membership on advisory councils, upgrades in company cars, reserved parking places, free lunches, and special business cards are just a few of the symbolic awards used to recognize individual outstanding performance. Offering a T-shirt or coffee mug to each employee who reaches a preestablished goal is an inexpensive way of gaining focus. Few would argue that this award is significant enough in financial terms to get people to improve performance, but there are a number of cases in which group dynamics and pride take over. The symbolic award is a way for employees to publicly display their accomplishments, and most companies have some form of individual recognition that can be exhibited in the workplace.

Hundreds of advertising specialty and promotion brokers supply symbolic awards. Full-service agencies offer them as an accommodation to their clients. They also offer artistic symbolic awards rarely available elsewhere. These awards are often limited-edition sculptures, designed and produced just for the company and/or event. As with the awards catalogue approach, these full-service agencies offer the design, communication, promotion, and distribution services that are not available with fulfillment sources.

Administration of symbolic awards is much the same as for the awards catalogue. Because the value of each item tends to be low, many firms stock the awards and handle most of the administration themselves, particularly if the awards are issued throughout the year. If the plan sends out the awards all at one time, it is considerably easier to have the full-service agency or fulfillment sources handle the distribution from a mailing list supplied by the company.

Generally, symbolic awards are valued at less than $25 each and are tax-free to the employee. Under certain conditions, such as with the cost of service awards, the tax-free allowance goes up to $600.

Make sure your symbolic award makes sense for the recipient.

The tax law tends to be interpreted differently over time, so be sure to consult your firm's tax attorney.

Here's a hint: make sure your symbolic award makes sense for the recipient. Giving a wall-hanging plaque to an employee without a wall is not a good idea.

Social Awards

Social awards include involvement, listening, pats on the back, respect, feedback, training, and activities (such as picnics, tailgate sales, and charity days). Most social awards are a function of management style and can be used to improve morale and acknowledge the value the organization puts on its people. Social awards should be an integral part of all management practices.

Noncash Awards and the Various Plans

Noncash Awards and Recognition Plans

Most recognition plans now use symbolic awards. They are also expanding to include award points. These points are being combined with point earnings from group incentive and project team incentive plans.

Noncash Awards for Group Incentive Plans

Group incentive plans create changes in an organization's culture. This can be one of the primary objectives of such a plan—and it requires excitement, focus, and involvement. Noncash awards help in creating those elements in a plan. Learning to step out of traditional roles, to understand new measures (or old ones in a new way), and to become involved enough to make a difference requires special effort and a special spirit. It takes a lot of cash to make that difference in a relative short time.

Concern is often expressed about using cash in a group incentive plan with a long LoS. As I have said several times before, long LoS plans run the risk of becoming a distribution methodology rather than a plan that activates people to affect the measures. Using cash can contribute to a sense of entitlement. Noncash awards can be used as a transitional strategy. Even with plans with a reasonable LoS, the transitional time can be used to shake out the measures and allow employees to get used to the idea of awards tied to performance. After a period of two or more years, the plans can convert to cash, if appropriate. The learning phase will be over, and the plan may need to be integrated into the "normal" media of cash awards. (Plans cannot convert from cash to noncash. Employees will consider it a reduction in compensation—variable as it may be.)

Noncash Awards and Project Team Incentive Plans

Most of the traditional project team incentive plans are being reinvented with noncash awards. All of the data on team idea plans discussed in Chapter Nine use noncash awards. The data on individual suggestion plans are primarily cash. Whether the better results from the team idea plans are due to the noncash awards or the unique design of the plans, I can't say. I do not know of any long-term plans that have converted to cash since 1980.

The fact that project team incentive plans must have their impetus from the employees themselves is probably the most compelling reason to use noncash rewards in these plans. Getting people to decide to take the step into involvement has to be a function of how motivated they are. If they are motivated by intrinsic reasons—the personal satisfaction of being involved outside their normal role—then only organizational barriers would have kept them from being involved in the past.

"What's in it for me?" is still an issue. In most organizations, project team incentive plans need an answer in addition to personal satisfaction. Noncash awards have proven themselves to be powerful answers to that question.

Conclusion

As organizations expand their thinking on how to design different recognition and group-based incentive plans to improve business performance, they need to consider a wider variety of awards. Almost everything works. It is a matter of return on investment. If you can motivate employees with enough cash to accomplish your objectives, cash may be your best option. It is certainly the most common. I am finding, however, that it takes more and more cash to get someone's attention and motivate them to make a contribution. You simply don't have to spend as much with noncash awards as with cash to get the same or better results.

CHAPTER 11

Implementation

At this juncture, I depart from my open-book management (OBM) friends. Not because I disagree with them. On the contrary. It is just that the essence of OBM—financial literacy, engaged and accountable employees, and a group incentive plan—makes this prescriptive implementation somewhat moot. In most OBM organizations, the design of the group incentive plan is very much an egalitarian effort. The rank and file are as critical to the design as management. The whole point of financial literacy is to enable employees to influence the very measures of the group incentive plan. Rank-and-file employee involvement on a daily basis in every aspect of the operation, including making and implementing decisions once reserved for management, is often espoused but rarely practiced in non-OBM companies. To speak of "implementing" organizational performance improvement plans in OBM is redundant. It all happens at once.

This chapter, therefore, is for those organizations that take a more traditional approach to doing business. It assumes a greater hierarchical structure than in OBM companies, the "usual" degree of financial literacy (meaning almost none), and some natural "push back" from middle management. In essence, this chapter is written for more than 99 percent of the companies in the Western economic block.

What You Will Find in This Chapter

I have addressed implementation as a step process that includes the following:

- Getting plan approval

- Management ownership, involvement, and education

- Introduction to all employees

- Operation

- Communication, promotion, and celebration

- Reassessment and renewal

Where appropriate, I have specifically described these steps for each of the three types of organizational improvement plans—recognition, group incentive, and project team incentive.

When the Design Is Complete

By the time a design team reaches the point of introducing a plan, they can be so tired of it that they quickly fall into the trap of expecting the plan to run itself. In some cases, they simply mail out the plan and hope the awards speak for themselves. That is the traditional way that plans emanating from the left-hand side of the reinforcement model are introduced, and it generally works there. (This is not to say that individual compensation plans couldn't benefit from borrowing some right-side-of-the-model methodologies to install a new base pay system or rejuvenate performance management. Recognition and group-based plan methodologies can be particularly helpful in implementing capability plans. The issues of education, ownership, and management involvement tend to be universal.)

"Implementation is 76 percent of the total effort." (Don Barry, Chase Manhattan Bank).

Recognition and group-based plans require a great deal of attention during the introductory stage. Implementation is where the real work begins. Don Barry, vice president of human resources (HR) for Chase Manhattan Bank, says that implementation is 76 percent of the total effort. He is the first to admit that he doesn't know where he got that number, but it makes the point, because implementation is the lion's share of the plan. So, once the design has been developed, you're 24 percent along the way.

Implementation must have strong financial support. However, while organizations often seem willing to spend the money necessary to design a plan, they seem less enthusiastic about putting the money behind it to make sure it works. That is probably to be expected. There is a passive awareness of compensation in organizations that only have individual compensation plans. They assume that because they have employees and pay them, any reward (seen as a form of pay) must be an individual compensation plan. Rewarding people has long been an administrative detail for most managers, who have always left it to the HR or compensation department.

Again, it's important to stress that any recognition or group-based reward is a business plan and not an individual compensation plan. You would not mail out a five-year business plan to your employees and then do nothing to sell it to them or train them in its implementation. That's because you could not rely on the mere existence of the plan and an innate understanding of its importance to motivate employees to do something different.

Plan Approval

For recognition and group-based plans to achieve their promise, they must be *marketed* first to your top management. There are two types of buyers: economic (they can buy) and technical (they can't buy, but they sure can stop the sale). The economic buyers are top management, including the CFO, and some influential line managers. The technical buyers are staff and line middle management and first-line supervisors. It is imperative that the plan be presented in a way that engages each manager's spirit, mind, pocketbook, and that makes it a tool to improve performance. That is the *content* of your marketing plan. The *context* of the plan is the attitude that what's good for your business is good for everybody.

The plan must be presented in a way that engages each manager's spirit, mind, and pocketbook.

Marketing Begins Before the Design Is Complete

If you have followed the guidelines for designing your plan, you have been marketing and getting input from top management all along the way. The last thing a team wants to do is tell top management it wants to create a self-funded plan that will improve productivity, customer satisfaction, and cycle time, get their approval to proceed, then not talk to them until the design is complete. You need to make sure that your decision makers, regardless of who they are, are conceptually and philosophically on board, and the earlier you do that, the better chance you will have of ultimately getting their approval. Keep them constantly updated, and constantly request their input.

It can be a sensitive matter to request input from top management without appearing to ask for direction. It is necessary to say clearly that you do not want top management to impede your creative process by giving you too much direction. There is a particular risk with recognition plans. If management's paternalistic (and control) genes activate, you may get a lot of helpful hints that aren't so helpful and are more than hints. Yet, you want them to let you know if the team is getting completely off track. This is a difficult balance, and constant reviews are necessary. The liaison between top management and the design team must be someone who has the ability to listen to what management says and to interpret and confirm it as input, not direction. Ideally, that person is the design team leader, in cooperation with the team's champion.

Recognition plans activate management's paternalistic (and control) genes.

Getting Top Management Ownership

Your first task once the design has been completed is to sell the plan to top management, set their expectations on what the plan can and cannot do, and receive their agreement to support the plan. Ultimately, nothing is ever sold in a presentation to top management. The presentation itself is merely a confirmation that top management wants to proceed with what it has been agreeing to throughout the process. It can be frustrating when talking with them to realize that they probably are not interested in the details of the plan, even though you've worked for months at getting it right. This is frustrating because presentation of the plan is such a great opportunity to tell top management what you have learned during the design process. They, however, are more interested in style, what the plan will accomplish, and what the return on their investment will be. The actual amount of education that you can deliver in a meeting with top management is limited. It would not be unusual for you to simply get sign-off on the plan without the people who approve it understanding even the most basic of its mechanics. (That isn't a bad thing at top levels. It is a serious problem farther down the management ladder.)

Preparing for the Presentation   To avoid getting into an endless group discussion going over ground you and your team have already plowed, you should prepare top management prior to the presentation by meeting with each of them one-on-one when possible. Often, top management does not allow enough time in a formal meeting to cover all of the details, so you should allow enough time in the one-on-one meetings to explain the plan fully and answer (or note) any questions or concerns. It is particularly important at this time to get across any necessary details of the financial considerations.

It is important to have an idea of who your audience is, how they think, what their patience level for details is, and what their hot buttons might be. It's also good to know to whom to pay particular attention and to whom not to pay so much attention, because not all voices are equal in these meetings.

The Presentation The presentation to top management should be done in a familiar style that parallels the way presentations are usually made to them for other strategic planning projects. The plan should be presented as a business decision, not as a new individual compensation plan.

The following is a generic outline you may want to consider. (Some steps are inappropriate for some plan types, but that will be obvious. The financial consideration step for recognition plans, for example, is very short: "This is the investment."):

1. Restatement of the design team's charter, mission, time line, and design guidelines.
2. Statement of need and how the plan meets that need.
3. Brief overview of what is already being done and how a plan should fill any gaps that exist—for example, "It will more effectively align people with the vision, mission, and strategic objectives."
4. Overview of the plan, including:
   Theme
   Objectives
   Measures
   Organizational units covered
   Employees covered
   Plan period and payout periods
   Reward structure
5. Financial considerations, including payouts, gains (if appropriate), and return on payout. All should have minimum, most likely, and maximum scenarios.

6. Plans for education, communication, promotion, employee involvement, management support, and assessment.

The reward structure for a group incentive or project team incentive plan is best explained through examples, just as if you were explaining it to the rank and file, using a chart that states the measures, baseline and goal (if appropriate), and the earning opportunity for each level of performance. Assume a level of performance for a payout period by measure, and calculate the payout.

You should provide top management with a financial scenario—minimum, most likely, and maximum.

Presenting the Financial Rationale of a Group or Project Team Incentive Plan   It is important that top management's understanding and expectations of the financial aspects of the plan be as realistic as possible. I strongly recommend that you provide a minimum, most likely, and maximum scenario. The financial member of the design team is the most appropriate person to present this message. Providing a minimum, most likely, and maximum gain, as well as payout and return estimates, reinforces the idea that the more you pay, the more you get. This tends not to be a hard sell in sales commission plans, but it is reasonably hard to sell a financial rationale to nonsales managers with backgrounds in fixed budgets.

Point out the risks, as well. If there is potential for cycling, make it clear and explain how you have allowed for it in the design. If there is a financial risk with a gain that has no dollar value, point that out, but explain why you made the decision. An important message to get across is that although the plan isn't foolproof, it is a lot less risky than the average business plan. You don't pay out until you have the performance improvement.

What You Want from Top Management   What you want from top management is their full support. That includes:

1. Agreement that the plan is acceptable and can be rolled out.
2. Agreement to spend the money necessary to educate, train, communicate, and celebrate in order to make the plan work.
3. Personal commitment from each manager to become involved in the introduction and operation of the plan (which could include making references to the plan in all speeches made to employees, stockholders, and the board of directors; being present at introduction meetings and at other times throughout the plan period when performance results are delivered and celebrations of particular events are taking place).

4. Commitment to walk the talk. This means that top managers are aware of the plan, can explain it, and will support it in word and deed. This is the most critical commitment. To the degree that it is career limiting, push to get that commitment. It will save you a lot of headaches later.

5. An understanding that the approval is in general terms. Be sure they realize that you intend to introduce the plan in a consultative manner to all levels of management and that during that process, you may learn something that will improve the plan. Be sure they understand that you have the right to tweak the plan, and that if there any major changes, you will ask for approval. All changes will be confirmed to the top management team before the official rollout to the rank and file.

Get a commitment to walk the talk.

Taking the Plan Down the Ladder

Once you have top management approval, you begin the process of educating the entire management team and developing their ownership of the plan. In most plans that affect employees, everyone hears about the plan at the same time. That is not the way to introduce recognition and group-based plans. In spite of the widespread flattening that has occurred in organizations, most still have a hierarchical structure. It is extremely important that each employee's direct manager be an authority on the plan.

Each employee's direct manager should be an authority on the plan.

Management Ownership, Education, and Involvement

The plan is introduced in a series of meetings with management. The type of meeting is a function of the plan type; recognition plans may not even need a meeting. I will discuss recognition plan introduction later in this chapter, but the following discussion will focus on group or project team incentive plan introductions. Meetings for these plans should be smaller (30 to 40 maximum) and in larger organizations, every attempt should be made to keep peer management levels together. Meetings with managers will vary in length, depending on how much you want to accomplish and what level of management you are addressing. Meetings commonly run about two hours for higher levels of management. For lower-level managers, meetings typically run for a full morning or afternoon.

Have your champion or her designate from the top management team introduce the plan at each level of management. This person should not be from the design team. After the introduction, a member of the design team can then explain the plan.

If you are going from location to location, it is important to engage local managers early in the process so they can become your on-site spokespersons. In organizations that have people in several locations, the general manager at each site needs to understand, own, and be involved in the plan so that he can be a viable local champion.

Organizations tend to over-explain plans at first. Give it time.

Give everybody a packet with the basic plan outline and places for notes. The explanations should be short and to the point and should include highlights of the plan, an explanation of the structure, and brief examples. You do not have to provide a complete explanation of the plan at this point. Organizations tend to over-explain plans at first. Give it time. It will take a few meetings for managers to really understand your plan.

The more you reinforce familiar key business drivers, the quicker the explanatory process will go. The critical point is to make sure that everyone understands the measures. How the plan will use measures and what those measures include are critical.

When the explanation is complete, use a blank flip chart and draw a line down the middle. On the left side write, "What I like about the plan" and on the right side write, "My concerns." Then ask people to volunteer their likes and concerns while you write them down without comment. This list should be as long as they can make it.

In the event that the group is made up of different levels of management, you can use a version of the nominal group technique. Give everyone a piece of paper and ask them to write down all of their likes and concerns. Have fun with this. You are looking for quantity, not quality. Now go around the room and ask each person to read something off their own list. If that concern also appears on anyone else's list, it is crossed off. The process continues until every list is exhausted.

The next step is to process the concerns. (You do not need to do anything with the likes.) There are three objectives:

1. To air concerns. Quite often they come from a misunderstanding of the plan. It is common for peers to convince others in the meeting that their concerns are unfounded or can be

addressed. You may discover problems you had not considered. It is better to find them out now and make corrections than to introduce a flawed plan.

2. To identify obstacles that will inadvertently be put in the way of the plan by the management team without their even realizing it. This is a subtle objective that requires creative listening. You may also find that a concern mirrors an obstacle created by the organization's culture, history, or management tradition, or by the nature of the business. I find that concerns of perceived loss of control are commonly expressed as, "How do I reward my outstanding performers?" These will have to be taken into consideration as time goes on.

3. To get a laundry list of messages that will need to be communicated to the organization. This is the most subtle objective. You are merely ferreting out educational needs and identifying obstacles that could get in the way of the plan's success. Examples are a previous bad experience with a reward plan; a lack of first-line supervisory communications skills; a lack of understanding of a particular measurement; and so forth.

After the concerns have been identified and most of them alleviated, you may find that you need an additional step in the training of managers to operate the plan.

If the project team incentive plan is in support of a team idea process or you are adding awards to existing ad hoc projects or continuous improvement teams, it will be necessary to train managers on the technical details of operating the plan. Team idea plans require training evaluation committees, resource managers, and team sponsors, each with their own unique responsibilities. Ad hoc or continuous improvement teams are continually beginning and ending. Generally, line management will work with the design committee to establish the measures and rewards for their performance.

In every case I've seen, people get more genuinely committed as they work through this ownership process. As they become more involved, you will need to put up another blank flip chart to record ways the plan can be used as a tool for management. When managers begin to connect with the plan, they see how they can use it to reinforce what they need to accomplish.

Once you have completed the process of looking at concerns and likes and uncovering management tools, it's time to ask people to work through some exercises. Give them an example and ask them, If this is accomplished, what will the payout be? Generally two or three exercises are enough to help them see exactly how the program will work. Don't skip this step. Everyone may understand the concept of the plan, but not everyone can work through an example. If they can't, they will not be able to explain it to others.

The Special Role of First-Line Supervisors

As you go through the education and ownership meetings, you are creating champions at every level of authority in the organization. First-line supervisors, however, are perhaps your most important client after top management. This may seem obvious, but data show that organizations tend to stop the educational process at middle management. First-line supervisors often hear about it when it is introduced to the rank and file. That is a mistake.

First-line supervisors are the unsung heroes of recognition and group-based plans.

The CARS data discussed in Chapter Two clearly show that first-line supervisors are some of the most influential people in any organization. In fact, they may be the unsung heroes of recognition and group-based plans. In nearly all cases in the CARS study, first-line supervisors were the least involved managers, but their involvement in plan results was strong. The CARS research is focused solely on group incentive plans, but it makes sense for recognition and project team incentive plans as well. To the majority of employees, the first-line supervisor represents the organization. If the first-line supervisor does not fully own and support the plan, employees are not going to see very much value in it either.

Introducing All Employees to Recognition Plans

Recognition plans also require management education and ownership development. Here again, the degree to which management education is required depends on the recognition plan design. Remember that the role of recognition is to reinforce all performance improvement processes.

Because recognition plans are after-the-fact, all-employee meetings are rarely held. The responsibility for these plans is primarily in the hands of management. General announcements of the various things to be recognized are published in the company's newsletter, and if necessary, forms of nomination are distributed to all employees with complete instructions.

Celebrating Objectives   The celebration of organizational objectives does not require a good deal of education. Celebrations are event-driven and organized and operated by committees. Reinforcement of activities demands only slightly more education to ensure that management understands which activities support the strategic objectives and how they can be appropriately recognized. These celebrations are usually handled by staff or the recognition plan coordinating committee.

Extraordinary People   Celebrating extraordinary people who happen to be employees requires a fair amount of management education, which is best handled through short, to-the-point, on-the-spot meetings with managers, or through written communications that explain that recognizing truly extraordinary people reinforces the whole process. Managers need to understand that this is not a typical employee-of-the-month plan. It is not time-based. They can nominate employees at any time for any reason—for their accomplishments both inside and outside the company.

If peers are allowed to nominate each other for recognition, the same type of education and tools are given to them. Managers must communicate with the selected employees to get their approval for public recognition. This requires education, since managers don't normally think that some people might find it embarrassing or uncomfortable to be singled out.

Spot Bonuses for Desired and Demonstrated Behaviors   Spot bonuses are easily integrated into performance management and special management development training. It is particularly common for spot bonus plans to be introduced at the same time as any of the other individual compensation plans, because they can be so supportive of those plans.

Managers need to be thoroughly trained to administer spot bonuses. When the spot bonus is delivered as a check or some other currency, managers need to follow all the rules laid out in the behavioral model (Chapter Five). They need to explain clearly and precisely why they are saying thank you, and they need to deliver the bonus personally. They also need to understand that they are reinforcing the process, and that it is socially acceptable for supervisors to thank employees, even though it has not been so in the past. Remember those tough-minded managers who thought people should assume they were doing things right until they were told otherwise? Spot bonuses reverse that management style, and in some cases the communication and education process is difficult.

Recognizing Service and Needs of Employees   These elements of recognition are generally mailed out as an introduction to the employee population and that's okay. They are elements of the plan that rely on awareness, rather than action. One exception is the introduction of flexible benefits, which requires much the same process as introducing a group incentive plan.

The 3M Company did an admirable job of rolling out a flexible benefit plan that provides a good example. Rather than introducing the plan with a three-ring binder mailed to each employee, 3M engaged an outside agency to provide technical backup. They involved educational and training specialists. Communications specialists wrote and designed the introductory package that explained the plan, overcame objections, and engaged people in the process. The agency made the communications fun and interesting. They helped improve the organizational design by creating a subset of the organization that was responsible for the plan in each of 3M's many locations to deliver the new flexible benefit process. They communicated and promoted the plan after the initial introduction as if it were a marketing campaign.

The 3M plan was immensely successful and far less error-ridden than most rollouts of this type. Now, each year when the plan is adjusted, 3M goes through the same process using the same specialists to create a sense of ownership in management and make it clear to them that the plan is a critical cost-management tool. The employee education process continually explains to people the greater flexibility and freedom that are available through the benefits plan. This has been a very powerful process for the 3M Company, one that they treat as a business strategy and not as a benefit plan.

Benefits are on the opposite side of the reinforcement model from recognition and group-based plans. If the 3M approach worked for an entitlement like flexible benefits, then creative education, ownership, and introductions will be even more powerful with recognition and group-based plans.

Introducing All Employees to a Group Incentive Plan

Just as in any other business strategy, the most important element of introducing a group incentive plan is educating and developing ownership in all managers. It is vitally important to take the plans to each level of management, explain them, answer concerns, uncover and meet obstacles, and discover management tools. People who are more comfortable with a "write it up and send it out" approach may find this introduction difficult, costly, and over-kill. However, if these plans are treated as another entitlement, they will never receive the kind of emphasis, focus, and engagement that are necessary for their successful implementation. With the proper support, they can engender ownership and engage people in the process of performance improvement.

In introducing a group incentive plan, you are likely to notice that the lower you go in the organization, the more time you will need for education on the measures—how they are calculated and how the baselines and goals were set. You may be concerned about explaining to employees how they can influence the measures, particularly in plans with a longer LoS. Managers will begin to take the plan personally—to own it—and see the value of engaging their people in it. The engagement has to occur at the first-line supervisory level.

Ownership takes place when all of management can say to their people, "Here are our objectives. Do we understand the measurements? Do we understand baseline and how we are going to be rewarded? More importantly, how can we affect the results? What can we do individually, as a work group, or as a department, to affect measurements that may not be rewarded themselves but that may contribute to overall performance?"

Group incentive plans are a statement of what influence the organization feels all employees can have in improving business performance. The importance of that message is reflected in the way it is introduced to all employees.

A conservative drug company used a passive approach to presenting a plan. The plan took more than two years to design. It was announced with a letter from the CEO and a brief description. The information packet was sent to all managers and employees at the same time. An 800 number was set up to answer questions. Out of four thousand employees, nine called. The company was committed to the plan, but the introduction reflected their unexpressed bias—this plan was a nice thing to do, and the rank and file can't really make a difference. And they didn't. Such plans fall into the dead squirrel plan category. A lot of noise, then a disturbing silence.

Eventually, in a more successful approach, the plan was introduced in a series of employee meetings, after the management education and ownership process was completed. The CEO made the formal presentation in twelve meetings to all three shifts. There was time for questions, which were answered by the CEO, the line managers who were present, and the design team representatives. Employees worked through an example using a bound notebook and pen that were imprinted with the plan's theme. The example was on the back of a commitment card. The commitment cards had room for employees to write what they thought they could do to make the plan successful. Each employee signed a card and dropped it in a barrel when they left the room. A drawing was held, and at the next break in the meeting, an announcement was made over the PA system about whose names were drawn and what they had won.

Kickoff meetings can be as elaborate or as simple as you wish. They may include video messages from an absent CEO; an audio-visual presentation reviewing the history and success of the company, complete with candid photos taken the previous week of employees at work; door prizes; drawing entries taped under the seats; coffee and doughnuts—whatever reflects your culture and the emphasis you want everyone to put on the plan.

The longest kickoff meeting I've seen was forty-five minutes, and it could have been done in thirty. You do not have to tell people every little detail of the plan. Ask yourself, "What do they need to know now? What are the five learning points critical to starting the process?" Usually, they are:

- The business reasons for the plan

- The measures, baselines, and goals

- What employees can earn at goal

- How often the plan will be measured and payouts made

- How committed the organization is to the plan

Everything else can be explained later. It is best, anyway, for the details to come from the employee's own first-line supervisor rather than from someone else.

First-line supervisors must go through the ownership process with their employees after a group incentive plan is introduced. The introduction and education process for first-line supervisors should therefore include training that teaches them how to engage their people in the discussion that will develop this ownership.

Presenting examples of measurements and earnings is the key to developing employee ownership of a group incentive plan. Once a measure is explained, the first-line supervisor asks her people to come up with their own ways to improve on the measurements. The supervisor needs to know how to lead them in that process and how to encourage them to step out of their individual job roles and see the measures from other angles. That's how they become engaged in the process.

In some plans, the supervisor uses a version of the nominal group technique to gather ideas from the employees. These ideas are captured on a flip chart and forwarded to the design team (or the on-site coordinating committee) after the plan is introduced. The team uses this input for ongoing communications and to remind people what they can do to improve. More about that later in the chapter.

You may have noticed that this process looks somewhat like the cascading MBO process (see Chapter Three). The difference is that this process is more meaningful and concrete, because you are going to reward for specific and measurable improvements. You are getting people to start thinking about how their behavior can affect results. If you can prepare and train supervisors to work with their people in this way, you will have come a long way toward implementing a successful plan.

Introducing Employees to Project Team Incentive Plans

I wouldn't recommend introducing two plans, particularly a group incentive and a project team incentive plan, at the same time. It is too much. If you decide to do both, introduce the group incentive plans first, followed by the project team incentive plan a couple of months later. Most recognition plans can be introduced at any time. I'll describe the most popular version of the project team incentive plan, the team idea process. Like any intervention that gives an organization a high return on its investment, this one requires a major introduction effort. The effort includes establishing teams, training, organizing for operations, and becoming familiar with the available resources. Whether short-term or long-term versions, the introduction of the team idea process requires the action and direct support of the first-line supervisors, who are usually assigned to team sponsor roles or to evaluation committees. The supervisors' role is to encourage their direct reports to participate.

The kickoff meeting is more of an informational rally than anything else. It is a time to crank up excitement and start people off in the right direction. The meeting focuses on the process of creating an idea and all the steps through implementation. Kits covering all aspects of the process are distributed. Questions are answered. The process manager, information coordinator, and team sponsors are introduced, and the members of the evaluation committees are named. The formation of teams, whether functional or cross-functional, is coordinated through the process manager and team sponsors.

Implementation of the team idea process tends to be somewhat more technical than implementation of group incentive or recognition plans. The education, engagement, and ownership issues are reasonably sophisticated because there are so many definitions of costs and how they are evaluated and what they affect. However, implementation is a process that generates, as I've said, tremendous returns for the organization. It also presents an opportunity to educate and to directly engage everyone in the organization.

Inside or Outside Job?

Some organizations work with consultants or outside agencies to implement group incentive plans, and some don't. Most use performance improvement agencies to administer project team incentive plans. It all depends on the amount of time, money, and staff the organization is willing to devote to the process. Project team incentive plans, particularly team idea plans, are probably about the only plans you should not try to implement alone. (There is little reason to reinvent the necessary support systems.)

I have found that almost everyone believes they can implement a plan themselves, and technically they can. They just need to make sure there are enough resources to facilitate the education, ownership, management involvement, and plan introduction processes. Staff organizations and human resource, compensation, organizational development, and communications departments are logical choices for implementation. All come with their own baggage, however, which often needs to be packed differently for a business strategy trip than one that simply tweaks entitlements. The biggest problem for participants is finding time to focus. Most people are loaded with work and special projects. If implementation of a plan is the fifty-first thing to do on a manager's list of fifty, it will not be properly supported.

Since recognition and group-based plans probably are not your core business, much can be gained from the cumulative experience of outside agencies and consultants that administer this type of plan on an ongoing basis. There are a number of capable and experienced consultants and agencies around. Finding the one that can package your plan and make it affordable and flexible is a challenge. Whether you administer the plan yourself or work with outsiders, expect to invest some funds into the implementation and operation of the plan. Nothing worthwhile comes cheaply.

If implementation of a plan is the fifty-first thing to do on a manager's list of fifty, it will not be properly supported.

And Then There Are OBM Organizations

I've already said that this chapter does not apply to open-book management companies. I include them here anyway to make a point about education—specifically, financial literacy, which is the heart and soul of OBM. Teaching everyone how to play the game starts with teaching them how to keep score. It takes some time. Jack Stack of Springfield Remanufacturing Company says that it takes a year. John Schewe, president of Merrill Distributing in Merrill, Wisconsin, did it in six months. Nothing accelerates adult learning like an incentive plan based on the very thing you're teaching. OBM companies introduce everything at once and spend the rest of the time working out the process—and counting the money.

In companies that don't practice OBM, education is equally important. The literacy applies to all aspects of the measures of success—lead, operational, and lag—and they must all be made crystal clear to all employees.

Operation of Recognition and Group-Based Plans

Recognition and group-based plans are marching orders, not paperwork systems. They are proactive from their introduction to their reassessment. They are a call to action, requiring flair and creativity. They must say to employees: This is the way we're going to do business. These are the things on which we're going to focus. This is management's role, and here is how employees can take advantage of this dynamic process.

No plan will run itself. Introducing the plan and expecting line management to integrate it into their daily work lives is unrealistic. Management's culture must shift, as must the culture of the rank and file. When it's everybody's job, it's nobody's. The most promising candidates for running a group incentive plan are the members of the design team, if they are not too burned out. Top management is clearly the steering committee for the plan, as they have been all along, but they won't make the plan run smoothly.

The CARS research reported that the group incentive plans are generally administered by the HR department, but I suspect they simply handle the mechanics—check issuance, and so forth. The plan needs an operational committee. In plans with a number of physical locations, the design team often takes responsibility for coordinating the plan, with site coordinating teams responsible for all the work for their site.

The model for project team incentive plans includes a steering committee because of the number of teams and the structure necessary to make them work. Even when team idea plans are integrated with continuous improvement teams, their administration requires a process manager and an information coordinator. Recognition plans are generally run by the HR department or a recognition coordinating committee.

Operating a Group Incentive Plan

Let's assume that the organization has appointed an operating committee for the plan, with representatives selected much like the design team was selected—if indeed it is not the design team itself. Most important, someone must be responsible for the measurements and collection of data, for turning it into performance feedback. People must know as often as possible how the plan is going, regardless of the number of payout periods. I recommend that someone from management information systems (MIS) be the performance-tracking person.

This person must be capable of collecting the information necessary to run the plan and delivering it back in an appropriate (immediate) time frame. This person's ability to gather that information and translate it into the earning opportunities or actual earnings of the participants is the heart of a successful recognition and group-based plan. It is not unusual for plan measures to be an accumulation of a series of other measures or excerpts from a more complex one. Therefore, all the components of the measurement on which the rewards are going to be made must be streamlined to flow into one measure for constant feedback and reinforcement.

Don't Delay Feedback   The collection of measurement data and the preparation of feedback have traditionally not been done with a sense of urgency. What gets measured gets managed, and what gets rewarded gets done—and gets a lot of attention. Measurement for reward purposes needs track shoes. Delay violates a critical element of positive reinforcement—immediacy; it reduces the performance-reward linkage, which in turn lengthens the LoS; and it reduces the ability to take immediate corrective action if there is a problem. The data are almost always in the system but are just being used for things other than performance measurements. Get into the system and short circuit it to get what you need. If you are measuring productivity, you just need the output and input numbers. Nothing else. They are generally available, in some form, soon after the measurement period, but they are being used for scheduling, performance against budget calculations and reports, inventory control, and so on. You don't care about all of that now. You just want what you need for the plan's measures. Get it quickly, and you've gotten your performance feedback.

> *Measurement for reward purposes needs track shoes.*

Anything longer than a week after the measurement period ends is too long. Set your turnaround goal, engage others in brainstorming how to get the information more quickly, process it, put it on charts or flyers, and get it out—all within a week if your payout period is monthly, two weeks if it is quarterly.

Don't Delay Payout   The same need for immediacy applies to issuing payouts. When the data for the payout period are ready to put on the charts, the checks should be ready to be cut. Whether cash checks from payroll or point checks from a special system or an agency, they should be in the hands of the employees as soon after the end of the payout period as possible—along with a communication piece explaining the results and how they were calculated, and a reminder of the rules. (All noncash incentive agencies provide these services, and companies are well advised to use these outside sources for this process. The agencies generally have computer software that will allow their clients to produce the checks themselves.) Obviously, the groundwork must be laid before the plan is introduced to the employees. Start buying lunch for the systems people early.

Sticking to the Rules   The operating committee often acts as an arbitrating body, answering questions and making rules concerning most aspects of the plan. It is important for people to understand that there are clear rules that will be followed. The following suggested rules include, but are not limited to, group incentive plans:

1. Decide how part-time employees will be handled. It is common to require them to work more than 50 percent of the time for the company and for their earnings to be prorated based on the number of hours they work.

2. Set rules for dealing with newcomers. Generally, people need to be employed for a certain number of months, usually three, before they can participate in the benefits of any incentive plan. Whether the company wishes to prorate their award based on their time served is up to the design committee. When in doubt, keep it simple.

3. Sometimes, suborganizational units such as departments or even work shifts have different measures. Decide ahead of time what happens if a person transfers from one department to another or moves to a different shift. Which measure should be used to award the individual? Having fought this battle until I lost my hair, I suggest that you stick by this hard and fast rule: Wherever a person is at the end of the measured period is where they get rewarded. It doesn't matter whether they have been there one day or all but one day of the period; they are measured and rewarded based on where they stand when the measure is taken.

4. Unique events (catastrophes or windfalls) can occur. Therefore, it is always wise to include a statement in the plan introduction saying that management reserves the right to change, alter, or stop the plan at any time for any reason, but *always within the context of being fair.* The statement should be made clear to everyone at plan introduction. The objective of the plan is to engage people in business performance. If there is an extraordinary situation that might affect those measurements, and the plan's steering committee decides to exclude the effect of the unique event, simply do not count those numbers in the measurement criteria for which you make payouts, but make sure you tell everyone what you are doing and why.

> *Wherever a person is at the end of the measured period is where they get rewarded.*

5. *Do not* change baselines during the announced plan period—or goals, or caps, or payout rates either, for that matter. Unless the baseline is designed to be a rolling average change during a program period, the structure in place at the time of introduction should stay in place throughout the plan period. Follow the rules absolutely. If the performance just misses a particular goal, do not pay out anyway. If the performance goes out of sight, pay out accordingly. If there is a windfall, handle it as I've previously suggested (in 4) above. The plan must have integrity and give people a sense of security. They must know they can rely on the consistency of the next iteration, if there is one.

6. Round off cash payouts to the nearest five dollars, or at least one dollar. Make sure you do not issue a cash check for anything less than what makes sense—I use twenty-five dollars after taxes. Of course, points can be issued without rounding; minimum amounts can be lower.

7. Any reward plan costs money, regardless of how much it may make for the organization. Therefore, it is necessary to regularly accrue for payouts. If there are monthly payouts, the accrual process probably is not necessary. Accruals for four months, six months, or one year are quite common, however. I suggest you accrue at the payout rate at goal performance. Don't get caught with your accrual bucket empty.

Accrue at the payout rate at goal performance. Don't get caught with your accrual bucket empty.

8. Make clear whether or not payouts are benefit bearing.

9. If you wish to exclude individuals on disciplinary probation or those rated at the lower end of the performance review scale, make it very clear to managers and employees alike. Do not bury it in the fine print.

10. After you talk to your lawyers about the language of the plan, a good phrase is, "The language used in this [booklet, plan explanation] should not be construed as creating a contract of employment between [the organization] and any of its employees."

11. Full disclosure is important for credibility. I like to end a plan document with a section called "Fine Print" in which I publish these program rules in large print.

Operating Project Team Incentive Plans

Many of the rules for group incentive plans often apply to project team incentive plans, but there are some significant differences.

Other rules that apply to project team incentive plans are:

1. Since project team incentive plans tend to be event driven rather than time driven, you must be able to produce checks for cash, points, or earned-credit to accounts at the time the events occur. Keep in mind that the award mechanism must remain flexible to meet the demands of the plan design.
2. Plans are commonly administered by quality improvement managers, staff managers, process managers, and sometimes HR departments.
3. If you use noncash awards, calculate the cost of taxes into the cost of the plan, as described in Chapter Ten. Do not have employees pay any taxes, and make sure they understand that they will not.

Project team incentive plans, particularly in support of a team idea process, require a significant amount of administration. It is an important process, considering that up to 90 percent of the employee population is serving on seven-person teams to create, research, and submit ideas and waiting on evaluation committees that approve or do not approve those ideas. There is software available for handling these chores. The software fee is usually calculated, however, into the cost of an agency turn-key contract for operating a team idea process. In the event that you are not working with an agency, do not underestimate the amount of paper that can be created when you engage people in making contributions. The paperwork system must enable rather than disable people. About 70 percent of the ideas and projects submitted are not approved or cannot be valued. Prepare those who do the evaluating to understand that the most important part of their job is to use the nonapproval of an idea as an opportunity to coach the team.

Operating Recognition Plans

Recognition plans have their own set of rules:

1. The HR department normally administers recognition plans, or they are controlled by people who have specifically been given that responsibility in the staff organizations—a recognition coordinating committee. If you celebrate events, make sure the event planners use an organizational objective as a theme.

2. Recognizing extraordinary people who happen to be employees requires the focus to be on communications. Because I recommend that these plans be event driven, not time bound, it is
   the responsibility of the person administering the plan to keep
   everyone—peers, both exempt and nonexempt employees, and
   managers—informed of the criteria on which nominations are
   accepted. In addition, people should be kept aware that they
   can nominate someone and people can be selected at any time.
   When there are enough nominations in the pipeline, the review
   committee chooses the appropriate people.
3. Beyond communications, administration of and accrual for
   recognition plan awards is simply a matter of cutting checks
   for cash or noncash awards.
4. Recognizing and reinforcing desired and demonstrated behaviors with spot awards work in very much the same way. In
   these cases, noncash awards are the norm and the dollar values
   are small. Simply attach a tracking mechanism to them so that
   when a check is generated (mostly by line management but
   occasionally from a central source in HR), there is some record
   that it has been issued. This way, you constantly know your lia-
   bility. An easier and more common procedure is to give each
   person a checkbook containing checks for equal amounts of
   cash or noncash points.
5. Since these plans tend to be relatively modest in size, keeping
   records for tax purposes is probably more effort than it's worth.

Communications and Plan Promotion

A recognition and group-based plan will become nothing more than
a methodology for distributing funds if it does not engage and
excite people. It will be budgeted and become an entitlement.

Communication and promotion are as important to a plan's success as is the plan's design. There is a clear distinction between
communication and promotion. Communication is a two-way
process. It answers people's questions, "What's needed?" and
"How's it going?" and it asks them the same questions. Promotion
is a one-way process that creates excitement, attention for the plan,
and the award opportunity.

Promotion and communications are ongoing. Sending out one
mailer a month just is not enough. People need to hear from you

*An annual state-of-
the-business meeting
with employees is not
enough. Quarterly or
monthly is better.*

at least every two weeks. An annual state-of-the-business meeting with employees is not enough. People need to be involved in group activities at least every quarter. Monthly is better. If that sounds overwhelming, just remember that you are activating another asset to improve the success of the plan.

Communication

Communications reinforce the basic tenets of the plan. Take every opportunity to re-explain it. Organizations assume that because a plan has been explained to employees once during a kickoff meeting, it is somehow deeply rooted in their psyches. All that needs to be done is to remind them periodically of what they already know. That has not been my experience. Employees may understand the plan, but being able to take appropriate action and connect with the measures is quite another thing.

What's Needed   A properly introduced group incentive plan does not give all the information at once. It takes the time to give people what they need when they need it. Focus groups and feedback from the supervisor's kickoff meetings can supply what else is needed; when teams need information, they have their team sponsors get it for them. Project team incentive plans, particularly in support of a team idea process, involve people to such a great degree that communication is natural.

With desktop publishing, color printers, and the multitude of agency reps available, there is no excuse for boring communications.

Most people think of company communications as simple, simply boring mailers in their in-boxes. You probably get so much business junk mail that most of it ends up in the trash or the recycling bin. I remember communications at General Electric many years ago being printed on a mimeograph machine. They were always slightly askew on the page, and there are probably still corners of paragraphs floating around out in the mimeograph ether because they never made it onto the page. These communications were difficult to create and seldom exciting to read. Today, with desktop publishing, color printers, and the multitude of agency reps standing outside the front door waiting to put together the perfect communications package, there is no excuse for boring communications.

Communications for recognition and group-based plans have to be attractive and easy to read. You are competing for a share of your employees' minds. Use color, clever design, unusual die cuts, or even simple black and white, but use them in a way that will attract people's attention in an in-box sea of dull gray.

- Use bullet points wherever possible.

- Fewer words are better.

- Write in plain language.

As for content, the bulk of communications should be dedicated to sharing with employees what they can do to improve performance. If the introduction has been rolled out as described earlier in this chapter, there should be a plethora of ideas from people on how they can affect the appropriate payout measures. Taking this information and translating it into project opportunities and individual actions provides more than enough fodder to continually remind people that they can make a difference.

Making Communications Interactive   Most writers of internal business communications complain that people do not absorb the things they read. People don't understand them, take them to heart, and make their ideas an integral part of their day-to-day work. There is the opportunity, however, with recognition and group-based plan communications to touch people. Interactive communications and feedback provide a chance for employees to absorb these day-to-day, week-to-week communications and make them part of their work life.

Create a mailer on a series of ideas for improving customer satisfaction. In it, you remind people of the plan rules and how customer satisfaction is measured. When you send out the mailer, you include a tear-off card that can be sent back. On the card, you print questions about the plan. Every returned card is thrown into a hat for a drawing. You include on the card any questions that reinforce the primary tenets of the plan: proper definitions of measurement, what the more global measurements mean to individuals at the work group level, and how much each employee will make if the current performance trend continues.

It is becoming more common for recognition and group-based plan communications to be sent directly to employees' homes. They get a good deal more attention that way, since they are one of the few business communications that are sent outside the work setting. What's more, they engage the family, particularly if the reward is a noncash award from a catalogue or a travel opportunity. The entire family has the opportunity to be involved in goal setting that has a powerful, if not so subtle, influence on the employed family member's contribution to the organization.

Communication and Culture: An Example

The spirit of these plans lies in developing a sense of corporate citizenship and teamwork. The role of communications varies based on how far and where the organization needs to go. Consider GS Technologies (formally Armco Worldwide Grinding Systems) of Kansas City. They had experienced a series of layoffs, and the relationship between management and the union was terrible. They were in such bad shape that there was even some question about keeping the plant open.

The need to reduce costs was of paramount importance, so management decided to introduce a team idea process, supported by a project team incentive. The process had little chance of success with the prevailing distrust. This distrust became a reason to launch a communications strategy, with the full cooperation of the union, to reduce the barriers among employees and between management and labor.

Many of the employees had been with the company for more than forty years. Old habits and attitudes ran deep. There was also a legacy of family members who had followed in their mothers' and fathers' footsteps into the company, and many of them had the same attitudes as their parents.

The first step of the communications plan was designed to help the people in the organization get to know each other on a more personal level. Photographs and a personal story, often written by a peer or family member, appeared in a special calendar. Each month, a different employee was featured and his or her story told, always with the permission of the individual. Some of the stories told of men and women conquering alcoholism. Others told of people mending relationships with family members. Still others talked about someone's dedication to the company, often a great surprise to everyone who knew the person. Many of the stories were very touching.

Employees began to see each other as more than just the woman who worked at the next machine, the man who shared a common break time, or the manager who was the enemy. The program also softened up management, which began to realize that they were dealing with people who just happened to be employees, people with many of the same concerns that management had. As a result of telling their stories and through their newfound ability to communicate with each other, the people also contributed ideas that were practical, intelligent, . . . and used.

As the process continued, there were meetings that for the first time were not battlegrounds; union and management fought less over grievances and more about mutual concerns. A "quality of work life" approach to business took hold in the company. Unlike the heavily ballyhooed programs of the early 1980s, whose primary claim to fame was to set up negotiations prior to regular union/management meetings on contracts and grievances, this process focused on creating a team of individuals for a common good. In fact, it worked so well that employees signed their names to a dedication-of-commitment document that was published as a full-page ad in the local newspaper.

A brochure was designed called "A Day in the Life. . . ." This was another effort to get people to know each other better. It included, again, photographs and stories. People told what they did and how they felt about the company, and shared their personal tales. Tensions between the union and management continued to lessen.

And then the company introduced the team idea process. It was designed to save money, save the plant, and improve the relationships between management and the rank and file. The company held celebrations and promotions. Communications increased, improving people's understanding of the business and why it did what it did. This prepared the way for a local management buyout in which the plant became its own entity.

The spirit created by this plan continues today. Both the union and management, as well as the few nonunion employees, agree that it was the dynamic communication and promotion process that helped to break down the barriers. And it was the project team incentive plan that showed the rank and file that management was serious about involving them in improving performance. Nothing dispels lack of trust like management saying they are going to do something and the employees seeing tangible results.

How's It Going?   It is common to have state-of-the-company meetings for all employees, usually once a year. A recognition and group-based plan provides an opportunity for those meetings to be more frequent. OBM preaches constant reviewing of the financial measures of the business to reinforce the financial literacy training and as a part of involving all employees in the business of the business. Monthly meetings with a review of sales, costs, cash flow, productivity, quality, and safety—focusing on those included in the plan—are face-to-face performance feedback. Information about the market, competition, projects, major sales, and losses is also shared. If a work group can carry the spirit and the data of those meetings into a follow-up question-and-answer meeting, they become even more powerful.

Employee performance feedback related specifically to the plan is relatively simple, but it can be delivered in creative ways. Performance feedback continually lets people know where they stand on measurements on which rewards are based, as well as other supportive measurements. Charts and bulletins can be used to tell the story. Post them in the cafeteria, e-mail them, include them in biweekly mailers, and ask first-line managers to share them with employees. A number of organizations use sophisticated videos to keep up an ongoing dialogue with employees. These systems are a great way to let people know what's needed, how they're doing, and how they can affect business performance.

The Other Half of Communications: Listening   The least practiced art in business is listening. It certainly is seldom practiced in recognition and group-based plans, which is a shame. Listening is cheap, effective, and educational. The two critical questions, "What's needed?" and "How's it going?" take on a whole new meaning when the answers come from the rank and file.

> *The least practiced art in business is listening.*

As a part of the regular supervisory meeting with employees to discuss how the plan is doing, the employees need to be asked the two critical questions. In group incentive plans, the answers are captured by the manager and fed back to the design or coordinating committee. In project team incentive plans, plan coordinators receive the information from managers and supervisors. In the team idea process, the team sponsors and, hopefully, mentors listen to what the employees think and feed it back to the process manager.

Focus groups run by an outside firm or the plan's management team can be used in any type of plan. They are particularly effective with recognition plans in which a more spontaneous, impressionistic input is necessary. Surveys are also applicable to all plans. In any case, there should always be a survey just after a plan begins and a couple of weeks before the end of the plan period. The survey does not have to be particularly complex, but it should be designed to capture the general feeling about the plan, how the organization is responding to the new employee citizenship, and how the plan can be improved.

Promotion

The objective of promotion is to keep the plans on the top of everyone's mind. Banners, displays, company product fairs, special events for charity, coffee cups, hats, pencils, imprints on cafeteria napkins, photos of teams at work, requests for help in a newsletter, all celebrations, and most meetings can contribute to promotion of the plan.

I find that getting a group of creative people together to brainstorm ideas for promotion is the fastest and easiest way. Have fun with it. Reward it. Use it. The promotion team can poll their peers, visit other operations, and do research in business publications and books obtained through the company or public library. They make out a list of promotion activities ordered by month, cost them out, and recommend action to the design or coordinating team.

Employees also can be asked to write newsletters or columns for existing communications about their experiences with and views of the plan. If they don't want to write, get a freelance writer (they are readily available at reasonable prices) or one of your communication people to do interviews and write them up.

One of the most creative promotions I've seen was done with homemade videos produced by employees on their own time. They told about what they were doing to influence measurements. The videos were shown in the cafeteria, and people had fun viewing them just as the creators did when they made them. Another company showed all of the videos in a large auditorium. Every group who participated in making a video was recognized and received a round of applause as well as symbolic awards. (If you do this, watch out. It is tempting to want to judge the best of the videos, or the funniest, or the most creative, but that is not in the spirit of what they are intended to accomplish. Remember, the goal is collective competition—employees as a group competing in the marketplace, not among themselves within the company. This plan is designed to unify the workforce toward common objectives. You might simply tell employees that anyone who submits a video—as long as it's in keeping with the style of the plan and not lewd—will get an award.)

Promoting the Award   Cash awards require a lot of promotion because they have a specific value in the minds of the recipients and it is difficult to make them exciting. As an example, promoting the reward at goal as the equivalent of a week's wage adds to its appeal.

Promotion of noncash awards is much easier and considerably more powerful. Noncash awards allow the promotion of VCRs, televisions, travel, dinners at local restaurants, or tickets to rock concerts. A catalogue itself is a good promotion device, particularly if it is sent to the employee's home so family members can browse through it, too. Catalogue buying has become quite popular, as you have probably noticed, based on the number of unsolicited catalogues you receive in the mail. People like shopping by mail or TV. Therefore, many award plans include not only the basic "wish book" of items, but they also include catalogues from popular companies like Eddie Bauer or The Sharper Image. Noncash awards appeal to a wide range of people, are limited only by the imagination of the plan developers, and can add considerable spice and fun to any plan.

At the Maritz Travel Company, employees regularly participate in theme days based on a particular destination—Ireland, Italy, or Australia, for example. They are served ethnic foods, watch folk dancers, or in the case of a Bavarian theme day, consume a fair amount of beer. Casual dress days, impromptu pizza parties, or afternoon joke breaks can all be used to promote the improvement process. Any activity that is different from "work-as-usual" changes the humdrum to fun and gets people involved. *1001 Ways to Reward Your Employees* by Bob Nelson (1994) has some great promotional ideas, especially in the "Fun/Celebrations" section. Check it out.

Make Payout Time an Event   Payout time is an opportunity for communication *and* promotion. By all means, give payouts in a separate check, statement, or award-point check. The award needs to stand apart from base pay compensation. Always put the award in a separate envelope. Give the envelope flair. Make it a different color. Put a message on it.

Set up booths for check distribution and combine it with a celebration, anything from coffee and donuts to a picnic. I know a CEO who has a stack of checks (in this case everyone got the same amount) and hands them out, with her thanks, to each of the people at the event. This is a great time for people to talk with top management. It is also an opportunity for managers to give informal state-of-the-company presentations and make people aware of the importance of the award mechanism.

Reassessment

Reassessment is a key element in recognition and group-based plans, for symbolic as well as technical reasons. Symbolically, reassessment sends a message that the plan is not an entitlement. Recognition and group-based plans have a communication/feedback/reward system built in that *makes* them—by definition—everybody's job. They have limited life cycles, and based on their success they can be reintroduced as is or modified, or they can be stopped altogether. That is understood up front. The reassessment process determines the fate of the plan.

Who reassesses the plan? I was surprised to find in the CARS research that HR was a major player in plan reassessment. While 83 percent of the group incentive plans were designed with the help of an employee design team, only about a third of the plans that were reassessed utilized the design team. It seems as if it would make more sense to give the reassessment task to the team that designed or operated the plan, since they are most familiar with it. Some organizations also appoint separate implementation and reassessment teams.

When should the plan be reassessed? Reassessment should be an ongoing process that constantly tells you how you're doing. If you pay out monthly, you can be reasonably sure of how your plan is working; but if you pay out annually, don't wait until the end of the period to assess your progress. Ideally, you should reassess, or at least review, your plan each quarter and keep constant watch on trends. The final reassessment takes place during the last three months before the end of the plan period. (Table 11.1 lists the types of plans discussed in this book and the reassessment timing recommended for each of them.)

Reporting Reassessment Results to Management

Reassessment is the only way to give top management the answer to the "Was it worth it?" question. The presentation to top management of the results of reassessment can be divided into three parts. The first part is a technical look at the plan. It should be based on hard numbers as much as possible—how did the plan measure up? The second part of the presentation revisits the reward plan effectiveness guidelines provided in Chapter Four. The third

TABLE 11.1. *Recommended Frequency of Reassessment.*

PLAN TYPE	REASSESSMENT
Recognition	Every year, although the intent is to run these plans continuously.
Group incentive	Every plan period, usually once a year.
Project Team Incentive:	
Short-term idea process	One year after the idea generation phase is over; usually sixteen months from kickoff.
Long-term idea process	Every year, although the intent is to run these plans continuously.
Continuous quality improvement teams	Every year, although the intent is to run these plans continuously.
Ad hoc project teams	Not necessary; assessment naturally occurs after the end of the project.

part provides anecdotal and survey feedback from managers and employees.

Introduce the presentation by restating the objectives of the plan. Include a look at the plan design and the financial rationale. You are reminding top management of what they approved.

The results of a group incentive plan are delivered as cost (payouts and other associated costs), dollar value of the gains, and a gross and net return on plan cost. Attempt to estimate how much of the gain is a direct result of the plan. That's a hard number to determine in group incentive plans, but ask yourself what else would have caused the improvement. What's different during the plan period relative to the baseline period?

The reassessment discussion is much easier in project team incentive plans. Gains can be attributed to the teams' efforts, including gains that cannot be valued in dollars. These improvements may be even more important than the return calculation.

It's difficult to know if gains from any plan will make it to the bottom line, but you should try. The degree to which you can relate the plan's performance to the performance of the organizational unit will determine how justified you can be in recommending continuing, changing, or stopping the plan.

Did the Plan Move You in the Right Direction? To prepare for the next part of the presentation, turn back to Chapter Four and assess the current plan(s) based on the guidelines presented there. The reward plan effectiveness model, you will remember, is a function of direction and power. Direction is defined as supporting the business objectives and desired culture. Power is a product of awareness, value, and performance sensitivity.

Has the plan moved the organization closer to its desired culture? Are you closer to what you want to be—more caring/paternalistic, integrative/high involvement, or exacting/demanding? This is a judgment call, but it can be validated through focus groups, surveys, and anecdotes.

Has the plan aligned employees more closely with the strategic objectives of the organization? Do employees understand more about the objectives and their measurements? Have they been able to affect the measures of a group incentive plan and/or a project team incentive plan? Again, the answers to these questions come from focus groups, surveys, and anecdotes.

Is there a high degree of awareness among employees about the plan? Is it top-of-mind? This is an element of the power of the plan. Awareness can be determined through surveys. For group incentive plans, it can be measured by the number of communication pieces created and distributed—and the amount of feedback received as a result of those communications. What was the participation in the promotions? Awareness of project team incentive plans is a pure function of participation and activity. Recognition plan awareness is a function of the number of objectives celebrated, activities reinforced, extraordinary people nominated and selected, and spot awards given out.

Is the plan valued by employees and the organization? Was the effort worth the reward to the employees? You've already determined the value to the organization in the financial and performance results analysis.

Is the plan's structure sensitive to performance levels? This is a quality of the design, but what is important is the perception of the employees. If they think it didn't reinforce increasing performance with appropriately increasing awards, that's information to use. Surveys and focus groups are the only way to gauge perceptions.

Anecdotal and Survey Feedback Are Critical The final part of the presentation gives top management anecdotal feedback based on input from managers and employees. This feedback is collected throughout the plan period. Examples include a customer satisfaction process changed by a continuous quality improvement team and how they were rewarded or recognized; the team idea that saved $100,000; a story like the one about Mildred and the storage company. These stories are the personal experiences of employees acting and talking like contributing stakeholders and showing a new concern for their internal and external customers.

Your goal is to find out what employees did differently as a result of the plan, and how change, if any, has occurred in their understanding of what is important to the company. The following topics, questions, and techniques are consistent with (and should be compared to) those considered in the assessment phase of the process, presented in Chapter Four. They are asked of all employees covered by the plan. Note that some items will not apply to certain plans:

- Request a list of the company objectives and the measures that reflect those objectives.

- Ask the following:
  Has the understanding of the objectives changed?
  Has the understanding of the measures changed?
  Has the communication with your manager changed?
  Has communication with peers changed on organizational issues?
  Has getting the information needed to do the job changed?
  Do people feel appreciated as contributors?
  Do people feel the plan was fair?
  Do people think others listened to their ideas?
  Has the trust level in management changed?
  Has appreciation of the internal and external customer changed?
  Did employees think they could influence the measures?
  Do they think their extra effort was worth it?

- What specific action(s) were taken as a result of this plan? To what degree are these actions outside the normal job?

- What was the best thing about the plan?

- What was the worst?

- What should be changed?

- Should it be continued as is or dropped?

- What do people want to know more about?

Most major consulting companies can give you a dozen ways of gathering this information along with your internal research person, if you have one. Surveys may be conducted by paper and pen, phone, or computer. All of the data can be compared to those collected in the initial assessment phase. They should also be compared to normative data, which are available from most outside consulting firms and a few internal research departments with expertise in employee and managerial research. The results of such a comparison can enable you to segment out employee reactions to the plan versus their reactions to their jobs, their supervisors, or events, so you can get a clearer picture.

I'm always surprised at what *isn't* heard about—positive or negative—until organizations go through the reassessment process. By reassessing every quarter, you can use this information to fine tune the plan. If you wait until the end of the period, you may well lose some good opportunities for improvement.

Renewal or Termination?

The CARS research showed that more than 70 percent of group incentive plans that reassess their designs make changes from year to year. The payout formula is the most frequently noted change. Modification of payout measures is second. Organizations tend to increase the number of measures rather than reduce them, reflecting a level of measurement literacy by the employees. Changes in business conditions or business strategies are the most common reasons for changes in plan design.

Of the 737 companies (updated from the 663 originally studied) covered in the study, 81 killed their plans or said they expected to eliminate their plans in the future. The primary reason they gave was lack of performance.

There are fewer substantive data on project team incentive and recognition plans. Generally, project team incentive plans continue until they run dry. In the case of the American Airlines team idea plan (IdeAAs In Action) discussed in Chapter Nine, the plan's success was a function of communications, education, listening to employees, the awards themselves, and the increasing support of middle managers. And the savings keep rolling in.

The main concept of continuous quality improvement plans is that the plan is a journey, not a destination. But it requires a good deal of "repumping" everyone involved or participation ebbs away. Regular reassessments are particularly effective in the repumping process.

Recognition plans are rarely killed. They probably should be sometimes, because they can get tired and predictable. Because there are so many types of recognition plans, refurbishing is not so much a matter of redesign but of constant promotion and assessment of effectiveness.

Renewing the Plan   Renewal is an opportunity. It offers people a chance to build on progress made in performance, communications, education, teamwork, and the understanding of the measures. Improvements in the design can be made to more directly affect this year's strategic objectives and perhaps to improve the LoS. People often see renewal as merely a continuation of what they did the previous year, with a few changes in the numbers. That is an entitlement trap. Renewal offers a new look at the performance improvement plan. It may have a new name, a new theme, or a whole new look. It is incumbent upon any design, implementation, and reassessment team to view this as an opportunity for a new beginning.

Part of the renewal process is to tell everybody what happened. The state-of-the-plan report to top management is a starting point, the place to look for the information that needs to be shared with employees. The employee version of the state-of-the-plan report should remind them of the objectives, how they were measured, and what the performance was. Recap the year for them. Talk about the peak in October and why that happened. Point out the market downturn early in the year and explain what you did to minimize its impact. Point out where you didn't succeed. Report the results from the surveys and focus group interviews. Tell them what you learned from those sessions and what changes, if any, are being made to the plan as a result. This clear and honest feedback gives the plan credibility. It tells people that this is an open, intelligent, and cooperative environment.

At this point you have set the stage to roll out the new plan. Tell them how it is different from the previous plan. Explain why and how you have tweaked an existing measurement, added a new one, or changed a baseline.

About Changes   In group incentive plans, changes tend to be the refining of existing measures or adjustments in baselines, goals, and payout rates. Measures that have been used for years in a company suddenly are pressured due to a plan. Accuracy becomes critical. More exacting reflections of what is really going on are demanded from both management and employees. The more exact and reflective the measurement, the better the LoS for the employees and the better the effect on operational and financial performance. Getting input on refining measures from all constituencies covered by the plan is an important aspect of renewal.

It may also be determined that a change should be made in the organizational level on which the measures are rewarded—to reduce the LoS or the effects of cycling. Organization-wide or facility-wide measures, particularly in group incentive plans, may benefit from moving some portion of the measurement to a lower level of the organization. This will reduce the LoS. Perhaps half of the total payout could now be based on a facility-wide measure, 25 percent on unit performance and 25 percent on work group performance. This is often a good way to give people a sense of power in affecting measures. Just be aware that the more you fragment the measures, the more you run the risk of increasing cycling.

Of course, the other side of the coin is an experience of cycling that negatively affected your financial rationale to a greater extent than you anticipated. It may be necessary to reduce the number of measures, move the measured level of organization up, or reduce the number of payout periods.

There is a rationale for lowering or raising a baseline on any measurement based on how it compared to the previous year. If you did worse and have to lower a baseline, find out why performance dropped (or why the previous year's performance was so high) before you make the change. Reducing baselines is very rare because if performance doesn't improve on most of the measures, the plan is terminated. But if the performance downturn is only in a single measure of several in the plan, baseline reduction is a possibility.

A common question is how to set the new baseline. If you are on a rolling average baseline on a quarterly or several-year basis, then the baseline is built into the plan structure. If you preannounced a set percentage increase at the beginning of the plan and the plan showed improved performance, your baseline adjustment is done.

If you set your baseline on the prior plan year's performance, then the renewed plan has all the improvement built in. Using it as your new baseline is a common practice, depending on how much improvement there was. If you've gotten a 15 percent improvement in productivity, think twice about increasing the new baseline by 15 percent. Such an increase will be regarded by employees as punishment for being successful. Some companies split the difference between the original baseline and the average performance. Some inflate the baseline by a minimal percentage.

Goal setting for group incentive plans is done just as it was described in Chapter Eight: gut feeling laced with data, including an average of the peaks of the previous year's performance.

In project team incentive plans, particularly team idea processes, the most common change is integration of the plan into the "normal" process of doing business. In team idea processes, short-term plans become long-term plans, which have lower participation and higher approval rates and more savings per idea. Ideas are often submitted through the normal hierarchical organization, although I do not believe that is appropriate in the first year or two of a plan. It takes longer than a year of success to get all levels of management on board, technically and in spirit.

Recognition plan changes are generally a function of the findings of the reassessment. I have no data on how or why they are changed other than what I have already mentioned.

Renewal Is a Time for Celebration!   The distribution of that thirteenth check from a reserve fund is cause for celebration. Annual payouts demand to be celebrated. Let there be hoopla! Tell people why they earned what they earned. Make it a big deal, especially if you pay out annually or it's the end of one plan period and the beginning of another one. An event celebrating the success of the old plan is a good springboard for introducing a new plan.

Conclusion

You wouldn't build a house and not protect it with insurance. Implementing a plan requires the same vigor you would need to implement any major business strategy. It is the insurance to your design and payout investment.

You cannot communicate and listen enough. Recognition and group-based plans are your opportunity to create and reinforce employee-management communications—and get a real payback for it. They can be a catalyst for educating the entire workforce on the business of your business. They can only become contributing stakeholders if you give them the right tools and knowledge.

Promotion and celebration are new to most plans, but promote and celebrate you must. Hold special events, hold drawings, and always position the promotions in the light of the plans. If you use noncash awards, you have an additional tool with which to promote the plan.

Reassessment asks the tough question: "Was it worth it—to the organization and the employees?" Data, anecdotes, surveys, focus groups, testimonials, and financial analyses are all used to determine the renewal strategy.

Handled properly, these plans can be critical in accomplishing such strategic business objectives as reengineering, new product development, or organizational design change. They need to be treated with the same kind of focus and support as any other business plan. You are literally establishing a process by which you can unleash the creative power of your employees to affect organizational performance. You are establishing a process by which management can begin to do what it should do—manage less and lead more. Employees working under the umbrella of recognition and group-based plans require less management because they are engaged in the process and have a sense of ownership. To treat these plans like an individual compensation plan would be like buying a Ferrari and trying to drive it in a cow pasture. You won't get the performance you deserve.

Summary and Final Thoughts

The longer I study reward plans, the more convinced I become of their power as agents for change:

- for making individual compensation more cost efficient

- for changing the language of development and evaluation from solely individual performance to incorporating competencies and skills

- for recognizing and celebrating events, accomplishments, and contributions in a way that makes performance improvement a positive, social business experience

- for engaging an entire workforce in improving an organization's performance

- for rewarding specific contributions made by teams that are focusing on unique opportunities for improvement

- for moving away from an entitlement mentality to one of rewards linked to performance

This book focuses on the plans themselves rather than the nature of the organizations for which they are designed. Reward plan design and implementation is an area of best principles rather than best practices, because it is driven by unique strategic objectives and the desired culture of the organization. The nature of the organization will be reflected in those objectives and cultural needs.

Most of us are tactical thinkers wishing for simplistic answers that will meet our unique needs with a minimum of time, money, and brainpower expended. Effective plans are not developed that

Those wishing for simplistic answers to meet unique needs with a minimum of time, money, and brainpower expended will be disappointed.

way. Questions of which plans work best in large versus small, job-shop versus process, privately-owned versus public, open versus closed, high-tech versus low-tech, manufacturing versus service, single versus multilocation, private versus public sector organizations are difficult, if not impossible, to answer satisfactorily. Too many combinations are possible for anything but superficial answers.

I have no doubt that books on plan design will be written for specific types of organizations. "Reward Plans for Small, High-Tech, Start-up Companies with Egocentric Owners" will probably hit the stands in the near future. It will suggest a minimum benefit plan, hiring for specific competencies, minimum base pay necessary to attract people, generous stock plans for wealth accumulation in the future, and a lot of recognition efforts to keep spirits high and protect the critical cash flow. Of course, those who follow the advice will still have to refine the plans to the organization's specific objectives and culture.

Trying to match a combination of organizational characteristics to specific reward plans is a trap that stems from traditional compensation thinking. Traditional compensation plans are generally transferable from one organization to another. They are customized to the extent that the organization's compensation philosophy is articulated and adhered to. The other plans described in this book are designed on the continuum from *adapted practice* (capability plans) to *completely unique design* (project team incentive plans). This is consistent with the "cost of doing business" to "business results" continuum included in the reinforcement model.

So, I will leave the organizational characteristics–plan design discussion for others. If the design and implementation principles I've described are followed, they will naturally take most of an organization's unique characteristics into account. Instead, in this final chapter I will step back from the details to share some general thoughts, organized by the primary subjects of the book.

How We Got Here — We've Discovered Another Key to Success

Organizations have been on a journey of discovering how to meet the needs of their stakeholders—financial, customers, employees, and communities. Most of their energy has been focused on financial stakeholders, and most rewards have been given to top management, who have traditionally served those stakeholders. The relatively recent "discovery" of the customer spawned the quality movement, which has added customer value to products and services. Unfortunately, however, employees and, subsequently, communities have not been well served. This century's dramatic improvements in technology have raised the productivity of the organization while reducing the workforce. The effect on communities—due to major layoffs—has been predictably negative. There are now more contingent workers, more entrepreneurial start-ups, and more lower-paid service employees than ever before in our nation's history.

Organizations are searching for the next silver bullet that will kill off the next spoiler to their success. *If there is a silver bullet, it is the employee.* If there is a catalyst for moving the employee from being a cost of doing business to being a contributing stakeholder for improving company performance, it is the precepts of open-book management (OBM)—education, involvement, accountability, and reward plans aligned with business objectives and desired culture.

> **If there is a silver bullet, it is the employee.**

What goes around, comes around. Frederick Taylor introduced scientific management to move independent craftsmen into a process that standardizes tasks so that they could work efficiently in jobs with individual measures. Now we are using capability processes to value craftspersons rather than jobs, and group incentive plans to reinforce direction and results rather than individual measures. Perhaps we will move into a work society of craftspersons in virtual organizations relying on technology to supply the glue of coordination and direction, with only pay for time worked and rewards for results.

Business Objectives—Broad Measures Have to Get Real

Generating a list of business objectives is not terribly difficult. But figuring out the measures that support those objectives is, relatively speaking. Determining measures and the organizational levels at which they will be most helpful is often a matter of what you *can* measure rather than what you would *like* to measure. Organizations often fall back on financial measures because such measures are supported by an existing system—accounting—but they are clearly not the sole measures of performance.

If you can devise a clear statement of objectives and a list of broad measures of success relative to those objectives, the rest of the performance improvement process is possible. If not, you'll just keep doing what you have been doing and hope it all comes out on the P&L.

I have been working with a huge service organization. One of the measures of their plan's success is financial, a variation of economic value added (EVA). The claim is that EVA is being measured at each organizational unit (branch) level and has been for four years. Top management assumes that all levels of management are using this measure, as one of four, to run the business. The intention is to reward for improvement on EVA as well as the other three measures at each branch's level.

Reward plans put the teeth of accountability in measurements.

It wasn't until we began to establish the baselines and goals for each branch's reward plan that we discovered that the EVA measure was accurate in only five of the company's forty-two branches. It has been used in all of the branches since its introduction, but since nothing (meaning rewards) was riding on it, it hadn't been taken seriously. Reward plans put the teeth of accountability in measurements.

You can't push a rope. It is better not to use a measure than to force it into a plan and find it has little credibility.

A couple of hints about developing measures for reward plans: remember to step back from the heat of the search and ask yourself, "Is this measure good for the *business* first and then for the reward plan?" Design teams often end up frustrated because the "perfect measure" has problems with tracking, consistency, or with accurately reflecting the performance of the people. Quite often, when a measure just doesn't feel right, you are measuring at too low a level in the organization. Even though it increases the LoS, moving the measure up one level makes it more reliable. Decide to work on shaping up that perfect measure for next year's plan, but for now move on to another. You can't push a rope. It is better not to use a measure than to force one into a plan and find it has little credibility.

The process of capitalizing on human assets always turns up things you should be doing anyway.

The process of capitalizing on human assets always turns up things you should be (or thought you were) doing anyway. It is an acid test.

Assessment of Opportunity Rather Than Readiness for a Plan

The first step in alignment is an assessment of what your organization wants and what it has now. I get frustrated by talk of "readiness." Are you ready for group incentives? For competency? For performance management? For education to create financial literacy? Of course you're ready. The assessment is not done to determine your readiness but to determine the areas you need to focus on most. Employee lack of trust in management doesn't make you not ready. It just tells you how to design your communications, feedback systems, and management educational process to improve the trust level. A management incentive plan that blocks the rank and file from submitting ideas for improvement doesn't mean you're not ready. It just means that a management incentive plan is a choke point in the system that needs some real attention.

Assessment is a diagnostic tool for finding out what to do, not whether or not you can do it.

The assessment process that determines the degree of alignment among your strategic objectives, your desired culture, and your existing reward plans tells you what has to be changed, kept, or discarded. The power of your reward plans depends on the degree of awareness, value, and performance sensitivity that characterizes those plans. Assessment is a diagnostic tool for finding out what to do, not finding out whether or not you can do it.

Most companies do not do an assessment before establishing capability, recognition, or group-based incentive plans. That is a mistake. Your plan will be significantly better because if you've done an assessment, and if you can discuss the results of your assessment with top management, you will have a greater opportunity to gain critical commitment and support for the plan. So many efforts to change rewards systems stall out because top management thinks it is just another reworked version of the base pay plan or that they are already doing a great job with their existing plans—although they rarely know the number of plans at work and what they cost. Showing them what they have now and what it is doing for them puts you in position as a partner working to improve the existing system of rewards to improve performance. If your intent is to change the way you do business through your employees, get that total commitment for support and leadership from top management at this critical initial stage with an assessment.

Individual Compensation, the Iceberg
That Has To Be Flipped

Compensation is an iceberg of cost.

Organizations simply have to make their individual compensation plans more cost efficient. Labor costs are being driven by the ever-increasing load of base pay (and its commensurate benefit costs) with little regard to the ability to pay or with the justification of improved performance. It is an iceberg of cost that has been accepted for so long that when it is recognized as a danger to the health of the business, management's action of layoffs punishes the wrong segment of our employee population. It is a time for good leadership and coaching rather than hacking away at the employee asset base. More often than not, layoffs reflect a lack of good management and utilization assets.

I think that organizations will eventually do away with merit increases based solely on the manager's perception of an individual's performance. Staying competitive in the labor market will be handled through adjustments of pay, and companies will pay more for those specific jobs the market values more highly. Variable entitlements (the yearly bonus you got but that you don't know why you got but you sure want it again) have to stop being a primary way to reinforce middle management and the rank and file. The focus must be on the customer who buys the product and service, not the customer who controls your bonus. For those outstanding performers who, for whatever reason, should be reinforced, I suggest carving out an expense category for special awards of significant size to be used at management's discretion—based on events or contributions, not on time schedules, and for truly outstanding performance. It is the exception, not the rule.

Instead of trying to measure the performance of each individual and to reward that performance with a limited amount of merit increases, we need to shift our energy to developing people. Competency development, combined with performance management (perhaps performance coaching would be a better term) and multi-source (maybe 360 degree) feedback on performance, is an important change in the way organizations deal with individuals. It is certainly more important than top management realizes. It is easy to sign on with a simplistic statement like "We are aligning our employee's competencies and skills with the core requirements of the organization," but such an alignment marks a profound shift in the business's culture.

This shift changes the language from micromanagement to person-based development. Do you connect pay to it? I don't know. It is potentially powerful and equally complex. I believe that a system can be built to support paying for competencies, but it will rely more than ever before on the employee's immediate manager to make it work. Computerized systems, zero-based budgeting for labor costs, and 360-degree feedback will help, as will HR professionals serving as consultants rather than as directive administrators. The process is difficult. The potential is significant.

> *A system can be built to support paying for competencies, but it will rely more than ever before on the immediate manager to make it work.*

Recognition, Group, and Project Team Incentive Plans To Improve Business Performance

Group and project team incentive plans have a simple and clear objective: improve organizational performance. Recognition plans reinforce the process of performance improvement. Combined with education, involvement, and accountability, these plans are the keys to making the company's employed assets work for them.

Recognition of Contributions, Behavior, Objectives, and Needs

People need to be recognized for their contributions. Lack of recognition takes their power away and threatens their self-esteem. The best way to recognize people's contributions is through a daily series of efforts of appreciation by the organization and all its members—managers to employees, employees to employees, and even employees to managers. Organizations recognize and reinforce employees for their service, contributions to the company, community contributions, and performance of desired behaviors. Companies also meet their employees' personal needs to a greater degree than ever before through ever-flexible benefits and service plans.

Organizations need to recognize and celebrate their objectives far more than they do now. If they are important enough to *be* objectives, it is in the organization's best interest to recognize and celebrate them.

Organizations also need to stop creating competition among employees through plans that publicly single people out, often without asking their permission. Based on some subjective, time-driven, administrative process such as "employee of the month"

> *Organizations should stop creating competition among employees through plans that publicly single people out.*

plans do more harm than good. Management needs to use that energy to give everyone the tools to improve as a team.

To make recognition plans work, organizations have to realize that it is more difficult for most managers and supervisors to show appreciation than criticism. If recognition becomes a formalized, "administrative" task, it will fall flat, and that increases the cynicism in the workforce. All managers need to be given the tools to tangibly show their appreciation to employees. Small spot bonuses, rather than large variable entitlements, given spontaneously and frequently are the most effective rewards I've seen. They can be integrated into the daily life of the organization and not be influenced by the petty disagreements or jealousy created by larger rewards.

Group Incentive Plans as Dynamic Management Tools

I think that group incentive plans are the great hope of improving organizational performance through people. They make sense. They can, and generally do, pay for themselves. They meet management and employee needs and share the risk and reward of performance. Properly designed, they meet the needs of all four stakeholders.

The longest and most detailed chapter in this book is on this subject. A group incentive plan is the most powerful way of getting employees to learn about finance and measures of productivity and quality. It is often the primary reason employees become involved in making a contribution and be accountable for improving performance, although it doesn't take long before the involvement itself and the pride it instills become equally compelling.

In their most simplistic form, group incentive plans provide an umbrella for the mobilization of the workforce to make the organization more valuable. They focus on the consistent, broader measures of performance. They are used by organizations to accelerate the change in their culture into one of performance improvement as quickly as they can.

In their most action-oriented form, group incentive plans are a dynamic mechanism for focusing everyone on the exact measure that, when improved, will make a difference and mean rewards for everyone. The problems for the year are identified, measures are found, employees are educated, and the reward plan is built. This is open-book management at work.

Here are some things to remember about group incentive plans:

1. These plans should be formula driven with a preannounced reward schedule and little or no management discretion in the distribution of the awards. Measurements are done by organizational unit. Either everyone participates or just management (including anyone with direct reports), but you don't carve out people because you can't figure out how they can directly contribute to the measure. This process is about teamwork, not micromanagement.

2. You have to be careful and, as Gerry Ledford of the Center for Effective Organizations says, nimble. Group incentive plans are powerful. You will get what you reinforce.

3. Pay attention to financial rationale and getting consensus on what "paying out when you should" really means to employees and to top management.

4. Do not overengineer. Pragmatism rules, certainly in the beginning. The key is to be objective about what you want, and then get out of the way.

5. Resist the tendency to drive down the measures and rewards beyond a reasonably sized facility (a physical location). You run the risk of management resistance to a perceived loss of control and the risk of relying on measures not originally developed for rewards. You also create the potential for cycling and suboptimization. Take the high ground in the beginning.

6. Reassessment is not a sometime thing. It starts in the first quarter and continues through the announced period. Reassessment sends the critical message, "This is not an entitlement."

7. Design and operate the plan as a business strategy tool. The awards in a group incentive plan are important, but they are not the dominant force. They are not another way to pay people but a way to engage employees and share with them both the risk and the reward.

Do not underestimate the resistance of middle management to change. The perception is often that group incentive plans take control away from middle management by establishing measures they didn't set or are not even familiar with. Plans telegraph what is important and how the organization will reward for improvement. Moving from king or queen of the hill to cooperative coach of a team can be a difficult transition. The implementation phase of developing management ownership can make or break a plan.

Do not overengineer.

Reassessment is not a sometime thing.

All of Chapter Eleven is about implementation, and it is perhaps the most important one of the book. Without proper implementation and follow-through, you cannot get the return on your plan investment you deserve.

Project Team Incentive Plans, Rewarding for Specific Contributions

If you need to reduce costs, improve customer satisfaction, enhance revenue, and improve processes, engage teams of employees to tackle those tasks. If the teams' contributions can be measured and valued, such as in cost reduction, reward all the team members according to a preannounced formula. If you cannot measure and value the contribution (or if it just doesn't make sense to try), show your appreciation through the recognition plan.

Most project team contributions should be recognized, after the fact. But when it comes to cost reduction and revenue enhancement, nothing works like a team idea process supported by a project team incentive plan. It is a major undertaking for any organization but one that gives a return on investment higher than any type of plan I've studied.

The General Trend, At Least for Reward Plans

Organizations cannot compete in the marketplace with overpaid, underchallenged, and passively involved workforces.

The time for paternalistic and apathetic organizations has passed. Organizations cannot compete in the marketplace with overpaid, underchallenged, and passively involved workforces. The problem was created during good times, and organizations have attempted to rectify it with the ax of downsizing. Treating people like a cost of doing business, to be reduced and controlled, is a sad waste of critical assets. Only by combining education, involvement, and accountability, and sharing with employees the risks and rewards of business, will organizations be able to turn their employee assets into ones on which they can get a return.

The employees are the system.

It has seemed, through the years, that organizations have continually come up with more ways to manage people into becoming greater contributors by providing yet another *system* for them to work *within*. Well, *the employees are the system*. They just need tools that will allow them to improve performance, and they need management to remove the obstacles. I see the process working time and time again in open-book management companies, and their performance outpaces that of most others. The challenge is to adapt the process to those larger, more bureaucratic, middle-management controlled organizations whose backs are not against the wall—always the hardest situations to change.

So, how do you get the attention of these organizations? Beginning with management, you grab them by the P&L, by designing and installing plans that give them a return on their plan costs of two dollars for every one dollar spent. That's a return that will get attention. For everyone else, you reduce the entitlement of regular base pay adjustments and variable entitlements—and maybe base pay itself. This is serious business.

Organizations need to introduce plans that allow people to get involved in order to improve performance, individually or organizationally. Control and information move from a few people to everyone, following the same appropriate direction from top management on what they must accomplish together. In most larger organizations, you may not be able to create a sense of equity (employee ownership), but you can share the risks and rewards of performance.

I started this book with a quote from Charles Handy. Here's another of my favorite quotes for the ending: "As organizations everywhere realign themselves around core activities and competencies, they are realizing that their people are their chief assets. Often this realization becomes apparent during a takeover or merger when the business, if it is any good, is typically valued at four to five times the value of its tangible assets. The difference is the potential added value of its intangible assets, the intellectual property residing in its people" (Handy, 1992, pp. 11–12).

I know that your intangible assets can be significantly increased, with no additional capital expense, by allowing your employees to become better educated, more involved, more accountable, and motivated through well-designed and implemented reward plans. And that makes work a lot more satisfying, fulfilling, and fun.

References

Beatty, D., and Ulrich, D. "Re-engineering the Organization" *American Medical Association,* 1991.

Bechtell, M. L. *The Management Compass.* New York: American Management Association, 1995.

Belcher, J. *Gain Sharing.* Houston: Gulf, 1987.

Berry, L. *Marketing Services: Competing Through Quality.* New York: Free Press, 1991.

Bryne, John N. "Management Meccas." *Business Week,* Sept. 18, 1995, pp. 122–134.

Case, J. *Open-Book Management.* New York: HarperCollins, 1995.

Connellan, T. K. *How to Improve Human Performance: Behavior in Business and Industry.* New York: Harper & Row Publishers, 1978.

Daniels, A., and Rosen, T. *Performance Management: Improving Quality Productivity Through Positive Reinforcement.* Tucker, Ga.: Performance Management Publications, 1984.

Deming, W. E. *Out of the Crisis.* Cambridge, Mass: MIT Center for Advanced Engineering Study, 1986.

Employee Involvement Association. *Annual Statistical Report on Suggestion Systems.* Arlington, Va.: Employee Involvement Association, 1994.

Gale, B. T. *Managing Customer Value.* New York: Free Press, 1994.

General Electric Annual Reports, 1992, 1993, 1994.

Handy, C. *The Age of Unreason.* Boston: Harvard University Press, 1989.

Handy, C. "Balancing Corporate Power: A New Federalist Paper." *Harvard Business Review,* Nov–Dec., 1992.

Handy, C. *The Age of Paradox.* Boston: Harvard University Press, 1994.

Hartline, M., and Farrell, O. C. *Service Quality Implementation: The Effects of Organization, Socialization, and Managerial Actions on Customer-Contact Employee Behaviors.* A Marketing Science Institute report. Chicago, 1993.

Hewitt Associates. *The Impact of Performance Management on Organizational Success.* Lincolnshire, Ill.: 1994.

Kanungo, B., and Hartwick, J. "An Alternative to the Intrinsic-Extrinsic Dichotomy of Work Rewards." *Journal of Management*, 1987, pp. 98–102.

Kaplan, R. S., and Johnson, H. T. *Relevance Lost.* Boston: Harvard Business School Press, 1987.

Kerr, S., "On the Folly of Rewarding A, While Hoping for B." *Academy of Management Journal*, 1975, *18*, (4), pp. 75–93. Kerr, S., and Slocum, J. "Managing Corporate Culture Through Reward Systems." *Academy of Management Executives*, 1987, *1* (2), pp. 99–108.

Knouse, S. B. *The Reward and Recognition Process in Total Quality Management.* American Society of Quality Control. Milwaukee, Wisc.: Quality Press, 1995.

Kohn, A. *No Contest.* Boston: Houghton Mifflin, 1992.

Kohn, A. *Punished by Rewards: The Trouble with Gold Stars, Incentive Plans, A's, Praise, and Other Bribes.* Boston: Houghton Mifflin, 1993.

Kovach, K. "Why Motivational Theories Don't Work." *S.A.M. Advanced Management Journal*, American Management Association, Spring 1980.

Kruse, D. L. *Profit Sharing: Does It Make a Difference?* Kalamazoo, Mich.: W. E. Upjohn Institute for Employment Research, 1993.

Lawler, E. E., III. *Strategic Pay: Aligning Organizational Strategies and Pay Systems.* San Francisco: Jossey-Bass, 1990.

Ledford, G. "Designing Nimble Reward Systems." Compensation & Benefits Review, American Management Association. July–Aug., 1995.

Mai, R. *Learning Partnerships.* New York: Irwin, 1995.

McAdams, J., and Hawk, E. H. *Capitalizing on Human Assets.* A research report of the Consortium for Alternative Reward Strategies and the American Compensation Association. Scottsdale, Ariz.: American Compensation Association and Maritz Inc., 1992.

McAdams, J., and Hawk, E. H. *Organizational Performance and Rewards: 663 Experiences in Making the Link.* A research report of the Consortium for Alternative Reward Strategies and the American Compensation Association. St. Louis, Mo.: ACA and Maritz Inc., 1994.

Nelson, R. *1001 Ways to Reward Your Employees.* New York: Workman Publishing, 1994.

O'Dell, C., and McAdams, J. *People, Performance, and Pay.* A Research Report from the American Productivity and Quality Center and the American Compensation Association; Houston, Tex. APQC and ACA 1987.

Oregon Productivity Center. *The Objectives Matrix*. Portland, Or., 1983.

Parker, G. M. *Team Players and Teamwork*. San Francisco: Jossey-Bass, 1990.

Parker, G. M. *Cross-Functional Teams*. San Francisco: Jossey-Bass, 1994.

Ross, T., and Graham-Moore, B. *Gainsharing: Plans for Improving Performance*. Washington, D.C.: Bureau of National Affairs, 1990.

Scanlon Associates, Seminar, Battle Creek, Mich. 1993.

Schuster, J., and Zingheim, P. *The New Pay*. New York: Lexington Books, 1992.

Sethia, N. and von Glinow, M. "Arriving at Four Cultures by Managing the Reward System." In R. Kilmamm, et al. *Gaining Control of the Corporate Culture*. San Francisco: Jossey-Bass, 1985.

Sloma, R. *How to Measure Managerial Performance*. New York: Macmillan, 1980.

Stack, J. *The Great Game of Business*. Rev. ed. New York: Doubleday, 1992 and 1994.

Taylor, F. W. *The Principles of Scientific Management*. New York: Harper-Collins, 1911.

Thor, C., and Christopher, W. *Handbook for Productivity Measurement and Improvement*. Portland, Or.: Productivity Press, 1993.

Towers Perrin. *Work/Life Programs: Supporting a New Employer/Employee Deal*. New York: Towers Perrin, 1995.

Tucker, S. "The Role of Pay in the Boundaryless Organization." *The American Compensation Association Journal*, Autumn 1995, pp. 51–52.

Walton, M. *The Deming Management Method*. New York: Perigee Putman, 1986.

Yasuda, Y. *Forty Years, Twenty Million Ideas*. Portland Or.: Productivity Press, 1991.

Index